North/South Calling

North/South Calling

Father Bob Ogle

FIFTH HOUSE in association with   NOVALIS

Canadian Cataloguing in Publication Data

Ogle, Bob, 1928-
  North/South calling

  ISBN 0-920079-31-8 (Fifth House : bound). - ISBN 0-920079-29-6 (Fifth House : pbk.). - ISBN 2-89088-297-7 (Novalis : bound). - ISBN 2-89088-296-9 (Novalis : pbk.).

  1. Ogle, Bob, 1928- 2. Legislators—Canada—Biography. 3. Canada. Parliament. House of Commons—Biography. 4. Catholic Church—Canada—Clergy—Biography. 5. Clergy—Canada—Biography. I. Title.

FC626.045A3 1987   328.71'092'4   C87-098045-9
F1034.3.045A3 1987

Published by
Fifth House   in association with   Novalis
406 Clarence Ave. S.   P.O. Box 9700
Saskatoon, Sask.   Terminal
S7H 2C7   Ottawa, Ont.
                                          K1G 4B4

Printed by
Gagne Printing
80 St. Martin Ave.
Louiseville, Que.
J5V 1B4

for my sister Mary Lou
and my 10,000 closest friends

CONTENTS

0

FOREWORD

I grew up on the prairie listening to stories about our family history. My father, mother, uncles and aunts had the Celtic impulse to turn ordinary life incidents into delightful tales. From a very early age, my brother and sisters and I would urge our father to, "Tell us a story, Daddy." And our imaginations would follow my father's memory to Quebec winters, asbestos mines, maple syrup, pioneer trains, breaking land on the prairie, steam engines, limitless hope, war, flu, bad times and alkali water. All became part of my life and sinew.

The Celtic impulse is in me, too — to pass on life experiences through the story, to record the event that spoke of bigger realities and bigger ideas. The idea of writing a book may have always been at the back of my mind, waiting for my retirement years. . .memoirs of an eventful life. But my own history was interrupted by serious illness. After a heart attack and the diagnosis of a blood disease, I began to write, using my experience of illness as a skeleton on which to hang my church and political stories. The anger I felt and projected onto hospitals and medical people so coloured the story that Caroline Heath, who had edited my first book, *When the Snake Bites the Sun*, cautioned that it was too bitter and suggested that I wait "until you heal a bit." But there was no healing in store for me. There was more cell destruction, more pain, cancer of the brain, and maybe no retirement years.

Another friend, Bede Hubbard, assistant to the director of Novalis press, came to visit me in hospital in Ottawa. He offered to send out to the media an article I had recently written about death and dying, about my completely unexpected joy of peace, contentment and freedom. He also pursued a suggestion he had made to me earlier about writing or having somebody help me write a book.

But would there be time? Radiation treatments were to begin in Saskatoon and I had no idea whether I would live another three days or 20 years. But I wanted to tell my story. Caroline Heath agreed to help. She sat with me through the weeks of radiation treatment as strength and memory receded, listening and questioning as I taped, then editing the transcripts, questioning and rewriting. Out of pain and weakness came *North-South Calling*. Caroline arranged to publish the book through her publishing company, Fifth House, in association with Novalis.

That's all this book is — my story, or some of my stories from the key experiences in my life's journey. Serious illness and death shadows bring freedom. They have allowed me to tell this much of the story. We don't know the future. Maybe there will be more time and more stories. But whatever the future holds, may peace and love be ours.

[signature: Bob Ogle]

Ottawa, January 1987

The editor wishes to thank Michael Hayden, Lloyd Rodwell, Grant Maxwell and Sister Ann Lafferty for their critical reading of the manuscript.

x

CHAPTER 1

CHILDHOOD

Having been born on Christmas Eve 1928 to Irish Catholic parents possessed of a powerful desire to ensure the salvation of my eternal soul, it seems hardly extraordinary that I was baptized on Christmas Day—even though this entailed wrapping me in blankets and whisking me across the way from the Rosetown Union Hospital to St. Theresa's Chapel in weather that was -40C.

The chapel was new to the world, too, having been opened that very day. The baptism was conducted at the font in the back of the chapel by Father Dubois. The only story I remember hearing about the event had to do with the stipend. The normal stipend at that time was $1, but my godparents had no money to give to the priest. My father, seeing this and having only one five-dollar bill in his pocket, took out the five and gave it to the parish priest. The priest pocketed the bill and we left the church.

My father, Henry Ogle, and mother, Annie Brennan, had both come from Quebec and spoke both French and English fluently. They met in the West and were married in 1926. They had, I think, one of the happiest marriages I have ever known. As a child, I never saw anger at home. There was a very strong sense of love in our house. I didn't realize until I was much older that not everyone grew up in such a warm and supportive environment.

Because we grew up in the Depression, I thought poverty was universal. Many memories of that poverty have remained with me, but two stand out. One is of people going by our house with convoys of starving cattle and horses and all their possessions loaded onto old wagons. They were leaving their farms, the dried-out land of southern Saskatchewan, and heading north into the bush. My mother and father would go out and welcome each group as it came by, sharing some of our meager supplies with them. Often it was only water we could offer, but even that was appreciated. The cows would all be bawling, as there was no water along the route.

The other is the memory of my father going for relief during the winters of 1935, '36 and '37. Almost everyone was forced to turn to relief, but that did little to lessen the humiliation. They were often treated like dogs by those who were distributing the relief supplies. Years later, I still couldn't forget how having to accept relief almost destroyed my father.

The farmers in our area would go together in the wintertime to the little town of McGee, where the relief supplies were unloaded. They got straw from other parts of the Prairies, apples and cheese—which sometimes were not fit for human consumption—from Ontario, and dried codfish from Nova Scotia. We didn't know what codfish was or how to cook it. I remember Mom trying various methods, but we never could eat it. In the end, my father took hay wire and made little snowshoes for us out of it. We kids wore these little codfish snowshoes until spring when they thawed and the whole porch filled with the smell of rotten fish.

The men would congregate at our farm early in the morning in the hope that they would be able to get to McGee about noon, load the supplies and get back the same day. After loading up, they would cross over to the Chinese restaurant, where they would go inside and warm themselves, eat their lunches and buy a cup of tea. Tea was five cents a cup and none of them had any money, so usually one of them would bring along four or five pounds of home-made butter and trade it for the tea. One time there was a raging blizzard. By the time they got to the Chinese restaurant their sandwiches were frozen and they were thawing them out on top of the old Quebec heater. Cecil Conlon, who had brought the butter that day, crossed over to the restaurant owner, put five pounds of home-made butter on the counter and said, "Let's deal for tea." The poor Chinese restaurant owner said, "I have too much butter already. I can't take any more. I can't give you any tea today for your butter." Cecil, who was the envy of the community because he had returned from the First War shell-shocked but with a $20-a-month pension, walked over to the door as proud as a man can and threw the five pounds of butter into the storm. They left that day without any tea.

Whenever I have to talk about aid, I think of that story. Giving aid is the most difficult, most delicate human act as far as I'm concerned. A person who does not have the money to buy the basic necessities for himself and his family is in an extremely vulnerable position. It is so easy to destroy his dignity. If we are going to give aid to another person, or another country, we have to remember that we are stepping into a crucial, sensitive area. If providing aid is the only solution in the short run, it must be done in a way that preserves self-respect.

During those Depression years, I was attending a small prairie school called Springville. It had seven students in seven grades, and had an extremely good teacher—Miss Margaret Hurst. The teacher's salary was $300 a year, but for two years the community could not pay her salary.

2

Margaret Hurst, however, was dedicated to teaching regardless of remuneration and she continued to teach. To her, teaching meant instructing children how to read and write and understand.

Because everybody was in the same room, we heard all the lessons. Even though you were in Grade 1, you knew all about the geography of Great Britain because Grade 7 was taking that. You also heard Shakespearean literature. Certainly, at the end of Grade 1 you knew how to read and write and count, because that was what you had gone to school for.

My father bought a Shetland pony, named Sparky, for me to drive to school. He was a cute little animal, with a spotted red and white coat. To look at him, you'd think he was the gentlest animal on earth. In fact, Sparky was the meanest son-of-a-bitch that had ever been born. We didn't know that when we got him.

My father took an old baby carriage that had been sent to us by our grandmother in the East, cut off the front wheels and added a set of shafts, transforming it into a small carriage that could hold two or three children. It was quite a smart outfit. Sparky had come with harness, so all we had to do was hitch him up to the little carriage and away we'd go. That was the idea. Sparky, however, had an absolute, unalterable resolution never to go more than half a mile from his feed box. The first day of school, I had Sparky all hooked up at least an hour ahead of time, being already a fiend for punctuality. When it was finally time to go, Sparky set off at a smart trot. After a half mile, he stopped. There was nothing I could do to entice him to go any further. All I could do was cry and allow Sparky to take me home again. Well, my dad told me I just didn't know how to drive horses. He said he would take me out the following Sunday and give me a lesson. That time it was my father who cried. He beat Sparky like I had never seen anything beaten before. He pushed Sparky. He pulled Sparky. He tried everything. But Sparky had gone the half mile and that was it. Sparky stayed with us for about three or four years, keeping within the half-mile limit. We finally traded him for four sheep, all of which died the first year. I'm sure if Sparky is alive today, he's still going the half mile and no more.

Prairie society in the Depression ran out of the school system. Most of the serious and social events took place there. For us kids the high point of the school year was the Christmas concert. It consisted primarily of recitations. My first recitation was a poem my mother had clipped out of the Western Producer. The only two sources of news that came into our house were the Winnipeg Free Press Prairie Farmer and the Western Producer. Their arrival with the mail was the highlight of each week. Around Christmas time, people would send poems in to these publications and they would find their way into the Christmas concerts.

The poem I recited in Grade 1 began, "The boy next door gives me a pain. He expects a great big aeroplane. Such children need correcting!"

At the end of the concert there was always a Christmas pageant. Mary in a blanket, Joseph in a blanket and the sheep in blankets—Hudson's Bay blankets—would all do their part. And then Santa Claus would arrive. Throughout the evening, messages came in, reporting on Santa's approach. Santa Claus was over Rosetown, they would announce. Then he was over Glen Payne, all the time getting closer. I could never figure out how they knew Santa's exact location. When I was in Grade 3, Santa Claus arrived wearing Dad's overalls and boots, and that was the end of the Santa Claus legend for me.

May 24 was also an important holiday for us kids. The Queen's birthday was a school holiday, the occasion of the annual Rosetown sports day. Since Springville had only seven or eight pupils, there were never enough of us to form a proper contingent, much less a band, for the parade. So the kids from Springville would catch a ride to town in the back of someone's truck and the teacher would try to line up some other school with only seven or eight kids. We would join forces at the back of the parade.

My first parade was in 1936, my first year at school. Mother had cleaned me up, my parents were going along for the ride, the teacher had arranged for us to join another small group, and there was to be a movie after the parade. The anticipation was almost unbearable. When we finally arrived in Rosetown, I had no idea where to go and I was really scared. A little girl at the parade site took me by the hand and marched with me in the parade down Main Street. It was quite a thrill, her holding my hand; I had no idea that this was humiliation in the making.

After the parade I saw my first movie, A Six-day Bike Race with Joe E. Brown. Later that afternoon I went back to the theatre and saw it again. When I got to my uncle's place, my cousins informed me that they had found out two things: first, that I had walked in the parade with a girl; and second, that I was wearing underwear my mother had made from one of her slips. They had overheard my mother telling my aunt about her remodelling. The cousins did not allow me to live down either of these alleged degradations until I was well into my 30s.

In our family life, prayer was extremely important. We said family prayers in the morning and the rosary and novenas every night. Scattered throughout the year were special prayers tied to my mother or father's private scheduling of religion, such as a novena to St. Ann, my mother's name sake, and novenas to other saints who had particular relevance for my mother or father.

The 16 miles that stretched between our home and the church might

4

as well have been 16,000 miles in winter. It was impossible to get there. So we celebrated Sunday at home with great devotion. Sunday prayers were special. And then there was catechism. My mother had a catechism book full of pictures—woodcuts of the prophets, the apostles, Jesus, the Last Judgment and devils—all the characters in this great drama called religion. On Sunday my father would spend an hour or two explaining these pictures to us. He always had a good story to go with every picture.

Every summer we had an intensive catechism course, given by the Sisters. In 1934, Bishop Gerald Murray had invited the Sisters of St. Joseph of Toronto to come West and operate the convent in Rosetown. It was to have been run by Sisters from France, but the adjustment to culture and climate proved too much for them. After their departure, the convent stood empty for several years until the Sisters from Toronto came. They stayed for almost 30 years. Part of their mission, which they took very seriously, was to teach catechism to all the children. They did this by running a ten-day catechism summer school. Registration was $2 a child and the parents supplied as much food as they could. The Sisters arranged beds for the girls in the dormitory upstairs and the boys slept in what would be considered the gymnasium below. The convent had next to no water. Its supply was from a well that was dry most of the time. We were not allowed to bathe or flush the toilets. The Sisters stood by with sour looks for any kid who dared to flush a toilet that had only been used five or six times. Where I came from, there were no flush toilets at all. To me, a five-flush toilet was better than no toilet.

Although I was impressed by the flush toilets, I was not impressed by the sleeping accommodations. The beds were very narrow and we were two to a bed. They put a big kid at the top of the bed and a little kid at the bottom. The first summer, my sleeping partner was a boy by the name of Herve Lebreque. He must have been about 14; I was seven. I was convinced he had the stinkiest feet in Canada, even though mine were no doubt just as bad. Everyone wore running shoes, which made feet stink and we couldn't wash. Every night those stinky feet pushed up to my face, just as every other big kid's feet pushed up to every other little kid's face. Herve landed on the beaches of Normandy June 6, 1944. He was one of the 19 Canadians captured by the Germans, tortured and shot as a prisoner on the opening day of battle.

There were different levels of catechism classes. They began very simply with questions and answers my mother had already taught me.

Who made you? God made me.

Why did God make you? God made me to know Him, to love Him, to serve Him.

How many persons are there in God? There are three persons in God.

And so on. Everybody knew all the answers.

My mother had been using a catechism she had brought from Quebec, a different one from the one with all the pictures. I had learned the acts of faith, hope and charity and the act of contrition from her catechism. The Sisters from Toronto had a different version of these four prayers and they made me relearn them all. At the end of the summer class, I made my First Communion. My mom bought me a little suit with long pants. It was my first suit and I wore it for several years. After my First Communion, we all went to one of the cafés and had a tomato and lettuce sandwich. It was the first time I'd ever eaten in a restaurant.

The shortage of water at the convent was not unusual in Rosetown. There just weren't many sources and the water they provided was so bad you couldn't drink it. On the farm we had two wells. One we called the drinking water well and one we called the farm well. Quite often, both wells were dry. Our house had a cistern built into the basement. In the springtime, my dad and Uncle Vincent would go out with borrowed wagons to collect melted snow from the sloughs. This water would be stored in the cistern. There was a hand pump in the kitchen connected to he cistern and we did our daily wash there. This supply would carry us through the summer. By fall the water in the cistern would be covered with floating dead mice.

To get water in the wintertime, my father used an old 45-gallon gasoline drum that had the top cut out of it. It stood by the stove and the last thing he did every night was fill it with snow. Of course that finished off whatever heat there had been in the kitchen, but it began the melting process so there would be water the next day. One time, when I was six or seven, my brother fell into the barrel. He might have drowned, had I not held him by the back of his pants and screamed until my mother came and hauled him out.

One of the greatest hardships for my mother in starting a new life out West was the shortage of water. She was used to living where there was an endless supply of fresh spring water. Here, everything that had to do with water became a major problem.

Washing clothes, in particular, was a major chore. Our washing machine was a wooden tub with a lever-action handle and rubberized wringer rollers. It was just a little too hard for Mom to run by herself; she had to have either one of the bigger kids or Dad help her with it. Doing the wash on Monday meant getting the water on the stove at least by Sunday afternoon. The big copper boilers covered two burners of the stove. When we had water, we would fill them, and when we had no water we melted snow. The washing would take all morning and was very hard work. Mom always insisted on three washes—hot wash, mid-

6

dle wash and cold wash—and then the laundry had to be wrung through the wringer three times. In winter the drying was done on a rack in the house and in summer on the barbed wire fences that ran outside the house. We had to be very careful putting the clothes on the fence and taking them off.

Communications in those days were fragile. We had an old radio that ran on three batteries—two B's and an A, each of which would have weighed 40 pounds. The radio had three dials. To get it functioning properly you had to have all three dials in exactly the same spot. Even with the dials lined up, it didn't function very well. So it was a tremendously exciting event in 1937 when our Uncle Vincent bought a radio at Macleods. The radio cost $39—$10 down and $2 a month. We had gone that day, as we frequently did on Sundays, on the stone boat, which skidded all over the roads, to a neighbouring family, the Rathwells, to spend the day there. That was a common thing for farmers to do—go out and spend the whole day with a neighbour. When we got home, we found the new radio—a radio that worked. We tuned in KSL Salt Lake City as clear as a bell. My dad was in charge of the radio from then on, because he knew the batteries would run down and we couldn't afford to buy new ones.

Certain programs were very important: Amos and Andy, the news and Monsignor Hunt, who spoke from KSL Salt Lake City every Sunday on a Catholic religious program. During all the programs we had to remain very quiet.

Uncle Vincent was one of my father's brothers. He was my grandmother Ogle's wedding present to my mother. Vincent had never married. Grandmother Ogle assigned him to our house so he would have someone to look after him.

Vincent had an unusual philosophy of life, particularly for those times. Work was never really that important, but the prairie was. Vincent loved walking on the prairie. He made a little whip out of some old harness and he would walk across the prairie, snapping this little whip against his leg, just enjoying the rhythm of it all. He used to go for long walks on Sunday. He would just walk off and be gone all day. Then he'd reappear. His going and coming that way suggested to me that there were no barriers. That's where I got the idea that you could cross the horizon. I carried that idea with me all my life—that there were no absolute barriers, every horizon was crossable, there were no mountains, it was all flat land when you wanted to go somewhere.

Vincent had a great feeling for nature. He understood sunsets and sunrises and he understood animals. He loved to break horses, or go and look for the cows, or just ride all day in the hills. He also loved to read Zane Grey. We had two books of Zane Grey and Vincent used to read me these stories. After a while he didn't have to read them because he knew them by heart. He used to just say them to me.

Vincent had the best memory of anyone I have ever met, but he only used it to remember things which most people didn't consider very important. Vincent knew the age of every cow, horse, dog, every animal that lived not only on our farm, but on every farm within 25 miles of us. He would go into a yard and list off the birth dates of all their animals. He had no memory at all for the cost of things, prices on the stock exchange or anything that most people would consider useful. He knew nothing about baseball or hockey. In fact, he thought they were a waste of time.

Even though we had a fairly nice house, the sleeping accommodation was limited and I was forced to sleep with Vincent. The house had been built by a man named Nixon, who thought the West was going to develop. It was the only house in the neighbourhood that had been wired for electricity. There was no electricity in the area, but if it had come, our house would have been ready for it. The house was heated in the wintertime by one coal stove and one Quebec heater. The house was cold all the time, but as soon as night settled the house became as cold inside as outside. Upstairs, where we slept, it was sometimes -40C and I would be forced to sleep under a buffalo robe with Vincent. I had to stay close to him to keep warm. Actually, I didn't have any choice. The bed was old and sloped into the middle.

My eldest sister died from an outbreak of diphtheria that ran through the neighbourhood the winter of 1929-30, killing a number of children. Dorothy died January 1, 1930. Because we believed that death does not take someone away, we always considered ourselves a family of five children. We said there were the four of us alive and then Dorothy. She was included in everything. Mother always spoke of the death of the eldest child as her greatest sorrow. New Year's Day was never a happy day in our house. It was never celebrated, because it was Dorothy's death day. I don't remember Dorothy. Her death left me the oldest child. The next was my sister, Marguerite, who was two years younger than me.

Our parents gave us no explanation of how babies are born. Sometime after Christmas 1933, Mom left the farm and a neighbour woman came to look after us. I couldn't understand why Mom would go away in the wintertime and leave this person to look after us. Then one day Dad went away and we heard that he was coming home with Mom and a new baby. There was exultation in the house at the news. We could hardly wait to see this new baby. When they finally pulled into the yard, there was Mom with the new baby in the sleigh. I ran to the door and my old Collie dog, Buster, got so excited he ran through my legs and knocked me down. That's my first childhood memory; be-

8

ing knocked down by the dog the day my brother Charles came home from the hospital. I was four.

My youngest sister, Mary Lou, was born August 22, 1936. We were much more aware of that birth. It was the depth of the Depression. Dad was away working at another farm because our farm had absolutely nothing on it. Mom had to go into Rosetown to stay with her sister-in-law for six or seven weeks before Mary Lou was born because she was not very well. We were looked after by a cousin, Marie, who was about 15 at the time. She really didn't know much about housekeeping and she never gave us a bath, which we thought was the best thing about that summer. For my sister, Marguerite, the best thing was playing cowboys all summer in the sand. George Ogle, one of our cousins from Rosetown who was the same age as me, came out and enriched our play. He'd been to lots of movies and could tell us about Ken Maynard, Tom Mix and all the great cowboys. He could even act them out. The one good thing about wind storms, as far as we were concerned, was that they left sand everywhere. All the ditches were full of sand, and it piled up against the fences. We played cowboys and Indians by the hour, riding our stick ponies, with George telling stories.

As the years went on, it seemed that our economic status deteriorated. The first car we had—a white-topped Model A Ford touring car—was actually quite a good car. In 1937, Dad went all out, trading in the first car and paying $175, or at least promising to pay $175, for a five-year-old Model A. It was really a good car. Good seats. Good everything. That year, however, there was absolutely no crop and the loan company was out to get the car back. For several weeks my father tried to hide the car in different places on the farm in case the loan company man came. I couldn't understand why we were hiding the car behind the haystack. The loan companies always sent someone you didn't know to take back what they had given you the money to buy. The person who took the car in could sell it at any price to make up the money owed and he could keep the rest. He made good money.

Some of our neighbours were better at handling the loan company men than my father was. One neighbour saved his car by picking up an axe from behind the door and threatening the loan company man, "If you touch that car I'll split your head." The guy left and the neighbour kept his car. My dad didn't have that kind of nerve and we lost our car. From 1937 until 1942 we had no car, which was always a humiliation for us, or for me, at least, because it seemed that almost everyone else had a car. Our next vehicle was a 1927 Model T. As far as I was concerned, it could not be classified as a car. It was a Model T. We paid $42.50 for it.

During the 30s, the farmers around us couldn't afford to buy licences for their cars, so one farmer would get a licence and everybody would borrow it and hang it on their car when they had to go to town. Everyone shared the cost of that plate. One year we had the licence and farmers would come and borrow it. I knew it was against the law and I used to worry about our involvement. They would drive to town, hide the car somewhere, buy their groceries and carry them back to the car, and get out of town before the police caught them.

In 1939 we lost the farm. My father had borrowed $600 to pay his threshing crew in 1928, and that debt had been hanging over our family all that time. For my father the worst four-letter word in the English language was *debt*. I can still remember him pacing the floor nights, because he couldn't pay back that $600. That year,1928, they harvested the wheat and then found out there was nothing in the heads. But Dad still had to pay the crew's expenses. In 1928 it was rust. And so it went, dismal year after year, always some disaster. The debt hung over our house, all that time. It was an insurance company in Omaha, Nebraska that got the farm in 1939. Surprisingly, we did get some crop that year and were able to buy a farm near Rosetown for a $500 down payment. My parents were very happy about the move because it meant we could all go to Catholic schools. This was terribly important to them. So we moved to the little house outside Rosetown where we lived for the rest of my youth.

My mother was a great one for naming things, and she always thought up cheerful names. She called our first farm Sunnyside. This one she named Pleasant Heights. I would have called it Little Shack on a Hill. We moved to the new farm on November 6, 1939. I carved the date into the trunk of a tree, which to my dismay, subsequently died. The last thing my mother did, when we left Sunnyside, was to go down to the basement and put new newspaper on all the shelves where she had kept preserves, so the next person would have clean shelves. But nobody ever came.

Our new home was about 1 ½ miles from town. The Catholic school was right in town. I was in Grade 6 when we moved. The transition from a school with an enrolment of seven or eight to one with 150 or 200, in which there were formalized classrooms, one grade to a room, with students sitting in rows, was quite difficult. In the beginning we hated it, but in due course we adapted.

Living close to town provided opportunities we hadn't had before. I was at the stage of wanting to belong to everything. I joined the Boy Scouts and I joined the Air Cadets. I joined the altar boys. I joined anything you could join. Since all these activities were at different times, I often walked the distance from our house to town three or four times a day. During Lent, I would walk into town early in the morning to serve mass, walk home, eat my porridge, walk back to school, walk home, milk the cows, eat supper, walk back for Air Cadets. I was always walking back and forth to go to something I had joined.

In the fall of 1942, it was decided that I would get a job. It was wartime and farm labour was scarce. I was eager to get a job because there were things I wanted to buy—like a new scout uniform and a bike. Actually, my mother had promised she would get me a bicycle when I finished Grade 8, and she did. She must have saved money from eggs and hens and who knows where. It cost $42.50. It was a wartime bicycle made out of the cheapest material. The handlebars broke the first day. I had wanted a bike since Grade 3 and had thought about all the different ways I could get one. When I finally got it, in Grade 8, everyone else was already thinking about cars. That bicycle taught me that there's a certain time in your life when you need something. If you can get it then, fine; if you can't, you might as well forget it, because it won't do you any good later.

I was 13 years old and not that big, but I knew how to handle most things. I had learned how to drive a tractor at my Uncle Mike's place on August 19. They were fixing the combine and there was nobody to drive the tractor for summer fallowing, so my uncle showed me how to drive the tractor and I summer fallowed all day by myself. When we came in for supper that evening, we heard on the news that the Canadians had won a major victory against the Germans at Dieppe. We listened to the unknown names, unknown places. Over the next few weeks the Winnipeg Free Press printed list after list of casualties. Gradually we realized that it had not been a great victory.

In the fall of 1942, I started working for Roy Hill, who was a neighbour and a distant relative. I was to operate the tractor in front of a big Holt combine. The job also included milking the cows before we went out to the field and after we finished at night. This meant rising at 4 a.m. and working sometimes till midnight. Although I hated milking and hated cows, I accepted this as part of the deal. Roy offered to pay me $5 a day, which was a huge wage for a person my age. When I arrived at the farm, there were a lot of repairs to be done to get the machinery ready, and harvest came in a little late. We didn't start harvesting until September 7.

The Model L Case tractor had to be started with a crank and I was too small to crank it by myself. There was a hired man who drove the truck and Roy ran the combine. We were pulling 16 feet of cutter bar and doing a lot of hill work, which meant the tractor was at an angle all the time. That was scary, but even worse was the fear of stalling the tractor. I knew if I couldn't get it going again, Roy would have to get off the combine and come down and crank it. It wasn't long before I was able to keep the tractor running most of the time.

My enthusiasm for the job was demonstrated by perseverance under very trying conditions. I got the mumps and my face swelled up the size of a potato sack. I couldn't eat for two or three weeks and yet I ran that tractor. When the harvest was finished, in mid-October, I had only earned $83. There had been so much wet weather, we'd spent days sitting in the house playing cribbage or just talking.

The first thing I bought with my earnings was a Scout uniform. I bought one that was too large, because the rule in our house when buying clothes was that you always bought a larger size than you needed so you wouldn't outgrow it too quickly. For the rest of my Scouting days I wore a uniform that was too big for me.

Because of the job, I missed the first six weeks of school that year. I had great difficulty catching up in some subjects, particularly Latin and French, which were new subjects for me. I had no difficulty catching up in mathematics, English or geography, but I never got a firm grasp on those two subjects.

As much as I had loved Scouts, in Grade 9 I was even more strongly drawn to the Air Cadets, which had been organized in Rosetown during the War. Now, my mother and father of course were very Irish. They associated military uniforms with the British oppressing the Irish. Despite the fact that all the other boys my age had joined, I had a very hard time persuading my parents to let me join the Air Cadets. I had to plead and plead and plead. I was the last one to join the Air Cadets that year.

Squadron 166 was run by Norman Smith, who was the O.K. Economy manager and who had fought in the First World War. The squadron was made up of about 50 boys from grades 9 to 12, from the public high school and the Catholic high school. We met two evenings a week. Even though I had to walk 1 ½ miles each way to the meetings, winter and summer, I think I probably had the best attendance record in the squadron. I loved everything about Cadets—the airplanes, the courses we took, the wireless, everything. We used to meet downstairs in the old community hall. It was a terrible room, but that made no difference to me, because above us, hanging from the ceiling, was the crashed wing of a Tiger Moth. As far as I was concerned, that wing meant airplanes, and I was going to be a flyer.

As Air Cadets we took part in several summer camps. They had a big impact on me. The first of these camps was in 1943 in Swift Current. My mother and my sisters had gone East to Quebec that year to visit Grandma and my father did not want me to go to camp. He was not that enthusiastic about my being involved in the Air Cadets anyway, but particularly didn't want me to go because it was haying season and he needed help with the farm. In the end, though, he gave permission for me to go to Swift Current for ten days. We were to go by bus. Dad drove me to the bus in the old Model T. I climbed on the bus with the other kids, all of us wearing our uniforms, and I was thrilled as could be, when Dad shouted up to the window where I was sitting, "Do you have any money?"

"No," I said, "I don't have any money, Dad."

"I don't have any money, either," he said. "The only money we have is a five-dollar bill at home. I'll go home and get it for you."

"I don't need any money, do I?" I offered, not wanting him to go, but he was already leaving.

"You'll need money," he said. He drove home and was back before the bus left. He passed the $5 up to me through the open window. I spent about $2.25 at the camp. It was a good camp.

On July 4, 1943, I had my first ride in an airplane. Cadets were not supposed to get rides in airplanes, but some of the English flyers who were training at Swift Current didn't mind bending the rules once in a while. They were flight-testing an old Oxford—"flying coffins" they were called— planes that had been used during the Battle of Britain and eventually brought over to Canada to be used as trainers. The turrets had been taken out of them and there were no seats except for the two pilots' seats. I sat on what was then the bomb bay, and held on. I had never been so scared in my life. After we landed, though, I could be cocky because I had one up on most of the other Cadets, who didn't get a ride that day.

The days at camp were filled with exciting activities. We marched and we drilled and we had target practice. We learned about airplanes and we learned how to be great flyers. We studied navigation and air-craft recognition, at which I excelled. Then camp was over, we were home again and it was back to haying.

Camp the following year was at Clareshome, Alberta. It was also a very exciting camp for me. By this time the British Commonwealth Air Training Plan had spiralled into one of the biggest operations that Canada had ever seen, with its air bases in almost every town. The program drew trainees from various Commonwealth countries. There were Australians stationed at the Clareshome base and I was very impressed by these 19 and 20-year-olds, who were men to me, drinking beer and singing. I only remember them singing one song—Long Ago and Far Away.

As the war was coming to an end, the enthusiasm at summer camp dwindled. One by one the training stations were closed and the airplanes burned. The summer of 1945 our camp was in Calgary, but I got little out of it because I was sick with hepatitis the whole time. By that time the fighting was pretty well over and everybody in the Cadets knew they would never get to the war. That was a terrible feeling for me. I had really believed that if I worked hard and did my cadet work well, I would be able to join the Air Force like all the other guys and become a bomber pilot and go off and bomb cities and win medals and become a hero. By 1945 it was quite clear that this was not going to happen and I can still remember the sorrow of knowing that I was going to miss the war.

My high school years were absorbed by the Air Cadets. We had some sports at school, but I was never a good athlete. I did, however, do well in the Air Cadets. That became my glory. At the end of my Air Cadet career, I was the flight sergeant.

During those school years in Rosetown, religion continued to be an important factor in my life. The religious atmosphere at home was reinforced by the school. Each school day began with mass, each class began with prayer. The day was punctuated by prayer breaks. We were expected to make private visits to the chapel, and there was benediction and confession every week. I became an altar boy, even though I was older than the other servers. The first mass I served as an altar boy was on December 8, 1939, the feast of the Immaculate Conception. There was supposed to be someone there to show me what to do. But that person didn't show up, so I stumbled through the role alone, humiliated by my ignorant blundering.

The Sisters of St. Joseph worked hard at encouraging vocations. They were always out recruiting someone for the convent or the seminary. Whenever the Sisters had visitors—Basilian priests from Toronto, or bishops, or relatives who were priests—they would invite me to serve mass and have breakfast with them afterwards. I was fascinated by these visiting priests, just as I had been fascinated by the priests who served us in the country. Our country priests were extraordinary men— mavericks in their own right, probably expelled from someplace because they were alcoholics or too unorthodox. They travelled through the hills south of Rosetown, stopping at homes of Catholic families. The neighbours would hear that there was a priest at a certain farm and everybody would congregate. There would be mass and confessions and afterwards a social. Many winters that was the only social event, apart from the Christmas concert. I can remember very clearly attending mass on the feast of St. Joseph in 1937. We knew from a flurry of phone calls that a priest named Father Billington, an Englishman, was going to say mass at our closest neighbour's, a mile away. The car had been in the garage since November. The roads were snowed in and someone had to stay home with my brother and sisters who were too small to walk that far. My dad became babysitter and my mother and I walked alone. That was a very precious occasion, walking alone with my mother and going to that mass. It was springtime and the crust of snow was breaking. As we walked, we kept breaking through the snow.

After that mass, Father Billington went on to Gunnworth, where he bought me a present—a little tool set with a hammer and a saw—and sent it back with one of the other neighbours who had gone to that mass. We didn't get presents very often. I kept that little tool set for years, not only because it came from him, but because it was just for me.

People wonder why I thought of becoming a priest. I suppose it was the fact that these men were so highly respected by everybody in the community. Later, when I read the lives of the English martyrs, I saw a similarity to our priests. Our priests weren't getting killed, but like the English martyrs at the time of Elizabeth I, they were itinerant priests, travelling alone through the countryside, from house to house, saying mass. It was a totally unstructured church. These priests went to the people and the people gathered around them. There was a tremendously good feeling about that. It made me want to do the same. I can't remember ever wanting to be anything but a priest—except maybe for the Canadian three-year-old's dream of being a Mountie and always wanting to be a pilot. But I wanted to be a pilot even after I was a priest. To fly. I've always been fascinated by flying. But I always said I was going to be a priest. So, when I graduated—one of two boys in a graduating class of 17—it was taken for granted that the next step for me was the seminary. It wasn't that my parents pushed me to go to the seminary, or that the Sisters talked me into it—although they were very happy about it. I wanted to go to the seminary. And so it was that on September 3, 1946, I set off for the seminary in London, Ontario.

CHAPTER 2

CLERICAL TRAINING

There was never any question about which seminary I would attend. Bishop Philip Pocock, who was bishop of Saskatoon at the time, had previously taught at St. Peter's Seminary in London, Ontario. Bishop Pocock just assumed that St. Peter's was the seminary for us and arranged for applications to be sent to us.

The only way to get to London was by train. There was a small contingent of young men from Saskatoon going off to the seminary that year. They booked a compartment on the train and invited me to join them. This became quite a dilemma for me—whether to get a first-class ticket and ride with them or get a tourist ticket and not be able to travel with them. In the end, I bought a first-class ticket, which probably cost 20 or 30 per cent more than the tourist ticket. The station agent in Rosetown gave me a piece of his mind when I bought the ticket, accusing me of wasting my parents' hard-earned money by buying a first-class ticket. I knew, too, that my mother and father had used all their savings to buy me new clothes and provide me with pocket money for the seminary. The diocese would pay tuition, room and board. This expense was considered a loan to be paid back in full if one left before ordination. Only half of the loan had to be repaid if one was ordained. When I left for London, I had with me a good suit and a good overcoat, and I was travelling first-class.

My companions on the train were Bob Pravda, Charlie Gibney, Norm Andries, Benny Provost and Des Leeper. They were all a little older than I was, having been at university or in the Armed Forces. They were taking me along as "the kid." Two others joined us in London, Jim Mahoney and Al Pich. We became a solid group in London, the Westerners at the seminary.

Our departure date allowed us a week in Toronto. Toronto was an exciting place for a kid from Rosetown. I stayed with an uncle and aunt and joined the others in visiting museums, taking a boat trip to Niagara and going to a lot of movies. We had a whirlwind seven days. My parents had given me $100 for the year, and my travelling companions assured me that if I needed more money they would help me. Before we left Toronto, some of them had run out of money and I had given most of my money to them. By the time I got to the seminary, I had hardly anything left except IOU's from my new friends.

The next year, there were 23 of us from Saskatchewan on the train going to the seminary. We took the cheapest fare. They put us in an old colonial coach that had been used to bring settlers out West. It had a charcoal stove at one end and wooden seats that doubled as beds. We all brought whatever food we could, and shared it. But the modest accommodation of that and subsequent years' train rides never tarnished the memory of that first grand trip.

St. Peter's Seminary was, for a person from Saskatchewan, an awe-inspiring building. It had been built by Bishop Francis Fallon in the mid-'20s and was an imposing neo-Gothic structure, set off by sweeping green lawns. The night we arrived we were met at the front door by Father Jim Carrigan, who later became the rector, and escorted to the living quarters. It felt like we were entering a prison. The place had a coldness about it, an institutional feel that it never lost.

We each had our own room and, although the room was sparsely furnished, it was luxury for me because it was the first time I'd ever had my own room. Here I had a desk. I had a chair. I had a place to hang my clothes. Over the years at the seminary, I became accustomed to hearing complaints about the food. But it was far better than the food we had at home. At the seminary we often had raspberries for dessert or other things that we never had at home. One summer when I came home for holidays, my mother brought out a jar of raspberries which she had been saving, because she wanted something special to welcome me home. For the rest of the family, those raspberries were a special treat. For me, they had become ordinary.

Life in the seminary was shaped by the rule. Our day started at 5:30 a.m. with a loud bell and it ended at 9:30 p.m. when another bell sent us to bed. In between there were prayers, classes, meals and recreational activities. And always there was order and discipline. Each day was the same as the previous one and the last year was the same as the first.

We had to maintain silence at all times, and we were not allowed to have another person in our room. Another person entering the room without the permission of the rector or senior staff meant instant expulsion. There was no smoking in the seminary. There were no radios. There were no newspapers. There was recreation for one hour each evening and Wednesday and Saturday afternoons. It was a very closed society, a very ordered life.

The seminarians came from a variety of backgrounds. There were young men from the Windsor area who had grown up with the Ford Motor Company. There had been a big strike at Ford that year. They talked about the strike and about the hardships their families had endured. Some of the seminarians came from mining families in Sudbury and another group of Polish descent from Pennsylvania also came from mining families. This mingling of people from varied backgrounds was a new experience for me. We didn't have much opportunity to talk, though. Most of our social exchange took the form of athletic activity—football, baseball, hockey. We had good playing fields and good players, so the games were stimulating and enjoyable. I began to learn these sports, but never became adept at them, much as I would have liked to.

Everyone at the seminary got a nickname, usually within ten minutes of their arrival. I was tall and lanky and must have looked like I might have fallen off a horse, so my nickname became Tex. My friend Al Pich and I had a stand-up joke which went like this: He would say, "Howdy, stranger. What's your name?"

"Tex," I would reply.

"Where you from, Tex?"

"Saskatchewan."

Our seven years of seminary training were divided into two periods: three years of philosophy and four years of theology. While we were studying philosophy, we could take a BA through the University of Western Ontario. The philosophy program included Latin, French and English. The Rosetown experience was back to haunt me. Our theological studies could not be applied towards a degree. They can now, but they couldn't at that time. After our four years of theology we were ordained.

The chapel was the centre of our activity. Each day began there. Each priest celebrated an individual mass and the rector celebrated mass for the students. We would file into our pews, wearing cassocks and surplices (with old ragged clothes underneath), to follow the mass of the day, in Latin, of course, and receive Holy Communion. After a 15-minute thanksgiving we marched down to breakfast. That was eaten in silence, while we listened to readings from books carefully selected by the rector. We took turns reading for 15 minutes, passages which we had diligently prepared. A mispronounced word or incorrectly inflected sentence could elicit a terse reprimand.

Each of us bought a set of books. The moral set was by Prummer, the dogmatic set by Tanquerry. The theology course was essentially a repetition of what my mother had taught me 15 years before. The seminary had a very small library. In one corner were shelves of books that we were not supposed to read. You had to have special permission from the rector or a senior staff member to get a book from this Index section. There probably wasn't much demand. We would have considered it sinful to read a book from the Index.

Scripture was one of our weakest courses. We had our first Scripture class during our first year of theology. The class was given by the rector, Monsignor A.P. Mahoney, and consisted simply of reading the Bible from beginning to end. We used the Douay-Rheims version. The following years of Scripture study were also very weak. All my life I felt ill-equipped because of the poor training we had in Scripture.

We also had very little training in liturgy or preaching. During seven years in the seminary, most of us probably only preached three or four times, and then only to our classmates, using a memorized sermon.

Spiritual direction was considered a very important part of our life. Every seminarian was assigned to one of the priests on staff, who directed him in his formation and spiritual life. I had Father Fergus Lafferty as spiritual director for seven years. I went to confession every week and saw him for advice and counsel once a month. He was kind and understanding and never pushed me too hard.

At the beginning and end of each year, and sometimes in between, there were retreats—a time of more intense prayer, more intense silence, more intense pursuit of spiritual goals. I was always a bit puzzled when these visiting retreat leaders preached about spiritual life. What did it mean, I wondered, to have a spiritual life, beyond the life we already had.

A few startling ideas popped up during our education. Most of them came from Father Leo Flynn, who taught a course in social ethics. One of his first assignments as a curate had been in Windsor, where he got involved with the labour movement. For his course he used Rerum Novarum, the social encyclical written by Pope Leo XIII in 1891, and Quadragesimo Anno, written by Pius XI in 1931. Rerum Novarum dealt with the conditions of people in the work force and the right to unionize. It dealt with the rich and the poor and condemned both free enterprise capitalism and atheistic communism. This was brand new to me. I had never heard of the social encyclicals, nor had it ever occurred to me that the Church had anything to say about this aspect of life. Yet here we were studying it in the seminary. It had particular impact because among us were young men from Windsor, who had lived in a situation where that social doctrine was very relevant.

In my third year of philosophy, I made the team for the annual debate. The question we debated was whether one was bound by communitive justice to pay a fixed amount of income tax. We lost the debate on a technicality, but it was an important event for me, not only because it was an honour to be chosen for the debate team, but also because it was the first time I was challenged on a social justice issue.

As a rule, we did not pay much attention to politics. I only remember voting once, although there must have been other times when we were eligible to vote. There was a special poll for the seminary and it generally went completely Liberal except for five or six Conservatives, depending on how many Morands were enrolled. The Morand family produced six priests and they were all Conservatives.

There may have been uniformity along political lines, but it ended there. The seminary had two distinct classes of people. There were the priests, who had their own daily order, who had different meals served at their own table, who had their own recreational room and their own cars, who dressed in full clerical suits and kept themselves apart from us. Then there were the students. Being ordained was like going from private to lieutenant.

We students were very close, like a team. We depended on each other. When anyone left the seminary, we were all affected. It was as if it were wartime and one of our squadron had been shot down. We thought of him as "lost."

Those of us who could get jobs worked during the summer holidays. Most of my summers were spent working at the Co-op store in Rosetown. One year my father wanted me to work with him on the pipeline where he was employed, but the bishop said pipelines were no place for seminarians to work and that was the end of that. I worked around home that summer at repairs and chores. Our farm was falling into disrepair, as my father had to earn a living off the farm.

During my years at the seminary, my mother was very ill. She suffered from polycythemia, a disease that I now have. She was constantly in and out of hospital, hemorrhaging and getting new blood. She had good days and bad days, but she was sick for seven years. Once I came home because they thought she was dying. One of the seminarians, Bernard Wall, gave me $100 to fly home. He had had a job as a salesman before entering the seminary and had saved some money. I'm sure he never expected to get any of that $100 back, and I've always tried to imitate that example of generosity.

Because of my mother's deteriorating health and need to be near a hospital, my dad moved the house into Rosetown during my last year in the seminary. Mother's hope was that she would live to see me a priest. It was my hope, too, but it was not to be. She died less than a year before my ordination, which took place May 30, 1953.

It can be gently spring or already decidedly summer at the end of May in Saskatchewan. But not that year. May 30 was a muddy, miserable day. It rained steadily all day, and rain in Rosetown in those days without pavement rendered roads and streets virtually impassable. Nevertheless, aunts, uncles and cousins congregated for the ordination, which took place in St. Joseph's Convent Chapel in Rosetown, and for the banquet that was held afterwards in the Legion Hall.

And so the seminary years had come to an end. I was ordained. I was a young cleric. I had the black suit, white collar, straw hat and shiny shoes. I said my breviary faithfully. I knew where the amices were kept at church. I knew how to hear confessions. I thought I knew all the things you had to do as a priest. Those seven years in the seminary had prepared us to fit into any parish instantly. It was like military training, preparing a soldier to fit into military operations anywhere. In looking back now on the seminary training we received, I see the gaps, the training we did not receive, and I see that the goal of our formation was not growth, it was obedience. We were taught to follow the rule, and the rule covered every occasion, every conceivable incident or decision from the beginning to the end of every day. If we broke the rule, we had to tell our superiors or spiritual director. When I think back on it, what amazes me is that no one seemed to mind. Everyone took it for granted. We were training to be something very special and we had been taught that it required this kind of discipline, this kind of obedience, this kind of total unquestioning acceptance of the rule, this acceptance of authority. No one seemed to worry about it. We just accepted it. In fact, we worked hard at becoming totally obedient. I certainly did, because if this was what I had to do to be a priest, then I wanted to do it. But it does strike me as odd, now that I think about it, that no one questioned this blind obedience to the rule. No one questioned whether or not it had any formative value. No one questioned whether it had anything to do with Church or Christ. No one questioned whether it had anything to do with community. It was the rule and the rule was supposed to make you into a priest.

The summer after my ordination was spent in the country parish of Milden, helping Father Denis O'Driscoll, an Irish priest who had been ordained six years. He had a tremendous load because of the distances he had to cover. I helped teach catechism and celebrate mass in parish chapels. But my career as a curate was short-lived. The diocese did not have a canon lawyer and Bishop Francis J. Klein felt it should have one. He decided that I would be the canon lawyer. So, in September 1953, I began three pleasant years of study at St. Paul's Seminary, University of Ottawa. Canon law fitted my whole style; I found it easy. There was a great camaraderie among the small group of students and I made a lot of lasting friendships.

The rule at St. Paul's was not as strict as the rule at St. Peter's. We were allowed to go out any time we wanted to. I used the freedom to catch up on all the movies I had missed during my seminary years. Sometimes I went to movies eight days in a row or to film festivals. I was also able to buy a small car, which I used to travel around the Ottawa-Quebec area to visit my relatives and go skiing.

At the end of our first year, we received a Bachelor in Canon Law; after the second year, a Licence in Canon Law; and after the third year, a doctorate. In the beginning, the bishop wasn't sure whether I should go on for the doctorate, but because I did so well the first two years, it was decided that I should complete the doctorate. For my thesis, I wrote *Faculties of Canadian Military Chaplains*, which was, in effect, a handbook for military chaplains. I thought it would be useful to them and could be sold to pay for the publishing. In doing the research for the thesis, I met a lot of military chaplains and became close friends with many of them. At the time, I saw no contradiction in priests being engaged in the military.

I defended my thesis, got my doctorate and headed home with some cousins in a new car, bought by my brother. The afternoon we arrived in Saskatoon, I burned my hands quite severely on the wiring and the car burned up. My hands were bandaged when I reported to my next assignment, which was the parish of St. Paul's Cathedral in Saskatoon.

St. Paul's parish was an inner-city parish. There were always several priests stationed at the old rectory. As a seminarian I used to stop by there, so I knew the priests. Joe O'Leary and Dennis Mulcahey were the two senior priests. Don Macgillivray was younger; he had been there for six years. Jim Mahoney, who was teaching at St. Paul's High School, had been there for four years. I knew how these priests worked. Their style was to be kind to the poor and the aged. All of them had a wonderful way of working with people. They had no official pastoral plan. Their understanding of their function was implicit in their activity. You said mass on time and you looked after the sick, the poor and the aged. The two senior priests gave me responsibility for the altar boys, the young people's club and the Catholic Women's League.

The year I was a sub-deacon, Bishop Klein asked me to drive him around the diocese when he did his annual circuit, administering the Sacrament of Confirmation and visiting all the parishes. Each community welcomed him with a gathering at which there would be alcohol. It was all perfectly normal, but it was very upsetting to me in the beginning because I didn't realize that priests ever drank.

Imagine my consternation, then, at discovering that the priests at St. Paul's had a drinking problem. Some of the laity of the parish probably knew what was going on. Later, I heard the term "the problem of Irish priests." But I was young and innocent, and for me it became a major problem—looking after two alcoholic priests, not being able to do anything about their condition and lying about what was wrong with them. People would ask where Father was or why he wasn't feeling well, and we young priests had to cover for them.

I plunged into the work that had been assigned to me. I organized the young people into a Marian Club, started a Business Girls' Association, worked with the altar boys and the Catholic Woman's League. I helped Bishop Klein with the chancery work and I helped with masses on Sunday. We all helped give instruction to prospective converts. The three young priests—Fathers Jim Mahoney, Don Macgillivray and myself—spent hours each evening in the parlours, giving instructions to people who wanted to join the church.

One lunch-time I was called to the phone to speak to someone who wanted to see me that night. We always carried our day books and I remember taking the book out of my black suit pocket, looking at it and saying, "I'm very sorry, but I can't see you tonight. I already have too many people to see." We worked out another time and I thought the incident was finished. When the meal was over, Father Mulcahey left the table early and went upstairs to his room. When I passed his door a few minutes later, he called out, "I want to talk to you," and motioned me into his room. I could see he had been drinking. He said, "You sit down over there. I've got something to tell you." I was absolutely petrified because he was an older priest, because I had never dealt with an alcoholic and because I could see he was angry.

"I heard you downstairs," he said. "I heard you tell someone that you didn't have time to talk to them. Well, let me tell you something. One time I used to be just like you. I was young and I was healthy and I used to have lots of people come to me. I used to have a lot of people who counted on me and I used to give great sermons at church. I was just like you. Well, now you think I'm an old bum, I know you do. You look down on me, but I want to tell you one thing. I used to be just like you and I don't ever again want to hear you tell anyone that you don't have time to see them." To this day I remind myself that I must never be too busy to see anyone.

The normal length of a pastoral assignment was five years, so I expected to be at St. Paul's that long. But during our retreat the following summer, I was called into the bishop's suite. "You know," he said, "we're going to start a seminary and I've decided that you'd probably be the best person to start it." That came as a complete shock. Because I was so young, I never dreamt I would be given such an assignment.

That year, 1957, there had been an unprecedented number of young men wanting to enter the priesthood. The big seminaries were full. In Saskatoon and Regina alone there were 12 young men who could not get into any of the major seminaries in the East or in Edmonton. In response to this situation, the bishop decided to convert the former St. Ann's Senior Citizens Home, an old brick house at 403 Clarence Avenue North soon to be vacant, into a seminary. I was to establish and administer the seminary and Father Joe Bisztyo was to act as the spiritual director.

Starting a seminary was not a small task, but I thought it would be easy. All you had to do was write the rule, get the rooms ready, make sure the plumbing was working, find someone to cook and buy the Corn Flakes, and you'd be off and running. During the month of August, I was able to contact the 12 young men and get them registered at the university. We bought some tools and started getting ready to fix up the old house. Renovations were delayed, however, because the house had not yet been vacated. On the feast of the Canadian Martyrs, September 27, 1957, the Sisters and the residents moved into the new St. Ann's Home and we moved into the old one with 12 seminarians. A very auspicious number. Just Joe and I, two lay-women cooks and 12 seminarians—that was the beginning of St. Pius X Seminary.

Our seminary didn't have the grandeur of St. Peter's Seminary in London or St. Paul's in Ottawa, but I set about making it a similar institution internally. We wrote a rule very much like the rule under which I had lived at St. Peter's. We would dress in black and everyone would wear cassocks. Strict obedience to the rector was of importance.

Our seminary was different from the others in only one major respect. The students were to take their philosophy classes at St. Thomas More College, which was affiliated with a secular university. Years later, another bishop told me that when Bishop Klein went to Rome for his *ad limina* visit after the seminary was founded, he was reprimanded by the Congregation of Seminaries who informed him that he had not obtained the proper permission. Bishop Klein didn't know you had to get special permission to found a seminary. When he went to see the Pope, John XXIII reportedly had a piece of paper in front of him which indicated that Bishop Klein had broken the rule by starting the seminary without the permission of the Congregation and by allowing the seminarians to attend a secular university. The story goes that Pope John XXIII was quite interested in this idea and asked Bishop Klein what it meant to the seminarians. Did they really study with other students? Did they take classes with other students, with women? Bishop Klein said they did and was bracing himself for another reprimand when John XXIII reputedly said, "I think it's a good idea, but don't tell the Congregation of Seminaries about it."

I was the rector of St. Pius X Seminary from 1957 until 1964. During that period of time I did a lot of carpentry, rebuilding the inside of the seminary so the old portion would be more comfortable for the seminarians. Each year new young men swelled the ranks of the original 12. They passed through a seminary training that was basically the same as the one I had gone through. Though I think I treated them in a very strange, overpowering way, I like to think that they saw through the rule, into the real quality that makes up the essence of human friendship. I certainly counted those men among my closest friends, both then and now. Although most of them had left the priesthood by the end of the turbulent 60s, I've always said they were the best seminarians we ever could have had. They were fine people; they had the right qualities for priests.

Bishop Klein was never short of jobs to do and he saw that I had the ability to do a lot of work. A few years after we'd started the seminary, he had a new idea. He was always getting new ideas. This one was to begin a Catholic Information Centre. It would offer instructions in the faith to adults, have a social action department that would raise awareness of social issues, and promote the Church through the media. Bishop Klein hired Grant Maxwell, a family man and journalist, as co-director of the centre and asked me if I would join Grant so there would be a cleric, too. I knew it was going to be a lot of work, added to my seminary responsibilities, but by this time I had also found that I could do a vast amount of work. Besides running the seminary I was already working in the chancery office—having been named Defender of the Bond of the Catholic marriage tribunal for the province of Saskatchewan. I was teaching ethics and religion to nurses at St. Paul's hospital and I was assisting at the cathedral every Sunday. There was no free time in my schedule, but I enjoyed work. I agreed to take on the Catholic Centre position. Over the next few years, that became a very heavy load.

Through the Catholic Centre, the diocese became very much involved in the social questions of the times. Grant and I worked together, trying to see how the Church should respond to these questions. One of the biggest issues we faced was the health care question, which turned into the medicare crisis of 1962.

In 1962, the CCF government in Saskatchewan announced that it was going to bring in a public medical insurance plan. A lot of people felt that this was the first step towards full-fledged communism and the plan was opposed by practically everyone outside the CCF Party. To be honest, I have to admit that I didn't have a clear position on the issue. I had heard some very important people call the CCF "Communists." My own bishop and other church leaders were unsure what position to take. Father Athol Murray from Notre Dame College at Wilcox, Saskatchewan, was violently opposed to medicare. He came up to Saskatoon and spoke to a huge crowd at St. Paul's High School, just behind the Catholic Center. He took off his collar and hinted at armed opposition to the government's plans.

Grant and I had no clear idea what the role of the Church should be in this debate. One person in our midst, however, had a very clear idea what should happen and what the position of the Church should be. Bob Von Pilis was an old Austrian who had been interned in Canada during the war as an enemy alien and had stayed here after his release.

He had a deep sense of social justice, acquired in many ways, but in particular through the Coady Institute at St. Frances Xavier University, Antigonish, Nova Scotia and through associations with Baroness De Hueck at Combermere, Ontario. He arrived in Saskatoon—a great lump of a man with a noticeable limp—to take on the editorship of a prominent farm paper. At least, that was how he earned his living. His passion was to get the Church involved in social issues. His position on the medicare question was unequivocal. Where he came from, national medical insurance was as ordinary as pure drinking water. There was no doubt in his mind that prepaid medicare should be available to everyone, and he was determined to see such a plan put into place in Saskatchewan.

In the summer of 1962, the seminary was quiet because the seminarians were on holidays. The Catholic Centre, too, was relatively quiet, although I was still giving classes there. The centre was in an old building on Spadina Crescent, where the Cavalier Hotel now stands. In the last days of the doctors' strike, the government negotiating team was in the Bessborough Hotel, across the street from the Catholic Centre. The doctors' group was in the medical building, just down the street. Lord Thompson had been brought over from England as a negotiator and Bob Von Pilis was escorting him back and forth, from one side to the other. He picked the Catholic Centre as their island in between and so, whether I liked it or not, I was in the middle of the medicare crisis. Those 23 days of the strike seemed like 23 months. The tension was tremendous, and for me the stress was aggravated by my own uncertainty as to what should happen.

By the 19th day, it seemed like the negotiations were hopelessly stalled and violence seemed almost inevitable. Any place else the kind of anger that was generated by this strike would have turned into violence, but because of our non-violent history, that didn't happen in Saskatchewan. Bob von Pilis wasn't about to give up, either. He kept shuttling the negotiator back and forth. On July 23 the strike ended, the Saskatoon Agreement was signed and the first public medical care insurance policy of North America came into effect. As everyone knows, other provinces followed and soon the whole country adopted the idea.

Through Bob Von Pilis and the medicare crisis, I got my first insight into politics and political power. You can pray all you want for changes, but before you can have a social change, someone has to make a political judgment. Someone has to decide that something will be done. That's what Bob Von Pilis showed me. I began to see the necessity of political activity and I saw that politicians take on tremendous responsibility, sacrificing privacy and freedom so that others may have a better life. The medicare experience shook me out of a very sheltered, com-

27

placent, clerical view of the world. I was thrust into the arena, where, even though I wasn't involved in the action, I was close enough to see how change took place.

Interestingly enough, after it was all over, we learned that all the media in Saskatchewan had opposed the government, except the Prairie Messenger, a weekly newspaper published by the Benedictine monks at Muenster, Saskatchewan. Their courage, too, showed me the importance of deciding that something needs change and then being prepared to speak out and put yourself on the line for your belief.

Bob Von Pilis was already ill during the medicare crisis. He wasn't that old, but he had cancer of the lungs and a heart condition. He once told me that he hoped he would die from the heart condition. He was mounting the platform to give a speech in Lloydminster when he collapsed. We buried him on February 29, 1964. In his will he left me his car, the only new car I had ever had. I was to have the pleasure of driving it for only a few months.

Until I was 30, the farthest I had travelled was from Saskatoon to eastern Canada. My first trip outside Canada had a profound impact on me. It was 1958 and I was rector of the seminary. The trip was the first large pilgrimage to Europe from Saskatoon. The tour was to go to Lourdes for the 100th anniversary of the great shrine, to Rome and to the world exhibition in Brussels. I organized the trip for 43 people, through Sinfonia Travel. Fred Sydow, who owned Sinfonia, accompanied me on the trip, but he was as green at this job as I was. The group was made up of people from around Saskatoon—married couples, seminarians, single women, old bachelors, children and university students. Fred Sydow's daughter was the youngest member of the group. She was 11. One lady in the group was 74. She was going back to see the Black Forest, where she had come from. The oldest man on the tour was Jim Stack, a retired farmer from Asquith who had a lot of money, but had never been further from Asquith than Delisle. It was a brand-new experience for him, a brand-new experience for us all.

The ocean crossing was the roughest the Homeric had ever made. I lost 11 pounds in eight days, all over the side of the ship. We arrived in Le Havre on May 10 and took the boat train to Paris. The French rail system was unlike anything we had ever seen in Canada. Trains left on time and went fast. If you weren't on the train at departure time, you missed it.

French hotels were equally surprising and mysterious. We had booked rooms in a very cheap, third-rate hotel on the Left Bank. Nobody knew how to go up the little elevator in the middle of the lobby and there was great consternation when we tried to get everybody a room.

From Paris we went to Lisieux, a town about 80 miles west of Paris.

The Allies had used the road to come up from Caen and Normandy during the summer of 1944, but our purpose in following it was to see the shrine of St. Theresa. Our guide that day was a Frenchman, an agnostic, and I remember being shocked by that. I had the group pray together that we might convert him on the way.

A few days later, my Catholic sensibilities were shaken again, this time by a visit to the Pantheon in Paris. Turning a Catholic church into a memorial to the French Revolution was an abhorrent desecration in my eyes. The soldier guide would click his heels and stop, point into a tomb and say, "Jean Jacques Rousseau." We'd stop for a moment, take a look at Jean Jacques Rousseau and go on to the next one, where he'd name another historical person and we would peer into the tomb. I don't know whether I was more shocked by the presence of these famous intellectuals and political figures in what used to be a Catholic church, or by this French soldier who was showing us along as though this was the way God had intended it in the beginning. Napoleon's tomb, too, was inside a church. It was positioned in such a way that visitors had to bow their heads on entering and I remember wondering if this was intentional. I also remember wondering why a whole nation had followed this man to their destruction, and thinking they could have all been good Catholics saying their prayers the whole time.

From Paris we travelled to Lourdes, which is a long day's train journey with two or three changes. When we arrived at a station, we had about 60 seconds to get all the bags off one train and onto another. We needed a system. There were 43 people and 76 pieces of luggage. We decided to divide the group into pitchers and catchers; this was going to be a great game. I was a pitcher. As I was standing in that French train throwing bags out, I looked down and marvelled at the 74-year-old lady catching bags as if they were baseballs. It took a few more days for everyone to really get in the swing of looking out for one another, but by the end of the tour those 43 people had become so close, so much of a family, that the separation at the end of the trip was very painful. We had several reunions afterwards, and it was always like a family reunion.

At that time, I was very caught up in the kind of devotion that we witnessed at Lourdes. The night-time processions of thousands of people singing hymns, illuminated by thousands of candles, and all the miracles and emotional expressions of faith were overwhelming. I remember looking up at the illuminated medieval castle above Lourdes, turning to the person beside me and saying, "It's just like heaven."

It was somewhere between Lourdes and Monaco that I had one of the best meals I've ever eaten. It was a long ride, about 14 hours. The guide we had then (Uncle Henry we called him) told us we had to take our lunch with us. We thought we could get off the train anywhere and buy lunch, because you could do that in Redpath, Rosetown and McGee. Uncle Henry knew what he was talking about. That train ran non-stop for 14 hours and it didn't have a diner on it. Uncle Henry had arranged for lunches to be packed at the hotel in Lourdes before we left. When we opened the brown bags and saw two pieces of hard black bread and two hard-boiled eggs, we were not impressed. But as the day wore on and there were no stops and no place to buy any food, it became clear that the brown bags contained our meal for the day. By the time we gathered round our brown paper bags, we were grateful to be together and grateful for that meal. Two hard-boiled eggs and two pieces of hard, black bread.

The train took us along the southern coast of France to Marseilles, through Monaco, then into Italy to Genoa and Milan. From there we went by bus and I can remember the thrill of descending through the Apian mountains into Rome, imagining that we were coming like Peter and Paul had come 2,000 years before, although from a different direction. Seeing Rome was an absolutely startling and wonderful experience for someone from Rosetown. We realized that the culmination of our visit to Rome would have to be an audience with the Pope, and we had not booked one. We knew that a French Canadian group that had been on the Homeric with us, had booked an audience—although they didn't want to admit it. They were our only hope. I can't remember exactly how we finagled our way in there, but on the Sunday that the French Canadians were to meet the Pope, we were standing beside them. When Pope Pius XII entered the audience hall we were filled with celestial joy. This was the peak of the Church, the triumphal Church that we had grown up in. Pius XII was a frail little old man. He was to die that same fall. But his entrance into that room had a powerful impact on the people assembled there. When he came to our group, Fred Sydow lifted up his 11-year-old daughter. The Pope reached out, touched her, then turned to go back to the front of the group to have a picture taken with the French Canadian delegation. I could see that we were going to be left out of the picture. I took out an American $5 bill and slipped it to one of the big guards dressed in papal uniform. He tucked it in his pocket, took me by the back of my suit and practically carried me through the crowd to the front. When the picture was taken, I was standing very close to the Pope. For the boy from Rosetown, now 30-years-old and a priest, it was the most exciting moment of a lifetime.

My cousin, Michael Fitzgerald, who was working for the Food and Agricultural Organization (FAO) of the United Nations in Rome, arranged for the men in our group to drive to Monte Cassino with a Major Ignatio. He was a Canadian with FAO, who had been the officer in charge of the chemical warfare unit at Monte Cassino during that long winter of 1943-44 when the Germans held the Allies at bay from the old Benedictine abbey. The day we visited was the 14th anniversary of the breaking of the Hitler line at that point. We visited the Polish and Canadian cemeteries, the monastery where Benedict had tried to save Western culture after the collapse of the Roman Empire and the place where Thomas Aquinas had done his preliminary studies. You could see Aquino, his home town, from Monte Cassino. Instead of joining the Benedictines as his family wanted, Thomas joined the Dominicans, but he had gone to school at Monte Cassino, as had many other people in my history books. Standing in Monte Cassino, I felt I was reliving Western European history.

The trip continued up through Italy to Ravenna and into Austria, where Bob Von Pilis' wife showed us the city of Strauss. Then we travelled back through Germany, up the Rhine by boat to Brussels, where we spent several days at the World's Fair.

The glory of Britain cast its shiny aura over the entire fair. The host Belgians were still trying to glorify colonial rule those few months before the Congo was to erupt. And off to the side somewhere was a little pavilion called the European Common Market. It was only about 30 feet square. They were giving out little pamphlets, promoting the concept of a single European market. I knew that would never work, so I didn't spend much time there. After the fair, we toured England. Then the rest of the group returned home on the Homeric, while I crossed over to Ireland and spent ten days touring the homeland of my forefathers and meeting relatives near Pettigo, the village my great-great- grandfather had left in the 1830s.

There was great sadness in London the day our tour came to an end. That disparate group of individuals had come together through sharing a goal, praying, living and eating together, and helping one another. They had become a community. I was to see it happen again in many other situations, but that was the first time I witnessed the formation of a community. For that reason, the trip was very important to me.

A second trip, which had none of the grandeur of the first one, nevertheless had a profound influence on me. It was in 1959. Father Al Pich and I went to South America primarily to visit my sister, Marguerite, who was then living in Brazil. Her husband was an engineer and had been hired by a Brazilian oil company to look for oil up the Amazon. It was also an opportunity for us to see a bit of Latin America and visit a number of friends, among them, Gillermo de Souza, a priest from Panama who had studied canon law with me in Ottawa. He had been sent to Canada by his bishop to study canon law and had never learned to speak English or French very well. He hated canon law, hated Ottawa, hated the snow, hated the winter and sometimes even hated me. He did like to play Hearts and I used to play the game with him every night. He was always saying he wished the course was over so he could get back to *his people*. I could never figure out what he meant by that.

Al Pich and I began our six-week tour by flying from Miami to Panama in an old DC 6, landing in the Panamanian jungle about 4 a.m. It was the first time I had ever been in a jungle, the first time I'd ever smelled tropical growth. Because it was all so new and different, I was nervous driving in from the airport through that jungle. Our hotel was a Hilton, the first hotel I had seen with no outside doors, just gratings. In the tropics, you don't need to keep out the cold.

There was a church across the street from the hotel. Early the next morning we communicated to the parish priest, with the little bit of Spanish we'd learned and the pastor's little bit of English, our desire to say mass, which he was happy to arrange. After mass, he took us to the rectory, a Spanish-style house, and offered us the cup of coffee that always follows mass in Latin America. I was fascinated by the sugar bowl, and puzzled by its four spindly legs standing in a trough of water. I soon learned that this was an attempt to keep ants out of the sugar. When the priest lifted the lid off the sugar bowl, the top of the sugar was black with ants. I took a spoonful of sugar, lowered it into my coffee, drowned the ants and sipped. I've had a lot of cups of coffee like that since then, but that first one was hard to swallow.

After coffee, we went back to the hotel and tried to get a taxi to take us to Gillermo de Souza's address. We couldn't get a driver to take us there. They all said, "You don't want to go there." Finally we persuaded a driver with American dollars. He said, "I'll take you, but I won't bring you back." I had no idea what that meant, but we got into the taxi. In less than five minutes, we were let off at the edge of the first slum I had ever seen. The two- and three-storey houses, teeming with women and children, had been built out of barrack blocks, salvaged during the construction of the Panama Canal. It was the first time I'd seen open sewers, the first time I'd seen naked children, the first time I'd seen swollen bellies.

As we stood transfixed by this shocking scene, some women approached who seemed to know, probably because we were wearing clerical clothes, that we wanted to see the padre. They took us down a narrow street, at the end of which was a little shack built out of cinderblocks. "This is the *casa de padre*, the house of the priest," they said, but there was no one in the house. From their hand signs, we gathered that he would be back and we should wait in the house. A barrier, about a foot high across the bottom of the doorway had me baffled. It obviously could not prevent anyone from entering and I couldn't imagine why it was there. Later I learned that it was there to hold out the sewer when it backs up in the street. All the houses have them. We stepped over this barrier into the darkness of the interior. The house was a cinderblock square, with a tin roof. Cockroaches crunched under our feet. That was a crucial moment in my life. Gillermo, the man I used to play Hearts with in Ottawa, had come back to be with his people. He lived in a room with one bed, one table and so many cockroaches that they couldn't escape his feet. Why would anyone do that?

Gillermo appeared shortly and greeted us warmly. He wanted to take us for dinner outside the slum, but I felt that we should see some of his parish. While he was taking us around, someone came to tell him there was a woman dying. We offered to accompany Gillermo. The woman, who had five children, weighed about 70 pounds and was dying from tuberculosis. She did, in fact, die that afternoon. We stood around her cot reading the prayers, in Latin, "Out of the depths I cry to thee, O Lord. Lord, hear my prayer." I had never been in the depths before. I had never seen anything dark before. I had never really understood those prayers before; in that place I understood them.

In Panama City, a 30-foot fence separates slums from luxury. It's like a country club on the Canal Zone side, where the Americans live. Inside that country club, the national security forces and the torturers of Latin America are trained by the American Army. In 1959 I didn't know that. I just thought it was awful to have the country divided like that. It was my first encounter with the North-South situation, which sets the very poor apart from the very rich as clearly as that fence.

In Colombia, Venezuela, Peru, every country we visited, we saw slums and brokenness. In Chile we experienced an earthquake and met Father Pat Peyton, who wanted us to help with his rosary crusade. After returning to Canada that year, I raised $50,000 to buy rosaries for Peyton's crusade.

After a few days in Argentina, we spent several weeks in Brazil, the last part of it with my sister in Belém, at the mouth of the Amazon. There again we ran into the Redemptorists, who were working along the Amazon. My sister and brother-in-law sent us home on a French Caravel, from Belém up through the Bahamas to New York. That was my first flight on a jet airplane.

A third trip that had a significant influence on me was a trip to Mexico I organized in 1961 for the Business Girls group of St. Paul's parish. My father, some seminarians and a few married couples joined us for the trip. We took a bus through the western United States into Mexico. It was one of the few opportunities I had to travel with my father and I was very interested in his observations. The first time we were besieged by beggars with their hands stretched out toward the windows of the bus, my dad simply said, "If we didn't have old-age pensions in Canada, they'd be doing that in Canada too." That's a profound observation. Unless there is a social system built into a country, there's only one way the poor can live and that's by begging.

Later, at the shrine of Our Lady of Guadalupe, my father had no difficulty going that last mile, praying and crawling on his knees to the shrine. The rest of us didn't make it. I saw stamina and a deep faith, tinged with Irish arrogance and guilt, in his perseverance.

I was fascinated to see traces of the civilizations that had existed in Mexico and had been destroyed by European Christians. The Spanish, I discovered, after beating Montezuma and the king of Mexico, had imposed on the people they conquered a foreign religion, a foreign culture, a foreign language—all in the name of Spain and Jesus. I had never been aware of this before and the revelation was most disturbing.

From Mexico City, the bus tour took us through eastern Mexico, crossing into the States at a place called Laredo. We went at least 500 miles out of the way so I could see the town named in my favourite song. I walked down the streets of Laredo singing, "As I walked out in the streets of Laredo, as I walked out in Laredo one day/ I spied a young cowboy all wrapped in white linen/ All wrapped in white linen as cold as the clay."

After my first trip to Latin America in 1959, I decided I wanted to go and work there. I paid off my seminary debt, cleared up my accounts and went to see the bishop. Bishop Klein just scoffed and said there was too much work to do in the parish. Two years later, when he went to Rome and met the 2,400 bishops of the world at the Second Vatican Council, he discovered that our diocese was very well off. He came back from that first session determined to send a team to Latin America. Pope John XXIII supposedly encouraged bishops in the northern world to send 10 per cent of their priests and religious to the South. I doubt if he ever said exactly that, but sending "papal volunteers" became an important gesture in the 60s.

In 1963, at the next sitting of the Council, Bishop Klein met with the bishop of Maceió, Brazil and arranged for a team from Saskatoon to go there. On Easter Saturday 1964, I was just leaving the Catholic Centre to visit a patient at St. Paul's Hospital when the bishop called me into his office, as he often did. We had just finished building the Catholic Centre and his new office was located there. "Sit down," he said. "We're sending priests to Brazil. Almost everyone has volunteered to go, but I've decided to send you, Father Don Macgillivray and Father Bernard Dunn." There it was. No discussion, no chance for the three of us to think about it or talk about whether we could work together or anything. It was decided for us and we obeyed. I was thrilled to be going and relieved that I didn't have to worry anymore about the seminary, the Catholic Center, or St. Paul's. In a few months' time, I would be starting a completely new kind of work. As I drove over to St. Paul's Hospital that day, keeping this secret deep within my heart because we weren't supposed to tell anyone, I felt tremendous excitement at beginning this new phase of my life.

CHAPTER 3

BRAZIL

On Easter Monday 1964, the priests of the Saskatoon diocese began their annual retreat. That was the first chance Don Macgillivray, Bernard Dunn and I had to talk about our assignment.

During the retreat, we heard on a radio which somebody had at the retreat house, that there had been a military revolution March 29 in Brazil. We knew nothing about the situation in Brazil, what a military revolution meant or how it was going to affect our work.

Over the following months, the team was expanded to include two nurses, Cécile Poilièvre and Ida Raiche. The five of us left Saskatoon August 2, 1964. Our first stop was Montréal. It was three years before Expo and Montréal's road system was being rebuilt. We rented a car to drive into the centre of the city, but it was almost impossible to drive on the muddy, unmarked roads. From Montréal we flew through New York to New Orleans, where my sister and her husband were then living. Stepping off the airplane in New Orleans was the first time most of us had encountered tropical heat. We were still wearing our black clerical clothes, of course, and the heat was almost unbearable. My sister and brother-in-law, who had lived in Brazil, told us what we could expect and what we should take with us—things we wouldn't be able to get in Brazil.

From New Orleans, we flew to Colombia. That was the first time we saw soldiers guarding every door in an airport. From Bogotá, we flew into Belém at the mouth of the Amazon. We arrived about 4 a.m., which I later found out is the usual time for North American flights to arrive. We were transferred through the darkness to the only tourist hotel then functioning in Belém. Today, Belém is a big, modern city with many hotels. My brother-in-law had told us that our hotel was the only place we would find air-conditioning, and we had to sit in a special corner of the beer parlour to find it. Don Macgillivray had never taken a drink of beer in his life, but that night he did. We drank beer in the corner of the hotel for at least an hour, trying to beat the staggering, tropical heat.

In Belém, we met the American Redemptorist priests who had already been working at a mission in the slums outside the city for ten years. Their pastoral style was traditional. They maintained a North American life-style and greeted us with open hospitality. Don, Bernard and I wanted to see the mission in Alagôas where we would be working. The two nurses decided to spend some time in Belém, working with papal volunteers in a health program run by the Americans. We were supposed to leave for Alagôas on a certain day, but the plane did not depart and we had to wait another day. We discovered such delays were common in Brazil. Finally, we flew down the north coast in an old Constellation, stopping seven or eight times. I rode in the cabin with the pilots. They were very friendly and one of them could speak English fairly well. They had to be good pilots because the airplane was not fit to fly. They had been told by the company that they couldn't use their brakes when they were landing, because the tires were too thin. So, they had to drop the airplane within 50 feet of the end of the runway and rely on gravity to bring it to a stop. They did that seven or eight times that day. We didn't have any flat tires. The airline, however, went out of business the following year.

We finally arrived in Maceió late in the afternoon and were met at the airport by two priests about our own age, Padre Pedro and Padre Solomao, who spoke some English. We were driven to the archbishop's residence—a huge uncomfortable old palace—typical of the Church that had prevailed in Brazil for centuries. We were received very warmly by the old archbishop, Dom Adelmo. We thought he was old, but his mother was there as well as his sister, who looked after the house. We were welcomed and asked the same questions by the archbishop, the mother and the sister: "Did your mother cry when you left? Did your father cry when you left? Did your brothers and sisters cry when you left?" Each of them asked us the same questions in French—a kind of French. We replied in our kind of French. They, of course, were just wondering how much sadness our departure had caused our relatives. We found out later that the family is the most important thing in Brazilian culture, so important that they couldn't imagine why we would leave our families to live that far away for so long. After the questions, the welcoming party turned to the cake—a huge iced cake. The archbishop's sister had a big knife and when she cut the cake it was just like cutting into an ant hill. Ants poured out of the cake, which they had literally hollowed out. We ate the cake, along with the ants. That's the way you do it. Then, the mother, the archbishop and the sister told us they had to go to another part of the state. They were leaving us in charge of the house, the three of us who had never been in the house before. We would have a week on our own to become acquainted with the area we would be working in and to talk to the two priests who had their own parishes.

We were each assigned a bedroom and shown the three toilets in the house. We didn't realize at the time that there was a rule about toilets in Brazil. You can't put toilet paper in the toilets, because it will plug them. A little pail sits beside the toilet bowel to receive the paper. Within 24 hours, all the toilets in the house were plugged and we were in dire straits.

After the archbishop left, we went to see if there was any food in the house. We opened the fridge and there was one sealer of water. That was all. It had been arranged that we would eat at a convent in another part of the city, but we were still surprised that there wasn't a single piece of food in the house.

During that week, one of our main objectives was to take the train up into the interior where União dos Palmares, the parish we were to work in, was situated. We were accompanied by the two priests and by an old man who lived in União. The train was called *Maria Fumasa*— Smokey Maria. This little steam-engine train took us 55 miles into the interior, through jungle, over rivers, past dug-out canoes and then up into the higher districts, where we saw sugar-cane growing on the mountain slopes. We had been told by Monsignor John Robinson, who had accompanied Bishop Klein on an earlier visit to the district, that the whole place looked like a golf course. I kept wondering where the golf course was. The only similarity between this terrain and a golf course was that it was green. And there were no clipped greens here; the sugar-cane all around us was 20 feet tall.

When we arrived in the village of União, we were certainly looked upon as foreigners and probably as oddballs. We were driven around the town in a jeep by Father Tertuliano, a Brazilian who had been looking after the parish, to see the little hospital and some of the schools. It was the middle of the rainy season and it was raining very hard. At the old pastor's house, we were again welcomed with a cake reception. There had been no full-time priest in the village for about four years. In spite of this, I had the feeling that the people were very skeptical about bringing in foreigners to do the parish work.

We spent the remainder of the week in Alagôas. During that time, one of the priests asked if I would give a lecture to the sociology class he was teaching at the university. He said he would translate it from English into Portuguese as I went along. I agreed and delivered an hour-long lecture on social services in Canada. Several years later, he told me that five minutes after I started to speak, he gave up on the translation and made up his own lecture till the end of the session. From Maceió we went south to Rio de Janeiro, where we met the two nurses who had flown down from Belém. That night we laughed ourselves silly telling about our experiences. That first week we found every situation and custom strange and funny because it didn't fit our patterns. On August 15, we started our orientation course at Petrópolis, the old imperial city outside Rio, where the emperor had lived. Petrópolis is very much like Banff, Alberta, a city in the mountains, cool all the time. In fact it gets quite cold when the clouds cover the city, as they often did that fall. In Petrópolis we met the group we were going to study with—64 people from 15 countries around the world. Everyone in the group wanted to be a missionary in Brazil. This course was one of the richest experiences of my life. We spent three months together learning about the culture and pastoral plan of Brazil, and learning Portuguese. Petrópolis was an extension of Fordham University and was under the overall direction of Ivan Illich, who was operating a similar school in Cuernavaca, Mexico, for the Spanish-speaking part of Latin America. The director of the school in Petrópolis was an American Franciscan, João (John) Vogel. John became a close friend of mine. He has since died of cancer. The purpose of the school was to prepare us to work within the Brazilian culture. They were not bringing in foreigners to impose a foreign mentality. For the first week, classes were conducted in English or French, mostly English. That first week had a tremendous effect on me. Of course, that week I understood it all. As we moved more into Portuguese, I absorbed less. One of the instructors at Petrópolis was a Jesuit priest from Fordham University, who lectured on cultural interchange. His perspective illuminated both the Gospels and the situation I was moving into. He gave the example of Peter the Apostle making a cultural transition when he went to meet Cornelius, the Roman centurion. Peter didn't want to go and Cornelius didn't want to meet Peter, because they belonged to two different cultures and two different religions. But Peter managed to pass through that cultural barrier and Cornelius became a Christian. I had never really understood that story before. Suddenly it had tremendous meaning for me.

Another instructor, a young doctor of sociology from Northwestern University in Chicago, gave us a week's course on communications. That was one of the most important educational experiences I ever had. Many of the ideas we learned that week I still use. He showed us how conversation can flow or be blocked, how misunderstanding a single word can change the whole emphasis of a conversation and mislead people. He demonstrated that facts rarely get past the first set of ears, that they almost invariably get distorted in the second telling. It wasn't an extremely profound course; it just brought home to us how faulty or free-flowing communication can affect the way people react and work together. Of course, at language school it was important to learn how language gets blocked. But he was also there to show us that as foreigners, our ears would inevitably distort what was being said. Then the Portuguese started. We were divided into groups of four, based on our ability to speak the language. We were assigned to one of these groups after a simple test, administered by one of the instructors. Each of us had to go up to her and repeat the question she would ask in Portuguese. The director of the school could tell what level we were at by our ability to repeat the phrase. The sentence was very simple: "O senhor tem um cigaro?" ("Do you have a cigarette?") I can't remember what I said, but I know it didn't resemble the original question. The director must have thought that anyone with a doctorate couldn't be that stupid, so they put me in the middle group. As the weeks went on, students were moved to appropriate levels according to their progress. Naturally, I kept moving down until I was in the bottom group with three other hopeless cases. That's where I stayed until the end of the course. I have never worked so hard at anything with so little success. During my years in Brazil I did acquire a good speaking ability in Portuguese, but it came slowly and painfully, and initially from children. Learning to speak like a child, in fact, was a great advantage. If everyone spoke like a child all the time, communication would be improved, because children are always clear.

In Petrópolis we learned that the Brazilian Church had already recognized the fact that the pastoral they had been following for the last 300 years was not working. As a result, they had developed a new five-year pastoral plan. The idea of having a pastoral plan was new to me. Nobody had ever thought of having a pastoral plan for the Canadian Church, as far as I knew. The Brazilian pastoral plan, in fact, was very similar to the planning already underway at the Second Vatican Council. We took two key concepts from this Brazilian pastoral plan for our work in União: Christian community bases; and the necessity of preaching the Gospel clearly, so that people would be changed by the word of the Gospel.

The theologian who instructed us in Petrópolis was João Segundo, who later became one of the leading liberation theologians of Latin America. At that time, he was a young Uruguayan Jesuit. He could not speak English, French or Portuguese, so he lectured to us in Spanish and it was translated for us. Now he speaks at least two of these languages. Petrópolis had also been set up as a place for liturgical experimentation. The liturgy of the Roman Catholic rite was all still in Latin, but in Petrópolis they had permission to say mass in the vernacular. The first mass I ever said in English was in Petrópolis, Brazil. That doesn't seem remarkable today, but at the time it was extremely radical. We trained at Petrópolis for 3½ months. During that time, our attitudes changed profoundly; we learned how to think and do things differently. When the course was over, we had to go to our mission. At that point, I was basically still unable to speak or understand the language. We arrived in União dos Palmares December 22. It was three days before Christmas and no one had thought to tell us that Christmas in Brazil is different. It's not that Brazilians don't know how to celebrate Christmas. They do. However, their form of celebration bears absolutely no resemblance to Christmas celebrations in Canada. In Canada it's wintertime and cold and there's snow. Christmas in Canada is, generally speaking, a quiet family affair. There are family festivities, maybe a church liturgy, a Christmas tree, presents and lights outside. But that's not how you celebrate Christmas in Brazil. Christmas in Brazil is the loudest, wildest, noisiest night of the year and no one would ever go home because they'd miss all the excitement in the streets. There's dancing and ferris wheels and gambling, and everybody, *everybody* comes and spends the whole night in the *praça*—the town square—because that's the place to be.

A jeep which we had bought in the south had been taken north for us. Driving into União in that jeep already set us apart. It showed that we had money. We were met by a bombardment of firecrackers, which is the way that the archbishop or the governor would be met. The mayor was there, as well as the town council, local celebrities, the judge and the police chief. There were welcoming speeches at the church and then we were taken to the house where we were to live. It was an old abandoned maternity hospital that had fallen into total disrepair. The people had completely rebuilt it. They had done a tremendous amount of work to make it livable for us. They had put on a new roof and installed plumbing and a stove. The two nurses were supposed to stay in the former priests' house. That house was not in good condition, so they stayed with us until repairs on the old house were complete. When we arrived at the house where we were to live, it was filled with furniture and household necessities—chairs, tables and dishes, utensils. It looked as if it had been newly furnished. After the festivities at the church, everyone came to our house, where the women had prepared *feijado*, a Brazilian meal. It's a bean dish served with sheep's stomachs, which takes a little getting used to, but is considered their finest meal. After the meal there was cake. Everyone was eating and drinking and having a grand time. We were feeling a bit lost, not knowing exactly what was going on. About 4 p.m. people started to go home. As they left, one would take a chair, another would take a table and someone else would take a plate. When the last person had left, the house was bare except for five beds, five chairs and five straw mattresses. The fully furnished house we moved into that morning had been stripped. The people had shared their goods with the house for the celebrations.

Our first big liturgical event, of course, was the Christmas liturgy, beginning with midnight masses on December 24. It was my 36th birthday. The priest who had been looking after the area had decided there would be nine midnight masses in nine places. My assignment was to help Father Dunn at the main church first. Then at 12:30, I was to be picked up by a group that would take me to another place for another mass. There must have been 30,000 people standing in the *praça* outside the main church for that first mass. All around the *praça* were ferris wheels, merry-go-rounds, gambling stalls and stands selling the local liquor. The noise of the crowd was periodically deadened by the explosion of fireworks and firecrackers. We found the commotion totally confusing, but it was obviously the way Christmas was celebrated in Brazil. Just before 12:30, I left the square to wait in front of our house for the ride that would take me to the next place where I was to say mass. When 12:30 had passed and no ride had come, I began to get annoyed. A young seminarian from our parish, Edivar, who became a great friend and help during our period of inculturation in the parish, was to accompany me. He arrived, but still no ride. Sometime later, probably a half-hour behind schedule, an old jeep came rattling down the street, one light beaming through the dark. The jeep pulled to a stop in front of us, and we climbed in. There were already four men in the jeep. Each of them had at least a three-day growth of beard and wore a revolver or a knife. One of them was known as a *pistoleiro*, a gunfighter. He had been in a number of gunfights in the northeast and, in fact, his mother had been shot in a gunfight on the streets of their village. He was known as a dangerous person by the people of the area.

We began driving to the place where I was to say mass, a little town called Roche Cavalcante that would be destroyed in the flood of 1969. The *pistoleiro*, who eventually became a good friend, helped with the reconstruction. We followed an old, dusty road along the river and then, at some point, veered off into the night, our one headlight moving through the thousands of people who were also on the road. It was quite eerie. They were all walking to a mass. Some of them were coming to União, some of them were going to Roche Cavalcante. When we arrived in Roche Cavalcante, there were another 10,000 or more people standing, waiting for the priest to come and say mass at a place that looked to me like a guillotine. It was a temporarily built scaffold with an altar on it. The seminarian helped me climb up on this platform, where there were some vestments and articles to say mass. He read the parts of the mass that were in Portuguese and gave a little sermon for me because I was unable to do any of this. After mass there was a celebration, a bombardment of noise from firecrackers and sky-rockets and a local band. All of this was making me more and more irritated, because this was not Christmas as far as I was concerned.

After the mass, the celebration and the cake, I was taken to a big sugar-cane truck, a Mercedes Benz, which was to ferry me through the dark night to the second place where I was to celebrate mass. This was on a *fazenda*, a big farm up in the mountains. There, at about 3 a.m., I celebrated my second mass, again with some 5,000 people crowded around in the dark. The people there had already had a bit too much to drink and a lot of them were lying on the ground. After mass there were more fireworks, more cake, and then the truck took us down the side of the mountain to a spot where we saw two mules with saddles. Experience would teach me that when you see two mules tied by the road, you're in for a long ride. This first time I innocently got out of the truck, the seminarian right behind me, and we mounted the mules. There were men to lead the animals and we started off into the dark, and I do mean the dark. Straining to see, the only thing I could make out was an occasional hint of the white shirt of the seminarian, who was on the mule in front of me. Then the mules started to slide frontwards down an embankment and we were in water. I deduced that we were crossing a river. The water came up to my feet, as the mules waded across the river and up the other side. The men had crossed on a nearby wooden bridge and they then took the mules by the heads again, to start them up the mountain. By the successive turns we made, I could tell that we were following a switchback road, up the side of what I later saw was almost a cliff. I could tell how steep the road was because we were riding in very simple saddles and my saddle was pulling back hard on the mule. I learned that these animals are so used to travelling up and down the mountainsides that when a long pack-train comes down loaded with sugar- cane, there's only one set of hoofprints. The mules literally follow in one another's footsteps. We climbed for half an hour or more, back and forth. The sound of the river wasn't further away, it was just further down, by the time we arrived at Aqua Fria, the last place I was to say mass. Again a group of people were waiting in the dark, but it was almost dawn and I was so tired I could hardly think or talk. We went through the celebration of mass again, following that had cake, and then I was taken to a little room at the back of the main dwelling, where I took off my shirt, lay down on a straw mat and slept for three or four hours.

When I awoke, it was bright daylight. The house had no toilet facilities, but I remembered having been directed to the backyard. I got up, walked through the kitchen where some women were preparing a meal, and went out the back door. After we had left, the seminarian told me that this was one of the most serious blunders I could have made. In Brazil, a man never appears in front of a woman without his shirt on. In fact, it's against the law to drive a car in Brazil without a shirt. Our seminarian used to laugh about this years later, when he felt comfortable enough with us to speak freely. He described how helpless he felt that day, when I broke a primary cultural rule on my first pastoral assignment. We were not warned about this at Petrópolis; it was assumed that everyone knew you keep your shirt on in Brazil.

Breakfast that morning consisted of foods I had never seen before and did not find very appetizing. There were different kinds of roots and meats, prepared in ways that were absolutely foreign to me. I couldn't stomach them that morning, but as time went on I came to like all these dishes. About 11 a.m. the mules were waiting again and the seminarian and I prepared to go down the mountainside. I was scared stiff when I saw the cliff we had come up in the dark the night before. The mules took us down very carefully, through the river and to the truck. We arrived back in União a half-hour later. I have never been so tired in my life; I could hardly wait to collapse into bed. When I got back to the *casa paroquial*, the house where we were living, there were the two nurses and a young man from Saskatchewan, Don Sirois, talking about the great evening they had spent celebrating Christmas. After Don, Bernard and I had described our ordeals, one of the nurses said in all seriousness, "I wonder what Christ would do if he were here?" I said, "He'd quit."

For the next four or five months, I struggled with the language, and struggled even more with the problems that confronted us in the parish. We found that the parish contained about 80,000 people compared to the whole diocese of Saskatoon, which had about half that number of people and 80 or more priests to serve them. A Peace Corps doctor told us that when he drove through the countryside around União he could see five chronic diseases in each person, without even stopping to examine them. The child mortality rate was more than 50 per cent during their first year. The illiteracy rate in the valley was about 80 per cent. As these facts began to sink in, we were almost paralyzed by the hopelessness of the situation. Not being able to communicate with the people about their problems intensified my frustration. The needs were so great, we didn't know where to begin.

Our first approach was borrowed from our North American experience. Within a few months of our arrival, we began visiting the people. Wearing white cassocks, which was the ordinary dress of Brazilian priests at the time, we would talk to people on the streets at night and go from house to house visiting families. This frightened people. They couldn't figure out why we were doing this. It was not something that happened in Brazil. The people who were most afraid were the *crentes*, the Protestants. They thought we were conspiring to get them. Although years later, people said the visiting was a good thing, its first effect was to create fear. As the months wore on, my language problem did not lessen, nor did my feeling of hopelessness. I had come out of a "successful" church and I was now in what I thought was a completely unsuccessful one. My anger and frustration with the situation made me so unbearable that the rest of the group finally told me I should go away

45

for awhile, take a rest and try to calm down. We had only been in União six or seven months. I thought it was too soon to take a holiday, but I accepted their advice. I packed a few books, bought a bus ticket and set out on a month's pilgrimage across Brazil. I kept trying to come to grips with this new situation and my place in it. One of the books I took along turned out to be one of the most influential books in my life, although when I read it now, it doesn't seem that extraordinary. It was called *The Advent of Salvation*, by Cardinal Danilieu, a French cardinal. The chapter on the spirituality of missionaries contained a staggeringly simple idea. Danilieu said that the missionary believes in the impossible. Great missionaries, he said, were people who cleared the way, who opened doors for people, and he gave as examples Abraham, Moses and Mary. God, he said, had told Abraham to create a mighty nation. Abraham had said it was impossible, he was too old. But Abraham believed in this impossible mission and he had a son, Isaac. Then he was asked to kill his son, which again would make his task impossible, but he believed. Moses, too, Danilieu pointed out, was given an impossible task—bringing his people out of Egypt. He knew he couldn't do it, because he couldn't speak well. He was a mumbler and he couldn't speak the language. I really related to that. Moses, however, believed in the impossible and he brought his people out. Mary was told that she was to be the mother of the Saviour, even though she was a virgin. That was impossible, yet Mary believed and it came to pass. Suddenly, as if a door had been opened, I had a tremendous spiritual experience. I realized I had to believe in the impossible. Until then, I had only believed in the possible. The impossible was that God had saved his people. Our responsibility was simply to be with them to celebrate that salvation. I returned to União with a completely new view of what had to be done in our parish. I also returned with a new faith—a faith in the impossible.

The Church had traditionally been one of the pillars of Brazilian society. The other pillars were political and military. At any official function, there would always be the cleric, the colonel and the local politician. The new pastoral plan for Brazil, although respecting the past and staying within cultural norms, nevertheless proposed that the Church had a responsibility to be more than a pillar of society. It had to teach the Gospel and work with lay people to develop Christian leaders. Today, that doesn't sound revolutionary, but it was then. The preferential option for the poor had not received the attention it was to get, after its endorsement in 1968 by the Latin American bishops at the first conference in Medellin, Columbia. The essence of it, however, was already there in the Brazilian bishops' first five-year pastoral plan, in the early '60s.

The Church in Brazil had become associated with old women. Men

46

did not go to church. Because Brazil is a very macho society, this identification with women meant that the Church had lost some credibility. We decided to work with the men, to try to get them involved in the church. Our first initiative, with this goal in mind, was a procession. Brazilians love a parade and church processions were part of their liturgical tradition. Some of the people we had met through our home visits were willing to help organize it. The procession was to be a celebration of the Vatican Council, which was underway in Rome. We had arranged for a Brazilian priest to conduct a simple renewal ceremony about life in general, about spiritual life, and in particular about the Council. But somehow a rumour started that we were going to take the statue of their patron saint, Maria Madelena, out of the church. Hostility began to build. Even though most of the men rarely appeared in church, except once a year for the feast of Santa Maria Madelena, they had the idea that we had come to destroy her church, their church. It is important to understand that a person's church is what he or she thinks it is. For them, church meant being sons of Santa Maria Madelena. In fact, that's what a man would say when you asked him where he was from. He'd say he was from the *terra*, the land of Santa Maria Madelena. That's how they identified themselves.

The procession began at various points in the town and was to converge at the church. We could hear bands and firecrackers going off in different parts of the city. Even though we weren't sure what was happening, we certainly were not aware that this celebration could turn into a lynching—our lynching. When all the strands of the procession came together, the church was absolutely jam-packed, the first time in its history it had ever been this packed. With men. Many of them were carrying a knife or a gun for the massacre of the gringos. But all that happened was the renewal ceremony, and afterwards they went home. The Archbishop of Maceió, Dom Adelmo, was in Rome attending the Second Vatican Council at that time. When the story reached him, he is supposed to have laughed and laughed at how the gringos conned all those Brazilian men into church.

That year was critical. We had to work out a pastoral form that would work in this situation. Having come to a foreign country gave us a kind of freedom. We looked at different pastoral schemes and methods. Then we began to read the Scriptures deeply to find out how Jesus had operated in his time. No one in the seminary had ever talked about modelling a pastoral plan on Jesus' pastoral plan. No one at any priests' meeting had ever suggested it and I had never read it in any book, either. But it seemed such a logical thing to do. If you were going to have a pastoral plan, start with Jesus' plan. As I understood the pastoral work of Jesus, the Church had to grow with the community, with committed people who would continue to do the work after the leader was gone. That's why He picked 12 close associates and another 72 that He called disciples. They were not as close, but were still very much attached to the mission. Then He preached to the multitudes. We could do the same. We could train 12, prepare 72 and preach to the multitudes. Father George Van Antwerp, an American priest from Detroit who had studied with us at Petrópolis, was thinking along similar lines. He was working in Recife and keeping in close touch with our group. He, too, picked 12 men and began to work with them.

I was given responsibility for the first 12. Over the next two or three months, I carefully recruited those men. I suppose today I would pick 12 men and women, but at that time I was still picking men. It seemed to me that picking those men was the most priestly act I had ever performed, the closest I had ever come to Jesus' mission. I looked for people who represented different groups and different classes. I picked a doctor. I picked a porter, a person who carried loads on his head. I picked a young man who worked for the department of agriculture, a man who ran the government-organized labour union, a tailor who could hardly read and who spoke in a dialect, a man who worked at the bank, and a *fazendeiro*—a landowner. Each man was chosen because he represented a certain segment of society. None of them was picked because he was more pious or holy or intelligent than anyone else. After picking the 12, I had to figure out what to do with them. No one had taught me anything about how Jesus trained his 12 men. Of course there were the parables. But, what did He do all day? What did He do between the parables? Most of the parables were aimed at the multitudes. What did Jesus do specifically to train his 12? How did He teach them to establish a church? That's an enormous undertaking. We couldn't know what He did, but I speculated that the first thing He might have done was teach them to talk to each other. The first problem you encounter in any church community is that people can't talk to each other. They talk at different levels or on different wavelengths because they belong to a certain class or because they have a university education. But, they lack the ability to really communicate. Our training in communication at Petrópolis had alerted us to this problem and offered some techniques for dealing with it.

Conscious of this potential communication problem, I began weekly meetings with the 12 men. I used techniques I had learned from the Young Christian Workers and from the Christian Family Movement. My objectives for the group were to study the Scriptures and talk about them together, to develop the ability to listen to one another, and then to select some problem in the community that they could work on as a group. We started with the Gospel of the week and it was unbelievable how they went at it. I often thought that they had the advantage of never having been corrupted by schooling. Their minds were still clear and they could respond personally to what they read. They often produced profound insights into the Scriptures.

In northeast Brazil, where people live in shacks without the necessities of life, the parables make more sense than they do to people living in comfortable houses. One parable that I had never understood made sense to me for the first time in Brazil. Someone knocks on the door and asks for bread to feed his visitors. The man inside says he's not going to help because his family has already gone to bed. That never seemed to me like a good enough reason to say no. It does seem like a legitimate reason, however, once you've seen a 10-by-10-foot Brazilian house with 20 people living in it. Some of those 20 people would sleep in hammocks hung from the ceiling and others would be sleeping on the floor. If someone knocked at the door after everyone had gone to bed, it would be a major problem to get to the door, much less to get food. From a North American perspective, the man who will not get up to give bread to his neighbour appears cruel. He wasn't hard or cruel. He just didn't want to disturb his whole household. But in the parable, the man outside persisted. It's really a parable about the power of prayer, and the man inside did find a way to bring bread to the door. Other parables, too, made more sense in the Brazilian context. For instance, I could really understand the one in which they let the sick man down through the roof. Houses in Brazil have roofs that are thatched or covered with tiles. If a crowd was standing around a house, of course you'd crawl up on the roof and take the tiles off to get in. For our Sunday sermons, we began to supplement the ideas we had been taught with the new insights, the new clarity that these mostly uneducated men brought to our study of the Scriptures.

Working with George Van Antwerp and other friends in Recife, we were able to organize over the course of the following three years special intensive courses using the model that had been established in Spain some years before—the Cursillo Movement. We adapted it to Brazil, calling it the Fermentista Movement. Fermento means yeast and we took it from the Scriptures—yeast put into the dough will make it rise. The goals of the Fermentista Movement were very similar to those of the first group I worked with. We were hoping that the original 12 would return to their communities and organize more groups. And indeed this is what happened. All through the parish, both in the city and in rural areas, groups began to spring up—groups of 20 or 30, frequently animated by one of the original 12. Our role in these groups was minimal. We attended the meetings and initiated the reflection on the Gospels.

My colleague, Father Don Macgillivray, had accepted responsibility for the 72, the disciple level. Many of the 72 were school teachers, most of them women. Father Don's mandate was to prepare them to teach the children better. The next level was the multitudes. The first time we preached to 10,000 people in União it seemed totally useless. But then we realized that this is what Jesus did. He preached to the multitudes. We believed, as the Brazilian bishops did, that if the word of God is preached clearly, in the idiom of the people who hear it so they can understand it, that it has the power to change social situations. I have actually seen it work in situations that seemed utterly hopeless.

By this time two Sisters of Sion, Sister Mary Ellen Martin and Sister Ann Murphy, had arrived from Canada. Later they were joined by Sister Diane Lieffers and Sister Joyce Sinnett. They all became active in our work. We were setting up *communidade de base*, base communities, which were often animated by men and women who had been in the Fermentista Movement. The people were taking responsibility for their own local church, rather than waiting for a 30-mile ride on a donkey to some *festa* in a big church far away where they would get their baby baptized. They were becoming a church people, responsible for the church of their area.

At the end of each *communidade* meeting, a question about the sick and the needy always arose. In the beginning, people only saw individual needs. They only saw the fact that this old lady was sick or this man had no job or this kid lost his foot. As time went on, they began to see a pattern to these individual problems. They began to realize that it was contaminated water that was killing their children. They began to understand that the only reason they didn't have electric lights on their street was because they didn't have a *politico*, a political person. Having identified the causes of their problems, they began to organize around specific issues. People are no threat as long as they are gathering to say the rosary. They become a threat when they start to organize and press for things they feel they have a right to. For this reason the *communidade de base* of Latin America, particularly of Brazil, have become a threat to government.

In my experience, people from the lower classes of society found it much easier to press for changes than those from the upper classes. The first person to leave the group was the banker. He was a good man, but the idea of becoming involved in social issues was harder for him than for a person who didn't have anything to lose.

Our favourite song at Petrópolis was "What has brought us together? It is love." The question however, always became *how* do you love your neighbour? In the beginning, people in the group would answer: talk nicely to them, look after them when they're sick and so on. But as we worked with the people, it became clear that if you loved your neighbour you had to acknowledge that he deserved a decent standard of living. This led naturally to social action. Even with this new answer, it wasn't always clear what we should do. How do you put the example of the good Samaritan into practice in a contemporary context? How do you pick up the guy and get him started again? For me, over the next few years, it had a lot to do with helping people get water and arranging to get electricity in places where there hadn't been any. It was simple things, such as making sure that the very poor had food.

During this whole period, Brazil was under a very strict military regime. Although many stories could be told about it, I think one might illustrate how serious the situation was. On December 13, 1968, the military government imposed what they called *ATO Cinco*, the fifth act. It was the strictest we had seen, virtually eliminating protection of human rights. Where we were living, some 60 miles from the coast, we only heard about it on the radio and read about it in the newspaper. There was no activity where we were, but we felt that could change. The day after the announcement, two American Sisters we knew from Recife, about 150 miles away, drove into the yard in their jeep and told us that some of the American priests in Recife had been arrested. It was thought that they would get life imprisonment or be expelled. This was very unsettling to us because we had worked closely with these priests in the Fermentista Movement. I went around União that day and talked to all the men I had worked with. I told them that if the police came for us, they should say nothing. They were to let us go and act as if they had not been involved, because they were far more likely to be killed or tortured than we were. Because we were foreigners there was a good chance we would just be expelled. Then all of our Canadian group went to see Archbishop Dom Adelmo, in Maceió. He had been through crises like this before, although never anything this serious. His advice was: don't get into any crowds, don't stir up any trouble, and hope the military doesn't come to the interior. We carried on until Christmas, without incident and without hearing anything further from Recife. It was impossible to interpret the silence. We knew that prior to the overthrow of a city, the gas supply was always cut off so that nobody could leave the city. The Sisters had left Recife with two or three gallons and had been able to borrow gas along the way. We were able to help them get back. But what happened in Recife after their return was anyone's guess.

We celebrated Christmas as usual in the parish and the next day we went to Maceió to celebrate Christmas with some Canadian friends. Then, with the permission of the group, I drove to Recife to find out what had happened there. I guessed that some of our friends, American priests, would be living at a seminary that had been built by American Oblates in an area called Boa Viagem, so I headed for the seminary. The streets were full of jeeps, armoured cars and soldiers, but I wasn't stopped. The Volkswagon I was driving carried a São Paulo license plate, which might suggest that I was a tourist. I turned off the main street of Boa Viagem into a side street, where the American seminary was. I had stayed there many times when our *fermentistos* were taking their courses there. As I approached the seminary, I could see soldiers and about 20 army cars surrounding the building, but also, inside the seminary yard, were the cars of all the Americans I knew in Recife. This was one of the biggest decisions of my lifetime. Should I drive past the seminary or go in? I drove past. After driving half a mile, I said to myself, "You were born a chicken. Let's go back and not be a chicken." I turned around. As I drove into the seminary yard, I knew it could be my last free act. The soldiers let me pass. I parked my car and entered the building. The old caretaker told me the Americans were being held there and where I could find them. The Americans—some 40 priests, nuns and lay people—had already worked out a system by which they could signal whether they were free to talk without the secret police hearing them. If one felt it was safe to talk, he would say "horse." The other person would reply "shit," if it was also safe for him. The priest who told me the code warned me not to talk if anyone was listening. I talked to the two priests who had been arrested—Dario Ruppiper, who had been in my class in Petrópolis, and Peter Grimes, who had been there later. They had been arrested because of what they were saying in church, basically criticizing the government for its treatment of the poor. They had been released from prison on good conduct the day before my visit and had been allowed to come to the seminary, which was being used as a holding ground for all the Americans. The rest of the American nuns and priests from Recife were also there under house arrest. Dom Helder Camara, the archbishop, had come on Christmas Day to celebrate mass. Several of the Brazilian federal police were billeted in the seminary as guards. I talked to one of them and he seemed innocuous enough. However, I'm quite certain one of those guards later killed a young Brazilian priest, Padre Henrique, who was secretary to Dom Helder. The guard I spoke to said he didn't think these people were Communists because he had enjoyed the midnight mass with Archbishop Camara and everyone else seemed to enjoy it too. He was glad he had been picked to escort the two priests to Belém because he had relatives there, whom he had never had a chance to visit. With this assignment, he was going to get a free ride to Belém and a visit with his relatives.

The two priests who had been arrested had been told they could leave the country or stand public trial. Anticipating a minimum sentence of seven years, they had elected to leave the country. About 5 p.m. the day I was there, an army officer came into the room and asked the two priests if he could trust them. If he could, he would not have to shackle them to take them from the seminary to the airport, which was about a mile away. This was a joke. The priests had no desire to escape. They were to be taken by car with a police guard to the airport. The whole incident was so Brazilian—some of the trucks wouldn't start; the batteries were dead. Today, of course, Brazil has new equipment, but in those days they had old, beat-up equipment. The soldiers came over and asked some of the priests if they would help push the trucks. For the next ten minutes everyone pushed.

The procession to the airport finally got underway. I decided to stay at the seminary and wait to hear what would happen. When the others returned, they described the events at the airport. Although there had been a strict order that no one was to come to the airport for the expulsion of these priests, the airport was packed with people from their parishes. When the priests walked in with their escorts, there was the general of the army, Dom Helder Camara and his associate bishop, an American from the embassy in Rio—who I was told was really glad to see these guys go—and four or five other high-ranking government officials. The people started to crowd around their pastors. The general ordered the priests to be taken into a side-room and threatened to return them to prison if the crowd did not disperse. At that, Dom Helder moved in and said that unless the general would allow the people to stay, he could arrest him as well. That apparently slowed the general down. When the two priests were finally marched out to the plane, all the people in the airport, thousands of them, began to sing the popular hymn we always sang with the *fermentistas*— "What was it that brought us here? It was love." It's a very rousing song. That was the last sound of Recife those two priests heard. "What was it that brought us here? It was love."

I stayed for a few days and then went back to Maceió and on to our parish. It was obvious that we'd have to be very careful or we could be arrested, too. My feeling was that accommodating the situation was preferable to confronting it and getting kicked out, because once you're out, you've lost. As long as you're there you may not be scoring very much but at least you're still in the game.

Before the Recife incident, we had been planning to have a development week in the valley of the Mundau, the valley in which we lived. There were four or five parishes in the valley. Over the years, we had worked with the priests and lay people in these parishes and we felt that what was really needed was a serious discussion about development in the valley. With the onset of the December purge, we could see that talk about development would be risky. Early in January, the local newspaper which normally carried no news about what was going on in Brazil, ran a headline which said the army was going to spearhead development of our valley. We had no idea what that meant, but chose to interpret it positively. With that bit of encouragement, I went to talk to the archbishop in Maceió about working with the army on this development. I didn't want to do anything that would get the Brazilian priests or bishop or anyone into trouble, but I was willing to work with the army if it meant development.

Dom Adelmo, the Archbishop of Maceió, and I always saw the world from two different angles, but we were close friends and he enjoyed my visits. I'd usually go with a new idea and he would say, "Roberto, come out and sit under the palm trees where we'll at least have a cool breeze to blow over us." He was saying that we could talk no matter how different our ideas were. This time, after I had presented my idea and we had talked it over a bit, I suggested we go to see the colonel. The way he looked at me, I could tell he was a bit afraid of that, and, of course, being a Brazilian, he had a lot more reason to be afraid than I did. "Okay," he said, "I'll make you a deal. You bring the mayor of your town, the president of the town council, the director of the high school, the leader of the local labour union, the local director of AN-CAR (the government development agency) and the state director of AN-CAR (who would be like a state minister, although at that time there were no elected officials in Brazil as they were all appointed by the central government). If you can get them to come, I'll go see the colonel with you." Well, he knew as well as I did that most of those people never even talked to each other. It was highly unlikely they could be persuaded to go see the army together. But I headed back to União and started politicking, trying to persuade them to come see the army with me. When I look back on it now, I think I had more gall than brains. I was determined to get those six people to the bishop's house on Monday afternoon, when the bishop had made a tentative appointment to see the colonel.

During that week, many of the professors at the State University of Alagôas were arrested. That made us more nervous. We didn't know how far this new purge was going to go. I spent three or four days talking to those six men, trying to coax them to go with me. You could never tell if they would or not. They agreed in Brazilian style. A Brazilian will never tell you he doesn't want to do something. If he doesn't show up, you know he was saying no from the beginning.

On the Monday afternoon, I headed into the city with three of the men. The rest were to be brought in by Jorge, one of our first *fermentistas*, in his jeep. I was praying they would show up, but it seemed almost impossible. The bishop was sure it wouldn't happen. At the agreed upon time, I was at the bishop's house with my three men and along came Jorge's jeep with the other three in it. There they were—the six men from

União, the six men I had to get. I can still see the look on the archbishop's face. He knew I had him and he was absolutely faithful to his word. He phoned the colonel and said that a group from the interior wanted to see him. Could we come over? The colonel said yes and before we had time to lose our nerve, we were on our way.

The archbishop got into the jeep I was driving and both jeeps headed toward the military compound, which was located just outside the city, as it is in all Brazilian cities. None of us had ever been inside that compound. We drove up to the gate and were met by two young soldiers carrying American-made rifles. I knew that if we got shot that day, we'd be shot by American bullets, too. The young soldier who stopped us didn't know who we were. The barrel of his gun was right beside my head.

"No," I said, "I don't want to talk to you. I want to talk to the officer of the day." I knew that in the army anywhere, but especially there, you have to give the impression that you've got more power than the guy pointing the gun at you. You have to ask for his commanding officer.

The officer of the day came out. He was very friendly, said they were expecting us, and to drive right in. The soldiers put their rifles away. We drove in, parked the car and followed the officer. My companions were very nervous, but I felt a certain familiarity. Soldiers are the same all over the world. They've been trained the same way. They talk the same language. They do the same things. As we were walking, the colonel came out to meet us. He was a little short guy. He looked like a retired barber, hardly a vicious man who could terrorize the region. I noticed he was wearing some war medals. I asked him if he had been in Italy and, he had.

"Do you remember the Canadians just to the left of you on the front?" I asked. Yes, he remembered the Canadians, and instantly we had established a rapport. He ushered us into his office— a big, wood-panelled room with carpeted floors and the first air- conditioning I had felt in three or four years. He sat us all down, the archbishop beside him, then me and then all the other people from União. He ordered coffee and after it was brought in, the archbishop began to introduce the subject of our meeting. He talked around the subject for awhile and then, although it wasn't really the proper protocol, I intervened.

"Really," I said, "we're very interested in the plan for development that we read about in the newspaper." He looked at me as if he had no idea what I was talking about. I continued, "We read in the Maceió paper that the army was going to lead the development of the valley. I've been working in development up in the valley with these men and other people and we'd like to help you if we can."

The colonel was stunned. He picked up his phone and a moment later a lieutenant colonel came in. He asked this big lieutenant colonel if the army had a plan for development of the valley of the Mundau. The question drew a blank from the lieutenant colonel, too. He went out and a few moments later returned and said, "No, we don't. We don't have any plan for the valley."

"Well," I said, "could we work at this together? I'm very interested in helping the people up the valley." The colonel said he'd be glad to work together on this.

"You have 800 soldiers here," I said. "What are you doing with them?"

"They're doing what soldiers do," he replied.

"Would you be interested in having them work in development?" I suggested.

"Sure," he replied, "but what can soldiers do in development?"

"I can show you 30 places," I said, "where they can build a bridge and if some of them can read and write, I can show you 30 schools where they could teach." These suggestions were obviously novel ideas to the colonel, but he didn't reject them. We agreed to continue our discussion about ways of working together.

The archbishop was getting up to leave. The others from the valley, not one of whom had said a word during the whole conversation, got up too. Before leaving, I had to ask one more question. "Colonel, we've been reading in the paper that a number of university professors have been arrested. Can you tell us why you did that?" The archbishop almost fainted. The colonel replied as casually as if he were telling that the wind was from the north. "Well, the general of the fourth army in Recife said we should investigate all the university professors, and this is the first time I'm getting my leave at carnival time. I want to take my wife to Rio at carnival and I want to get this done before I go." Instantly, my view of the purge changed. It became a very down-to-earth matter that had to be dealt with quickly so the colonel could take his wife to carnival in Rio. We parted amicably. He asked me to come and visit him at his home and I invited him to visit our parish. As we were walking back to the jeep, the ANCAR director apologized to me for the state of the army. I told him the army is the same everywhere.

Heartened by our meeting with the colonel, we proceeded with our planning for the week of development. Because I was due for a leave and because the wet season was about to start, we decided to hold the study session in September, eight months later.

We had hoped to start the week by having Dom Helder Camara speak to the people. He's very good at talking to groups about how the Gospel leads to development. I went to see him, accompanied by a Belgian Sister who had studied with us at Petrópolis. Dom Helder had moved out of the palace and was living in one room behind an old church. The place was machine-gunned several times during that period, but he remained there. When we arrived, he was visiting with a doctor friend of his, discussing the Gospel and the liturgy for the next Sunday. After the doctor left, I presented our invitation. I knew he had just come back from the United States, where he had talked in New York and at Harvard, and I said, "Our little development week is no big deal. We're just going into a little municipality in the interior of Alagôas." He said, "Roberto, this is not small, this is big. Until Brazil can start doing this in every municipality, there is no real hope for development." He regretted, however, that in all likelihood he would not be able to join us. He was blacklisted by the army and he didn't think that the fourth army in Recife would let him go, nor did he think the colonel in Alagôas would be free to let him come, and he was right.

As it turned out, no one came for the week of development. On March 14, 1969, a devastating flood swept through the valley, destroying three or four towns, including several in our parish. Hundreds of people were killed. All thought of a development week was forgotten.

That day, March 14, I was scheduled to leave for North America. That morning, the road to Maceió was cut. People were pulling bodies out of the water, but at this point we had no way of determining how serious the flood would be. I didn't know whether to stay or leave. The rest of the team said they thought I should leave. My friend Jorge said he would drive me up over a mountain pass and get me onto the highway. The drive over the *serra* took two or three hours. We got to the highway and into Maceió. Then the news started to come in about how bad the flood was, how much damage there was and how many people had died. I boarded the plane for Recife. I felt terrible about leaving, but there was no way back into the valley. The only way you could get in was by helicopter and the army was using all the helicopters. I decided the only thing I could do was go home, talk about the flood and raise money to start rebuilding. I did spend my time at home that spring talking about South America and the flood. Our assignment to Brazil was to have been for five years. As we approached the end of the five years, I felt I was just ready to start. I could speak the language fairly well. I knew everyone from the governor down in the state and everyone from the bishop down in the church. I was well-known throughout northeast Brazil. I felt that the people accepted me and I could now begin to work effectively. While I was home, the bishop told me he wanted me to come back to Canada the following year. I found that very difficult to accept.

When I returned to Brazil, I knew I had only one year left to work there. When a time frame is shortened like that, it changes the way you act. When I arrived back in Maceió, the reconstruction had not yet started. The flood had been followed by rains and there were still hundreds of people living in total misery on the banks of the river. Roche Cavalcante had been wiped off the face of the map. Temporary sheds had been erected and hundreds of people were still living in the mud. The first day I got back, Sister Diane Lieffers, who had worked with me in that section of the parish, and I drove out in a jeep to see the refugees. There was a woman lying in the mud, giving birth. Diane helped deliver her little girl. Amazingly, she didn't die and whenever I go back to Brazil, she's always the person they bring out, as a symbol of that year.

We never knew how many people were homeless. The refugees and the people who had lost their homes in the flood were everywhere and there was no way to keep track of them. They were all sugar-cane cutters, most of them poor. The first objective had been to get food and blankets for them. Our team had worked very hard all that summer, doing basic refugee work.

The army brought in supplies from all over Brazil and the police chief in our town was put in charge of the local refugee work. All the supplies that came in, the blankets, the food and dishes and other supplies went to him. One day he was gone and so were all the supplies. We were outraged at the thought of somebody stealing relief supplies from refugees. But the people weren't angry. In Brazil, because many of them have always been poor, they feel that if you ever get a break you should take it. Their attitude was: "Well, if I'd had that chance, I'd have taken it, too."

The archbishop had received $50,000 in emergency relief aid from Pope Paul VI. When you have a limited amount of money and everyone needs it, it's very hard to know how to divide it. In this case, the archbishop gambled on my being able to transform that $50,000 into houses for the people in Roche Cavalcante. In fact, he had gambled to the point of buying a train carload of cement in Recife. Cement was hard to get. Everyone was looking for cement. He had secured a carload and told me that it was for me to use in building houses. He set up an account with the $50,000 and put me in charge. I was to buy land, construction materials, line up workers, develop a plan and build the houses. The government had already begun building houses for refugees in other places, but much of that money was lost and the houses never got built. I took my job very seriously. The first step, finding land, was very difficult. Although there were thousands and thousands of acres with sugar-cane on them, the land was all owned by one man. Taking land out of production was unthinkable. Nevertheless, I started negotiating with the man and his grandson, who ran the sugar factory up the line from where these refugees worked. At first they wanted me to build houses among the squatters in the village. I kept insisting that these were going to be good houses and we should find good land. In the end we only got seven or eight acres. It wasn't much, but it did take some cane out of production. We cut down the cane to put up the houses. Next we had to get the materials and the workers. The area has good clay and bricks are easy to make. We got people started making bricks and tiles and building window frames. We paid their wages out of the bishop's money. That was the first time I saw how an economy actually works. I would give out the equivalent of $1 to a person who had made bricks. That same day, the money would pass through ten hands and turn into $10. The brickmaker would give it to the man who sold beans, the bean man would give it to the woman who made clothes for his children, the woman would spend it on dishes and it just kept moving along like that. You could see that $1 of aid money become $10. The valley started to come alive again. In Brazil, bricklaying is a common profession. All the houses and other buildings above the level of straw construction are made of bricks. Bricklayers generally worked in pairs — a bricklayer and a helper, who made the mortar and passed it to the bricklayer. Because there were so many people out of work, I decided to expand these bricklaying teams into three. That was a mistake. It broke a cultural pattern. They didn't know how work in threes and after a week or two we had to go back to twos.

We staked out the houses and put Manuel, one of the *fermentistas*, in charge of the construction. He was a bricklayer and was respected by the other bricklayers. They worked two men to a house. The houses were all the same and were set in rows on streets. They were to have electricity, and a very primitive kind of plumbing. During that next year, I spent 90 per cent of my time at the houses, working with the men, digging wells and setting up a pumping system. Eventually the whole town was able to use the water system. On March 14, one year after the flood, we officially opened the houses. The governor of the state came from Maceió by special train. He didn't dare go any further because the state was to have rebuilt the next village and those houses never got built. The Apostolic Nuncio came up from Rio for the opening. The Alagôas director of development was there, along with other dignitaries and many local people. There was a big party after the official ceremony, and much rejoicing.

The minister of education, who had accompanied the governor, suggested that if we could build houses that fast perhaps we could build a school, too. He actually provided the funds and we built the school during my last month in Brazil. Sister Diane and I had always wanted to paint a big picture and the school offered a chance to do that. When the school was finished, we painted a mural on one of the outside walls. It was a very primitive picture, but the people understood it. We painted cane cutters working on the cane and oxen pulling the cane wagons. One evening I was standing in the *praça*, which they named after me, and there was a man there, a cane cutter, standing with his little boy. I heard him tell the boy, "That's me up there. That's me cutting cane. But if you go to this school, you'll never have to cut cane." During that last year, we built 50 houses and the school. They're all still there and in very good condition. They have all been repainted, even the mural. The school is still functioning. The teachers are paid by the state and they are part of the community now. I left Brazil June 1, 1970 after an unforgettable farewell ceremony. With three months until my next assignment and an unexpected inheritance of $1,000 from an aunt, I decided to spend the summer travelling in the Third World.

From Rio I flew to Senegal where I began a trip through West Africa—Senegal, Guinea, the Ivory coast, Ghana and Nigeria. I had about $10 a day to live on, but I stretched it by hitchhiking from one mission to the next. Going to Africa from Brazil, the first thing I discovered was that I had been working in an African culture in Brazil and didn't know it. I learned that although the United States and the Caribbean had imported many black Africans, Brazil had by far the largest number of slaves of any of the sugar-cane producing countries. That accounted for the African origin of most of the people in the area where we had worked in Brazil. They had mixed with the Portuguese, but retained most of their African culture. I heard it in the music in West Africa, saw it in the clothing, tools, houses. In fact, I know exactly where one group of people that lived near us in Brazil must have come from. They had a unique type of house and I found the same house in Ghana. All this came as a shock to me. Here I had thought we were dealing with Latins in Brazil, only to discover that we were basically dealing with Africans, people who had come from West Africa.

Leaving West Africa, I travelled through Zaire and South Africa to the inland country of Lesotho, where I witnessed the installation of a black bishop and met the queen of Lesotho and all the archbishops and bisops of South Africa. I later spent some time with Archbishop Dennis Hurley in Durban. I could see that some of the bishops were very distant from the black Africans. Many of them had never been in Lesotho before. Two Sisters who were in Lesotho for the first time for the bishop's installation were quite upset because the black Sisters didn't allow them to go first in the reception line. Apartheid is so ingrained in their culture that the white Sisters took it for granted that white people always came before black people, even when they're Sisters.

After the bishop's installation I wanted to go to Kimberley, where the Canadian Oblates had a mission. The bishop of Port Elizabeth, Bishop Green, said he could drive me part way. He drove me out of

60

Lesotho, through Maseru and towards Bloemfontein, which is a large town in the eastern part of South Africa. When we were still 50 or 60 miles from Bloemfontein, he said, "Well, I take a turn here and go south now. Do you want to come with me or what do you want to do?" I didn't know what to think except that going with him was going in the wrong direction. I said I would get out and hitch another ride.

It was about 5 p.m. and it was July, which is mid-winter in South Africa. I was wearing only a light jacket I had borrowed from a priest in Johannesburg. I got out of the car and waved goodbye to Bishop Green. Then I was standing alone beside the road. It was cold. Two or three cars passed. The darkness started to descend. It became totally dark and I was still standing there. Cars went by with their lights on and I could hear animals in the darkness. I didn't know how far it was to the next town. Finally a car slowed down, backed up, stopped and a door opened. In the car were five black men. Only one could speak English. I told them I wanted to go to the nearest Catholic mission or the nearest town. They talked back and forth in their own language and finally said that they would take me. The one who spoke English was driving. He tried to make conversation with me as we drove along, but it was hard with the rest of the people talking too. After we'd gone about a mile, they turned off the main highway and it seemed to me then that we were in darkest Africa. I started thinking that the small amount of money I had on me was probably more than all of these five people put together had and we were in the middle of nowhere. But my fear was unfounded. After an hour or so the lights of a town appeared ahead of us. They'd never heard of a Catholic mission in Ladysmith, but they found out where it was and drove me to the door. I wanted to give them some money but they wouldn't take any. That was the most perfect enactment of the good Samaritan story I have ever experienced.

The priests at that mission were Dutch. The next morning they had to minister in their parishes, one of which consisted of about 30 Catholics in Ladysmith, and another which included 7,000 blacks in one of the townships outside Ladysmith. I said mass with them in the little wooden church in Ladysmith. It was a strange feeling, knowing that these priests lived with that tension all the time. Half of their work was with 30 whites and the rest was with 7,000 blacks. I could not imagine working in South Africa, with the total contradiction between Christianity and apartheid. After mass they said they'd leave me on the highway if I wanted to hitch-hike. There are no trains on Sunday and no buses for white people in South Africa. I accepted their offer and was soon out on the highway again, this time in the morning and wearing my clerical collar. I wondered what would happen if a cleric was seen on the road. I didn't have to wonder long. One Mercedes Benz after another stopped on its way to church. Each driver cursed me for standing there on the highway—a white man standing on the highway like that—and then went on to church. After a while, two surveyors picked me up in their Mercedes and drove me into Bloemfontein.

From South Africa I travelled up through Tanzania, Kenya, Uganda and Ethiopia. I crossed the Arab states, entered Pakistan and India, where I spent several weeks in four or five major cities. I touched down in Burma, Thailand, Singapore and Hong Kong, and stopped for the World Fair in Japan. The World's Fair in Osaka stirred the same feeling of anger in me as the World's Fair in Montréal had in 1967. People couldn't understand then why I was angry. I said, "You can't call it a World's Fair. Call it the rich people's fair. Call it anything, but don't call it a World's Fair because most of the people of the world aren't represented here." I got to Osaka, and it was the same thing. I had just spent three months travelling in the Third World, observing poverty. When I got to Osaka, there was the First World, the rich world, celebrating, calling it a World's Fair and ignoring the fact that most of the world's people were hungry. And I was angry again.

By the end of that journey, I couldn't help reaching the conclusion that if you're poor, you really haven't got a chance. It doesn't matter where you are born—Saskatoon, Addis Ababa or La Paz. Without a financial base to work from, you just can't get ahead. Without money, you can't even get the essentials of human life. I had seen how many people around the world are trapped in that state. During the six years I spent in Brazil, I had grown attached to the people. Because of that I could no longer ignore the questions of poverty and underdevelopment in the world. Also, during the time I was in Brazil, the Second Vatican Council was shifting the Church towards an identification with the poor. For me that meant a major shift in my understanding of the role of the Church in the world.

Even in our remote village in Brazil, we were reading the documents that came out of the Council almost as soon as they were presented. Somehow the Brazilians managed to get the Council documents translated into Portuguese and published in the newspapers almost the day after they were printed in Rome. The document that influenced me the most was the Pastoral Constitution on the Church in the Modern World, the document that developed during the Council. It begins with the statement: "The joys and hopes, the griefs and the anxieties of the men of this age, especially those who are poor or are in any way afflicted, these too are the joys and the hopes the griefs and the anxieties of the followers of Christ." For me, that was a radical, new understanding of what the Church should be. The Church was to identify with those who suffer, who bear the hopes, griefs and anxieties of this age, especially those who are poor or in any way afflicted. Their joys, hopes, griefs and anxieties are to be those of the Church. It meant a major shift from a hierarchical, power-based Church, to a Church of the poor. This new concept of Church dovetailed with my own experience in Brazil. The conjunction left an indelible mark on me.

The most visible and immediate effect it had was to move me away from clericalism. The shift occurred naturally in Brazil. When we arrived in that country, the Church there was still very clerical. We had to wear cassocks all the time. It wasn't long, though, before we dropped the cassock for non-liturgical work and changed to a sort of army-type shirt, with a cross on it. We felt that clothes were irrelevant. You were a priest and your mission was with the people. That's what mattered.

On one of my trips home, I went to see Bishop Klein, who was then bishop in Calgary. He was very upset by the fact that I was wearing casual clothes, not clerical garb. I was saddened by the visit, because we had been quite close and I couldn't understand why my casual clothes should come between us. I found out later from another bishop that he thought I had lost my faith.

De-emphasizing clericalism was not, to my mind, synonymous with abolishing hierarchy. I did not think the Church's hierachical structure was wrong. Christ founded His church on the apostles and they were essentially the first college of bishops. I see the hierarchical structure as necessary to provide leadership. The aspect of hierarchy that I object to is the abuse of power associated with a position.

I saw Dom Helder Camara as a model leader. Even during the four or five years the army had him under surveillance in Recife, he walked openly on the streets every day. He visited people all day long. He went to churches, convents, schools and homes. He was always walking on the street and he always had 500 people walking with him. He was really a teaching bishop. He spoke the truth of the Gospels, many times even at risk of death. That to me is the role of a church leader—being part of the people and speaking a clear gospel message in favour of the poor. Dom Helder never used his position to seek privilege for himself or the church. He used his position to speak for the poor.

Dom Helder used to talk about the role of the missionary priest. I questioned whether it was right for us foreigners to be there. "This is a Brazilian church," I said. "It should be Brazilians who determine its direction." He used to say, "If you are part of the people, Roberto, you are part of the Brazilian church." He agreed that if a missionary came and tried to impose a foreign culture on the people, that was wrong. But, if you respected the people, their language, culture and way of understanding, and if they looked on you as one of their own, it was all right. Eventually I agreed with him. Unfortunately, the missionary tradition has all too often confused Christianity with European culture and done considerable damage by obliterating a culture in the process of implanting Christianity in a European form.

Another important lesson I learned in Brazil came from an unlikely teacher. A section of the parish of União which Sister Diane and I ministered to was in the valley of the Pelada. The valley of the Pelada was one of the most beautiful places I have ever seen. It always seemed to me that God must have reached down and scooped out a 20-mile chunk of the mountain to form that perfect valley. It had 45 degree walls and was maybe 1,000 feet deep. To get into it, we had to go up over a mountain which was impassible most of the year, except on foot or by donkey. Jorge and I tried to set up a development scheme in that valley. We went in every Wednesday, no matter how bad the road was. We'd go as far as possible by jeep and the rest of the way by mule. We never missed a Wednesday.

The only crop in the valley was bananas, miles and miles of bananas. We would meet with the banana workers at the home of Anisio, an old black man who was accepted as a teacher by the farmers. He had a mud house with a tiled roof. We used to carry in a little blackboard and a few little things for teaching and I would start the meeting with a prayer in my weak Portuguese, and then Jorge would explain his new method of growing bananas.

These farmers had been growing bananas for many years without ever planting new ones. Banana is a grass, which grows to the size of a tree. Every year the tree is cut down, leaving a big stump. Next season, a shoot comes up beside the old stump. A banana stump could accumulate to a width of 15 feet. This method of leaving the stumps wasted a great amount of land and water. Jorge was trying to convince them to plant new shoots every year in rows, so they could be cultivated and retain water. But they were farmers and the hardest people in the world to change are farmers. Every meeting was exactly the same. We'd go in and say the prayer. Jorge would go over again how they should change their banana-growing practices. Finally, one day, Anisio saw that Jorge's plan might have some value to it. If what Jorge said was true, they could reclaim a lot of land and plant more bananas. He turned around and said in the dialect of the valley, "I'm going to change. I'm going to do what Jorge's telling us to do." Then he turned to me and said something I have never forgotten: "God divided his wisdom and knowledge and the Holy Spirit distributed it among all the people." To me, that meant that everyone has a bit of the wisdom and knowledge of God. I have to respect that and look for it. Anyone you meet could have the bit of wisdom you're lacking. From that time on I was convinced of the necessity of community, based on open dialogue.

Anisio was a remarkable man. There had been missionaries in the valley some 300 years before, but he said there had never been a priest in the valley during his lifetime except me. Yet he knew the New Testament by heart. He could recite all the Gospels. They had obviously been passed down from one generation to the next.

Anisio was recognized as the religious leader of the people in the valley. I had no trouble according him that position. I admired him greatly. One time I was able to get him to Recife on a *fermentista* course, at which Dom Helder was speaking. I got Dom Helder and Anisio talking together, and I just listened. I knew there were two extraordinary sources of wisdom in the same room that day.

CHAPTER 4

ST.PHILIP'S

On my return to Canada, I was assigned to St. Philip's, a parish in southeast Saskatoon. It had been established by Bishop Klein and the first parish priest had been Father Don Macgillivray. After his term at St. Philip's, Don was one of the first mission team to Brazil. Monsignor John Robinson succeeded him and I was the third pastor. The parish had a tradition of lay involvement, which began with the fund-raising, planning and overseeing of the construction of the church building.

The parish was predominately middle class. There were a good number of university people, some business and some working class. Within the parish boundaries, there were churches of 12 other denominations. About 25 per cent of the population was Catholic.

When I arrived September 1, 1970, I was 25 pounds overweight from improper eating during my trip around the world, and I was having considerable difficulty readjusting to life in North America. This was strange, because it had only been six years since I left. Many of the people I talked to in those first few weeks had not noticeably changed during the six years I was away, whereas my perception of the world had changed drastically.

When I arrived, the parish was in the hands of a young priest by the name of Father John Owens. John was very active in social movements in Saskatchewan, particularly the Indian movement. He had taken down the crucifix in the rectory living-room and replaced it with a huge poster of Che Guevara. Soon after my arrival, John decided to leave the active ministry and return to the lay state.

Having worked as a member of a pastoral team (*equipe*) in Brazil, I was eager to set one up at St. Philip's. The first week I was there, I advertised for a Sister to work in the parish. Only one Sister applied and she left after eight days. Later, I was told that no one applied because I had asked for such high qualifications. It wasn't until the second year that Sister Arlene Boulanger and Sister Mildred Strauss came to work in the parish full time. They worked with me and the assistants who were assigned to St. Philip's over the next five years—Fathers Emil April, Denis Shirley and Benno Burghardt, and a deacon, Mike Bedard. We worked as a team—planning, doing, revising, planning, doing, revising.

We marked out our areas of responsibility according to individual skills. One was in charge of music, another in charge of the children, and so on. The team approach seemed to come naturally to some, and not to others.

Shortly after arriving at St. Philip's I learned that a small group of priests, who were later joined by sisters and lay people, was planning to meet each Monday from 7 a.m. till noon to pray, study and work out a pastoral plan for the coming week. The formation of this group, called Monday Seven, had been suggested by a number of priests, sisters and lay people who had attended summer sessions at the Ecumenical Institute in Chicago. The purpose of the institute, which was an outgrowth of a meeting of the World Conference of Churches near Chicago some years before, was to draw people from all denominations into a communal situation in which they learned how to plan and organize their pastoral work. I was very happy to join the group in its formative stage and become part of this intense strategic planning team.

Surprisingly, St. Philip's had no parish council when I arrived. There had been one, but when its last term expired Monsignor Robinson recommended that it be dissolved. He wanted the next pastor to be free to set up whatever structures he felt were necessary for the time. This had the advantage that you could start from scratch, and the disadvantage that you didn't know where to start. I began visiting people in the parish, many of whom I already knew from earlier years, asking them what they thought the parish needed. My own preference was a team approach, using the parish council as the basic structure.

Although I had worked extensively with lay people in Canada, particularly as director of programming at the Catholic Centre, my appreciation of working with lay people grew in Brazil. Through my work with the *fermentistas*, I discovered how capable people were of assuming responsibility for pastoral work in the parish, and how their taking on that responsibility transformed the parish.

There was one big difference between St. Philip's and our parish in Brazil. In St. Philip's, men as well as woman were already actively involved in the church. I felt that the parish structure should reflect this and that couples should form the core of our parish council. Our parish plan at St. Philip's, however, could be the same as it had been in Brazil, pursuing the same three goals: to preach the Gospel clearly, to form community, and to celebrate this coming together around the Gospel with good liturgy and social action.

People in the parish associated strongly with the separate schools within the parish boundaries that their children attended. It seemed logical, therefore, to allow the council to reflect these three sections of the parish. At a general parish meeting, I proposed a parish council based on couples, three of which I would pick, one from each section of the parish, and three the parish could elect, also one from each section of the parish. Young people, seniors, and other individuals could be added later. Two couples would drop out each year and two new couples would be elected. Seventy-three people came to that first meeting and, as I recall, 72 supported the proposal.

As a means of involving people in the preaching of the Gospel and in the building of community, we began a program which we called Meet the Padres. We met once a week in the home of a family. That family would invite others from their neighbourhood—Catholic families, but also families from other denominations, whoever they considered to be their Christian community.

After introducing ourselves, we read the Scriptures for the following Sunday. Then I asked the people what they felt the theme for the sermon should be and what they would say if they had to preach. It was the first time many of them had ever been asked that kind of question, and they often had tremendous insights to contribute. At the end of our discussion, I would ask if they had any stories that could be used in the sermon. People would tell about their own experiences or about something they'd heard and, invariably, there were good stories.

People began to listen more attentively to the Sunday sermon because they knew that some of what was going to be said was theirs or they might be asked to do it for the next Sunday. They began to see that one had to prepare for the preaching and hearing of the Gospel. You couldn't just come to church on Sunday and expect to grasp it all immediately.

Lay readers were becoming the common way of announcing the liturgy and they had to know how to read. Good intentions alone do not make a good reader. We brought in a radio broadcaster to conduct a workshop with our readers. He selected the participants he thought had potential and worked with them. The goal was to have the Scriptures read clearly so that whoever was listening could understand them.

Our preparation for the Sunday liturgy reflected the way we thought about the liturgical year. I imagined waves hitting the shore, 52 waves a year. Just as a wave starts far out, builds to a peak, crashes onto the beach and flows back out, I saw a week in the parish starting to build on Tuesday with our Meet the Padres meeting. The rest of the week, it should build to a peak, which would be reached on Sunday with the celebration of the liturgy. Then on Monday, the wave would slip back out to rebuild for the next week. That image helped me, and perhaps others, to see the church week as a continuous dynamic. It culminated with the celebration of the liturgy on Sunday, but that was only the result of preparation during the week. As the wave went back out to sea, so the people were carried back out to their world. The Sunday liturgy would have to sustain them until the next wave peaked the following Sunday.

Having just come back from South America and a trip around the world, I was very aware of the Church in other parts of the world, with the result that concern for the Third World and the notion of universal Church pervaded my work at St. Philip's. I stressed that we had a relationship to the rest of the Church, and a special relationship to the Church of the poor. Stories from my Latin American experience crept into my sermons and surfaced almost every time I spoke at meetings or gatherings. I was convinced that we could not ignore what was going on in the rest of the world. It wasn't something separate, something out there. It was related to what was going on here and it was our concern. Maybe people absorbed my belief by a kind of osmosis or maybe they began to see it for themselves. It was just a question of becoming aware of another reality, learning how other people lived, thought, prayed and suffered. Once they were aware, the response followed.

During my first Lent at St. Philip's, I made awareness of the Third World a strong part of our Lenten lives. The Canadian Catholic Organization for Development and Peace (CCODP) Share Lent program helped stimulate awareness and giving. Although I never directly appealed for money, the money started to come in. The generosity of the people in St. Philip's was astounding and that same generosity seemed to sweep the diocese and the country.

An invitation from the CCODP to be one of their project assessors gave me the opportunity to keep informed about Third World development. I also used my annual three-week holiday in January to go back to the mission in Brazil or visit Peace and Development projects. It was very important to me to return to the Third World, to get back into the world of the poor and the weak. It's very easy to get away from it and forget it.

In our efforts to build community at St. Philip's, I began to be bothered by the role of the schools. The separate or Catholic school system in Saskatchewan had been established in 1905, to allow Catholics to have their own elementary schools and carry out the formal education of their children within the Catholic faith. Full tax and grant funding through Grade 12 were approved in 1964. When I arrived at St. Philip's, I found that the schools were well organized and doing good work, but not focusing their efforts on the parish, the local church community. In my view, anything that was not helping build the local community was an obstacle. I also objected to the schools demanding that the parish priests give a good deal of time each week to carry out school programs—instruction of the children and celebration of the liturgy in schools. In short, I felt that the schools were serving their own ends and not helping to sustain the parish community.

My first discussions with principals and school board officials were a bit heated. Gradually, though, I did get the educators' co-operation and the schools became part of the parish. Each school took on the responsibility of bringing the children to the church and preparing them to lead a children's liturgy. Each school led the children's liturgy once every three weeks. As that progressed, I felt the teachers, the children and their parents were growing in their understanding of community.

The children's liturgy was celebrated on Saturday night. It was directed towards children and designed for them to participate. They did the music and the readings. I used to ask the children to come up and be near me at the altar during the celebration, so they could really feel they were in the Father's house. In South America, people looked upon the church building as the Father's house, where everyone had a right to be and where you could feel at home. You could bring your baby and change the diaper, bring the dog, eat your lunch and talk to your neighbour. The church on Saturday, when they came to market, was noisier than any place I'd ever been, outside of a factory. At first, I found this very disturbing, because I was brought up to think of church as a sacred place, where you were supposed to be quiet. But, after I was there awhile, I realized that they were probably closer to understanding what church is about. It is the Father's house and the Father wants everyone, no matter how poor or old or weak, to be totally at home there. I tried to develop that sense of being at home in our liturgies at St. Philip's. It seemed essential to help the children become familiar with the building and with what went on in the church. I think they came to feel they were part of it all, and that was important in building community in St. Philip's.

The Saturday night children's liturgy was one of four distinctly different liturgies held in the parish every weekend. We felt we had to respect the form of celebration people wanted. And, since not everyone wanted the same form, we tried to provide a wide range. We wanted everyone to feel at home at the liturgy they attended.

The first liturgy on Sunday morning was very traditional, a simple format, for people who still liked to pray the rosary or pray quietly to themselves. The second liturgy on Sunday was like the old high mass. We tried to have good traditional music and liturgy, and at the same time bring in little changes that people could accept without difficulty. The last mass was a youth mass, with a folk band, good young singers and many innovative liturgical practices. The youth mass was by far the most popular liturgy. The church could never hold all the people who came to it.

The last year I was at St. Philip's, we celebrated the 25th anniversary of the parish. We stretched it a little, because the parish hadn't physically existed that long. However, 25 years earlier the first inkling of a new parish had been felt. During the time I was at St. Philip's, parish collections as well as money for international development increased. The parish was never in any bind for funds and we were able to pay off the mortgage. Someone suggested that we burn the mortgage as part of the 25th anniversary celebration. Father Don Macgillivray, who had taken out the mortgage, happened to be home from Brazil and took part in the mortgage-burning. It was a good celebration. That day, we put up a first-class relic of St. Philip Neri, which we had received from the pastor of the church of St. Philip Neri in Rome for the church of St. Philip Neri in Saskatoon. It was to symbolize, in a way the more traditional people in the parish could relate to, the universal Church, the Church community.

Part of the long-range plan we developed for the parish was to try to make the celebration of each sacrament a parish event, involving parishioners as much as possible. We felt, for instance, that baptism, which is the call of new members into the church, should be done publicly and that the parents and godparents of those being baptized should be properly instructed before the sacrament was conferred. A team of lay people took on the responsibility of visiting the homes where there were infants to be baptized, arranging and delivering communal instruction, and continuing contact with the parents to make them feel welcome after their children had become part of the parish. The sacraments of penance and first communion were also celebrated as parish events. Many parents were involved with our team in the preparation for these sacraments. We introduced lay communion distributors, which was uncommon at the time, and we began relying on them to take communion to the sick. We felt that it was the community's responsibility, not just the priest's, to see that the sick, the old and everyone else were being looked after.

Another innovation, which hardly seems remarkable now, but which had tremendous significance at the time, was the handshake during mass. When people overcame their northern reserve, actually touched their neighbour, shook hands and wished them the peace of Christ, another barrier to community dissolved.

We also introduced communal penance, a practice which was just beginning to spread. The parish council and the pastoral team of priests and sisters put a lot of work into preparing a communal celebration of the sacrament of forgiveness. I felt it was very important for us to recognize that besides being sinners individually, we were also sinners collectively, that we were as a group living and doing things which contradict the justice and goodness which must characterize the kingdom of God on earth.

The sacrament I found increasingly difficult to witness was the sacra-

72

ment of marriage. Many of the people who came to be married were not really part of the community. It was almost as if they walked in off the street sometimes, wanting to be married. I was very concerned about the breakdown of so many marriages and worried about marrying kids whose chances of making a go of it seemed awfully slim. Often the young people who came to me had no interest in looking at the serious side of what they were about to do. I wanted to say to them, "Look, I don't think you should get married. You're not ready." I found it hard to officiate at some of these weddings in good conscience. I felt as if I was collaborating in something that was wrong. I knew that in many parishes the sacrament of marriage had become a filling station type of event. People line up, set a date, spend three months making arrangements for the hotel and the banquet and the cars and a thousand things that have nothing to do with their future life. They're caught in a culture that's so materialistic that they have a difficult time thinking about what's really going to take place. These kids weren't entirely to blame, though. The responsibility for preparing the next generation of married people, I felt, rested with the community. Why couldn't one couple, I thought, take responsibility for one or two new couples and help prepare them, help them understand what they were entering into, so the wedding could be a celebration of their union and their future and not just a social event. That's the approach we moved towards.

In my first few months at St. Philip's, I encountered some resistance from the traditional forces. That first fall, I was asked to reconvene the Catholic Women's League and informed that this would require my attendance at an executive meeting and a members' meeting each month. I knew that other parishes had a CWL and that St. Philip's had always had one, but I couldn't see how I had time to do this for 17 people who were already good, active Catholics. So I went to the first executive meeting and said, "If you can come back next month and tell me what reason you have for existing here in this parish, I'm prepared to listen." I felt that the traditional organizations—the CWL, the Knights of Columbus and so on—often worked against the community and the parish without realizing it, by splitting people off from the parish. In my view, groups in the parish should be formed as parish groups and should be parish-oriented. The next month, the CWL told me they hadn't come up with a reason for existing independently and so the group was shelved.

The good work the CWL had been doing wasn't dropped. We found a way of doing it which involved many more people in the parish. We called it the Love Your Neighbour Group. Volunteers put their names on a list and took responsibility for one week a year. If anyone in the parish needed assistance, in any form, these volunteers would see that they received it. Hundreds of people volunteered—men, women, children, and youth. The Love Your Neighbour group basically became responsible for looking after the needs of people in the parish.

One of those needs was the care of families around the time of a death. Whenever there was a death in a family in the parish, the Love Your Neighbour group helped sustain that family—from the moment of death, until they had dealt with the practical matters and the grief and had worked their way back into another way of life again. I was very happy that the parish took this on as a serious responsibility.

Other activities with a broader scope were also undertaken by the parish during the time I was there. During my first year at St. Philip's, the synod of bishops in Rome announced plans to study the priesthood. In conjunction with the bishops' study, St. Philip's decided to conduct a study within the parish to determine the parishioners' understanding of the priesthood and the ministry of the priesthood. The study was directed by Dr. Frank Vella, a university professor and member of the parish council. It was done with a good deal of seriousness and according to academic standards. We gave the results to the bishop to add to the general pool of information being gathered in Canada in preparation for the synod. I don't know how much effect it had, but it was good for the parish to see that they had a responsibility to address major Church issues. Several years later, another study was done on the role of women in the Church. Again, a comprehensive study gathering the opinions of the parishioners was conducted. I felt that this also helped the parish move from a narrow focus on its own problems to a more universal perspective.

In 1972, I was elected president of the Western Conference of Priests, which entailed responsibility for hosting a major conference in Saskatoon in 1973. The parish sustained me with practical and moral support through an exhausting year preparing for this conference. Over 300 priests and 15 bishops from Western Canada gathered in Saskatoon. The main speakers for the conference were Father Dick Hanley, who was the general of the Oblate Fathers at that time, and Father Richard McBrien, a leading North American theologian from the University of Notre Dame.

The theme of the conference was How the West is One and the thrust was to build Church community. Some progressive resolutions came out of the conference, including support for new ministries for the Church in Western Canada and opening the ordained priesthood to women and married men. The archbishop of Winnipeg, Cardinal George Flahiff, was among those who publicly supported all six resolutions that came out of the conference. The priests and bishops at the conference passed resolutions which they felt were necessary for the ministry of the Church in Western Canada, knowing they did not have the power to effect those changes and knowing that what they thought was necessary would not take place. The power was still going to be centralized and exercised from the top down—the top being the Vatican—and the Vatican would not budge on these issues. It was very frustrating, and I think it was this frustration and feeling of powerlessness and futility that led to the demise of the Western Conference of Priests a few years later.

Although we knew we could not expect major changes, some of us continued to introduce practices we felt would be allowed. At St. Philip's, we invited women to distribute communion. It was a natural step in our parish, because the parish council was comprised of couples. They became the first lay distributors. The bishop came to confer on them the mandate to do this. At first it caused some consternation and a bit of confusion. I made sure there was always a priest giving communion too, because some people simply would not go to a woman. In due course the practice was accepted and, in fact, has become very common.

Another change we made early on was the removal of the altar rail. It was made of beautifully finished wood and had been built into the church, but it symbolized the separation of the lay people from the altar. I talked it over with the parish council and they didn't know what to do. Finally, we just took it out and kept it hidden for a year or two. It was eventually given away. By then the altar had become the heart of the church community.

Changing people's expectations of their church is a sensitive matter. I had a good lesson in that one Christmas. It was 1973. We had prepared for Christmas in the traditional way. The crib was set up and the liturgies and the sermons were ready. On the afternoon of Christmas Eve I got a phone call from Ben Smillie, a United Church minister in Saskatoon who is very active in social ministry. Ben said, "The Americans are bombing Hanoi tonight, on Christmas. What are you going to do about it in your mass?"

"Well," I said, "what can I do about it?"

"Well," Ben replied, "I think you have to address it." I let Ben's phone call stop there, but afterwards I thought maybe he was right. If we really believed in social justice, how could we celebrate an innocent Christmas when a horrible thing like that was happening to other people, many of whom were Christians as well. Without going back to the liturgy team, I changed the homily to include the idea that on Christmas we have a responsibility to think of the whole world, just as the infant Jesus had been sent for the whole world. I spoke about the bombing and said we really did not have a right to be tranquil while this was going on. The homily changed the tone of the liturgy. At the end of the mass I changed the usual dismissal, "May the peace of Christ be with you," to "May the peace of Christ disturb you."

When mass had ended and most of the parishioners had filed past,

I noticed a woman with three children, whom I did not recognize. As she approached, I could see she was quite distraught. When she reached me, she exploded: "You have spoiled my Christmas. I am a separated parent and I have very few days in which I can celebrate. We have been getting ready for this Christmas for several months, the children and I, and we were expecting a peaceful sermon here and you come and totally disturb everybody, just upset everybody and I am very, very angry at what you've done." She was gone by the time I finished saying I was sorry. The last person in the church was also someone I had never seen. He came up to me, shook my hand and said, "I'm here by accident tonight. You will never see me again. I work for the World Bank and I just got caught in Saskatoon tonight because of the air traffic tie-up. I'd like to tell you that that was the best liturgy and sermon I have ever attended in my life." That sequence of reactions was the best example I've ever had of the impossibility of following a middle road. If you take a stand, it's going to upset some people and win support from others.

Because of our diocesan rule of the "flexible five," referring to the usual duration of an appointment, I looked upon my appointment from the beginning as a five-year operation and planned it as such. My last year there, 1975, we designated a year of reconciliation. Fourteen homes were selected as stations for the celebration of reconciliation, which we held on a Sunday in April. The parish team visited all 14 stations. The parishioners were invited to visit any one or more. People did go from one home to another and there was a tremendous feeling of warmth and unity. The idea was that we were coming together in reconciliation with one another, with the universal Church and with the world. The symbol was to act as a reminder that this reconciliation had to go on all the time.

During that reconciliation year we also organized two pilgrimages to Rome for ten days each, both of which I led. They were done on an economical, co-operative basis and many people got to Rome who would never have been able to afford it otherwise. Again, the purpose was to experience something of the international Church and grow in our sense of Church community.

I viewed my five years at St. Philip's as an opportunity to build Christian community and to live, not above, but with the community builders. Although my role was to be their priest, I did not see that role as putting me above them. To me, it meant living and walking each day with people in the community and helping them to find a better way to preach the Gospel, form community and celebrate both.

Over the years I had come to see the role of the Church as the cutting edge in society, working its way into the future clearing a pathway for people to follow. If the Church is not doing that, if it remains silent, uncontroversial and inconsequential, it is not fulfilling its task. The

Gospel has to be proclaimed and lived in such a way that it breaks down barriers and clears a way for people to get through.

Christ's life shows us how to be the cutting edge in society. He rejected what his society stood for and laid down a new path for people to follow, a pathway of love and service. Christ was extremely concerned about this world, about feeding the hungry, clothing the naked, housing the homeless and visiting the sick. Even though He talked about another life and another kingdom, He issued very strong directives about how one was to live here and now. I felt that Christ's Church had to go through that same process today, that it could not stand still, could not accept the status quo. It was to preach the truth of love and community for the present and the future. It was this concept of Church as a universal, Christian community and as a cutting edge in society, that informed my work at St. Philip's.

CHAPTER 5

ENTERING POLITICS

As my last year at St. Philip's was drawing to a close, the bishop informed me that I was due for a sabbatical. Having been ordained for 22 years, I welcomed the idea. It was an opportunity to try a totally different form of ministry. I looked into the possibility of going to a prison and living for a number of months with the prisoners. On the advice of some parishioners, I also applied for a scholarship being offered by the International Development Research Center in Ottawa for middle-aged people with an interest in international development. When I received notification that I was one of ten people selected to receive the scholarship that year, I decided to do the research project. It involved travelling and studying the long-term effect of projects funded by Canadian non-government organizations like CCODP, CUSO and the YMCA. I presented my observations in a book, which was entitled *When the Snake Bites the Sun*.

It was September 9, 1977. I had just delivered the last chapter of my book to the printer. I can remember feeling relief as I drove across the old black bridge up to St. Francis, where I was part-time assistant to Father Denis Shirley. After eight months of steady work, that job was done. I was making myself a sandwich for lunch when the phone rang. That phone call changed the course of my life.

The person on the phone was Mary MacDonald, an active New Democrat, a graduate of the Antigonish movement in Nova Scotia, a leading battler in the medicare crisis of 1962 in Saskatchewan, an ardent Catholic, and a wife and mother. Mary MacDonald was calling to ask me to let my name stand for the New Democratic Party candidacy in the federal riding of Saskatoon East. This new riding had been created after a re-division of seats following the 1974 election and no one had yet been nominated in the riding. It was part of what had formerly been called Saskatoon-Humboldt. Saskatoon East and Humboldt-Lake Center were the names of the two new ridings.

This invitation came completely out of the blue. Nothing could have been further from my mind than entering politics. I had never been at a political meeting. I didn't even belong to a political party. I said it was nice of her to ask, but I was not interested. "We feel that you have the qualities to do this and we'll give you some time to think it over,'' she said. "In fact, you have four days to think it over and I don't believe you should drop it that casually. I think you should look seriously at this possibility." She went on to say that Father Andy Hogan, who came from Nova Scotia, from her own territory, was an NDP member of Parliament. There was a precedent.

That afternoon, I couldn't get the matter out of my mind. I kept thinking of the visit I'd had the year before in Brazil with the Benedictine contemplative nuns who had studied Portuguese the same time I did at Petrópolis and who had become close friends of mine. Whenever I was in South America, I would spend some time at their house in prayer and contemplation and also talking with them about the world situation. Of all people I knew around the world, even though they were contemplatives, they seemed to have the best grasp of what was happening. That last time I was there, while recovering from a bout of altitude sickness that struck in Bolivia, we talked about my future. It was not clear to me, so they promised to pray in a special way for what they called *Projeto Roberto*. They used this term because I was always talking about the development projects I was visiting and studying in Latin America. Mary MacDonald's call triggered that memory. After I hung up, the thought flashed through my mind: could this possibly be the *Projeto Roberto*? Was my project being directed to me? During the course of that afternoon I decided I had better give it some serious thought. I phoned Bishop Mahoney and invited him over for supper. This was not uncommon. The bishop was always willing to come and discuss matters of concern to his priests. The bishop was very open on this occasion too. After talking for three or four hours about my entering politics and what it could mean for me and the diocese, we left the matter open. He said he would think about it and take counsel and suggested that I do the same. There was, however, a 96-hour time limit on the deliberations.

I phoned my brother and sisters to see how they would react to the proposal. My brother, Charles, was quite cool to the whole idea. My older sister, Marguerite, thought it would be fun to try it. My younger sister, Mary Lou, said, "It would be a long shot from a standing start."

On Friday I went to visit some New Democrats—Olie Turnbull, director of the Cooperative College of Canada, a man who had helped bring about funding for Catholic schools in Saskatchewan; and Herman Rolfes, a former parishioner from St. Philip's parish, who had sought my advice before entering provincial politics. Neither of them was enthusiastic about my taking this step. After talking to them I was pretty sure I wouldn't do it, but I felt obliged to seek further counsel. There was little time, but I felt I could consult the parish priests in Saskatoon East, the teachers at the Catholic school in the parish where I was living, ten or 12 couples my age whom I had known for many years and talk to 25 or 30 parishioners.

On Saturday I phoned the parish priests. On the whole, they were cautiously open to the idea. A couple of them were openly enthusiastic. They thought I might be able to carry out a mission in this new role. My close friend, Grant Maxwell, happened to be in Saskatoon and I turned to him for advice. He was prepared to support whatever decision I made, but he was leery of the idea.

On Sunday, which was the third day of the deliberation, I asked people at mass to come into the rectory and spend a few minutes with me. I said I needed their help in making a major decision. At the first mass, I asked people in the first two rows and at the second mass I picked five couples at random. At the third mass I asked the last dozen people who remained in the church at the end of the service. When we were in the rectory, I asked them what they thought about priests in politics. I was surprised that there were so few objections. What would they think about me in politics? The response to that was almost universally affirmative. Then they asked, "Which party?" My reply dampened their enthusiasm, but they had already committed themselves on principle. Only one couple actually opposed the idea. At the end of the consultation with my parishioners, I had the impression that I could enter politics without causing too much consternation in the local church community.

That same day, I made a number of local and long-distance calls to other couples I had known for many years. From them came almost universal acceptance of the idea. In fact, the last couple, Joe Campbell and his wife, Rosemary, said, "Why not?" I was left at the end of the third day with that question—Why not?

The Liberal incumbent in Saskatoon-Humboldt was Otto Lang, who at the time was Minister of Transport in the Liberal government. Because I knew Otto well, I felt it was only proper to tell him what I was considering. A mutual friend, John Hardenne, arranged the phone call. I told Otto that I had been asked by the New Democrats to stand for the nomination and asked him what he thought. He said, "You'd make a very strong candidate."

On Monday I talked to the teachers at St. Francis School. Of all the people I consulted, their response was by far the most reactionary. Most of them rejected the idea of a priest in politics. They felt that a priest's place was in a parish.

When I ran into Caroline Heath later that day, she asked if I had reached a decision. I described the consultative process and told her I had decided not to run. Caroline said, "That's fine if you don't run, but I'm concerned about your reasons. I think the basis for the decision should be what you feel is the right thing for you to do."

From that chance encounter I went to Jean Hardenne's, to meet with some of Otto Lang's supporters who had called and asked to see me. There was a handful of people at Hardenne's, all Catholics, all friends of mine. They were there to offer me the possibility of a Liberal nomination. My reaction was not what they expected. Going into that meeting, I was not prepared to accept the NDP nomination. They turned me right around. I had never been interested in politics and I certainly wasn't about to deal with anyone for a nomination. But the Liberal meeting made me think that maybe I had what it takes, maybe I should do it.

On leaving Hardenne's that night, the question came back: Why not? Why are you doing it or not doing it? I was to meet the bishop in the morning and I still had no answer. It was terrible, not being able to make up my mind about something so important. I decided to spend the night in prayer. I went into the church and began a night of desperate struggle. Sometimes I refer to it as my agony in the garden. I was forced to appraise my life, what I stood for, who I was and what I really meant by talking about social justice. That didn't provide an answer. I looked at the question of whether or not I should enter politics. Both sides had good arguments. I knew I could continue to utilize my skills as a parish priest. On the other hand, I could probably also do something as a member of Parliament. I still could not decide between what looked like two good alternatives. Out of desperation I decided that I would solve it by what the breviary, my prayer book, would tell me at dawn. I don't ordinarily live my life like that. I'm not a charismatic prayer person. But I could find no other way of making this decision. There was no one I could ask to help me make it. I had already done that and I had both support and opposition. So, as the dawn broke that morning in the church, I opened my breviary to the early morning prayer for Tuesday, the 24th week of the year. The reading was a sermon on shepherds by St. Augustine and in it were these words: "They are after all to be like lambs. Gird your loins and light your lamps. No one lights a lamp and then puts it under a basket. He puts it on the lamp stand that it might shed light on all in the house. In the same way, let your lamp shine before men so that they may see your goods and glorify your heavenly Father." The reading seemed to suggest that I had some light to show and that I should go ahead. I began to cry, to weep, and I never do that. But the dam of tension and indecision had broken. I knew, suddenly, that I was free to go ahead, if that is what was to be decided for me by my colleagues and bishop. Or I was free not to. That was possible, too. I also knew at that moment that if I took this step I would never have the safety of being a cleric, a church man, again. From now on I would be a political priest. I'd always be on the front line, always in danger, always under attack. I can still remember how I felt as I left the church that morning. I was leaving behind the safety of the church. I was leaving behind a very safe life. I was walking out into the darkness that was the future.

That day, September 13, there was to be a regular meeting of the Saskatoon parish priests and others on the pastoral committee with the bishop at the Catholic Centre. I drove to the bishop's house, where he was having breakfast, and we talked. I said, "I am now free," and I started to cry again. I remember wondering why life had to be so hard. The bishop had also taken counsel, but still wasn't sure what to do. He suggested that we present the question to the pastoral committee. At the end of the pastoral meeting, he presented the situation to the 15 priests present. The discussion was extremely serious and open. At first some did not support the idea, while others were very supportive. Two and a half hours later, after everyone had spoken, there seemed to be a consensus that the bishop should give me permission to go into politics. When the meeting was finished he simply said, "You go ahead, Bob. You have our permission to do this." Again I started to cry, which is completely out of character for me, but I couldn't stop it. Then the bishop and the priests worked out what my life should be like for the next little while, whether I should preach on Sundays, where I should live, how I should dress, etc. It was decided that I would continue to live in the parish and carry out my duties there. As soon as the election was called, I would move to the seminary.

Although I was unaware of it in those days of deliberation, opposition to my political career was building in another quarter. In Rosetown. My aunts and uncles never did accept it. During the years I was an MP, they would barely acknowledge my existence and never say anything to acknowledge my work in Ottawa. One of the hardest things about political life for me was being rejected by part of my own family. They were all Liberals, of course. I think they were more upset by my going NDP than by my being a priest in politics. They had been very anti-NDP and I suspect the neighbours had a good laugh at their expense. My family did not suffer embarrassment graciously.

For me, the question was whether or not I should enter politics. It was never a question of which party. From what I knew and what I had read, the New Democratic Party, apart from the question of abortion, was the party that followed most closely the encyclicals and other church teachings which embodied my social principles. The next thing that had to be done was to tell the New Democrats that I was willing to let my name stand. At that point I didn't even have a party membership. Buying a membership made me eligible to be a candidate. Then I had to find someone to nominate me. I went back to my old friend, Olie Turnbull. Olie scrutinized my motives, then accepted my decision and agreed to nominate me. Pat Lorje was asked to second the nomination.

The next step was to write a nomination speech. Since I had never been at a nomination meeting, knew nothing about the process, knew none of the other candidates and none of the delegates, I didn't know where to start. Turnbull and Lorje gave me some suggestions. I knew I could talk a bit about medicare and a bit about the labour movement, but I also had to say something that was distinctly mine. Interestingly enough, the topics I chose were to become the two key issues of my political career.

The nomination meeting was held on a Saturday in Our Lady of Lourdes School auditorium. I didn't know what to wear. I had only a few clerical clothes and an old green suit. I wore the green suit and a turtleneck sweater. I had prepared a flyer about myself and I arrived at the school, by myself, carrying these flyers. There was a fair amount of commotion in the auditorium, but I didn't know what was going on. It was all new to me. I was taken up to the front, membership card in hand, and informed that I couldn't vote because I hadn't been a member long enough.

The meeting opened and they called for nominations. There were three: Margaret Fern, who was president of the association, a young lawyer by the name of Bob Borden; and myself. We drew straws to determine order of speaking. Fortunately, I drew the third spot, which meant I could at least see what the others said and how they did it. When it was my turn, I got up and looked at the crowd and realized this was just a crowd and I had spoken to lots of crowds. From that moment on, I felt right at home. I talked about serving, about working for people and working to bring about world justice. And then I said that if I was to be their candidate, they had to accept three conditions. The first was that I was going to defend human life from its conception until its natural end. That meant I was against abortion, euthanasia, capital punishment and anything else that killed people, including famine, violence and war. That hung in the air for a minute, because the New Democratic Party convention statement called for abortion to be taken out of the Criminal Code. These people could see that I was demanding to be allowed to hold a dissenting position.

The second point I wanted to make clear was that I was going to remain a priest before, during and after the event. I specifically said "event" because I knew this could be over in five minutes. The third condition was that I didn't want anyone who worked for me in the campaign to ever make a personal attack against Otto Lang or any member of his family. That hung in the air for a minute or so, too, but I said, "No. That's the way it's got to be." Then there was clapping and I sat down. Next came the election and the counting of votes. When the announcement was made, I had taken 218 out of 305 votes, winning the nomination on the first ballot. It was all over. Lorne Nystrom, whom I had never met, was the guest speaker, but I didn't hear much of his speech. I was already at the back, trying to find out what to do next. I was looking for the organization that would win this election, but I began to discover that political associations do not necessarily have the tight organization that parishes do. You can't assume that someone will step forward, ready to do all the work. I found this a little disconcerting. As I was leaving the meeting, Roy Romanow said to me, "You're good, but you've got a lot to learn about speeches." He thought my speech was too long and I had a lot to learn about policies.

We expected the election in the spring of 1978, which would give me about nine months to get ready. My intention was, as in anything else I had done, to go all out. I hadn't gone into this to lose; I was out to win the election. I had no inkling what that meant or the amount of work that would be required.

During the next few months I struggled to meet the people in the party and get a sense of the organization. It became clear to me that there was a lot of organizing to be done and I was hoping to get a good campaign manager to tell me how to do it. I envisaged a campaign working like a wave, building so fast and so high that no one could stop it. Reaching that pitch, however, would take an enormous amount of effort.

In those early days, I dealt with a number of mundane affairs, such as clothes. I had only my clerical garb and my green suit. I had to find a way to look more like a candidate. Bud Sarich, the husband of Margaret Sarich, one of my campaign workers, offered to lend me a suit for the filming of a television advertisement. While we were doing the shoot at the YMCA, where I generally swam for a half hour every day, some Liberals arrived and they became really angry because I was wearing this nice suit. I couldn't see why they would get angry about my wearing a suit, but they did. That's when I decided to get lots of new suits. The cry went out in the Saskatoon New Democratic Party that I wore a 44-tall and any suit that looked good would be used one day a week, whenever the owner could let me borrow it. It began to look as if I had an extensive wardrobe, which I did, but it hung in many closets.

Early in the campaign I felt that I had to get my name known. To accomplish this, we planned to have a full "drop" of the constituency. Before Christmas we dropped leaflets at every house. Later we developed what came to be known as my "holy" card. It was a little card, the size of a holy card, with my picture on the front and a short message on the back: "To me the NDP offers the best chance we have in this country for economic and moral justice." I gave these cards to people personally. No one got a card except from me.

Then I started knocking on doors. There were more than 25,000 doors in that constituency. I had maps of the constituency with the polling districts and I set out as if I were trying to paint the map by coloring the districts I visited. When the election was called, 577 days later, I had knocked on every door in the constituency at least once, some more than once. I learned that a visit to the door, even a very short one, has impact. This came home to me very forcibly as I began to run into people I had visited 25 years earlier as a young curate in another part of the city, and they described those visits in great detail.

When I asked people what their political problems were, they almost invariably said they had none. If they did talk about a problem, it was usually the same kind of problem they would have discussed if I had been there visiting as their priest. In one home, someone didn't have a job. In another, someone was sick. My experience as a priest had taught me the necessity of reacting to people accurately and quickly. Meeting people at the door simply required quicker reactions.

If someone told me to get lost, I never bothered them again. I instructed my campaigners not to bother them, either. I kept records of every person I had seen, who was supportive and who was not. After knocking on that many doors, I concluded that it was worth the effort. People want to have whoever is working with them or for them know who they are. What surprised me was that the visits did not have to be long. A visit could be very short, but it had to be marked by a thought or phrase that the person would remember me by.

After knocking on 25,000 doors, I also reached the conclusion that dogs play a significant role in the lives of Saskatonians. At many houses, when someone opened the door, all you could hear was the dog. I'm not that fond of dogs, but when I saw how important the dog was, I talked about dogs. One day I was campaigning with a Lutheran minister, Mark Koenker. Mark was born in the United States and knows American politics. He also knows how to campaign and we were a good team. Ordinarily, four of us would go down a street; Mark and another person on one side, my sister Mary Lou and I on the other. This particular day we were in a poor part of the city. Mark was going down his side and he came to a house that was just barely a shack. The front door was open. Inside was a Great Dane standing on his hind legs, with his two front legs up against the screen door. The owner of the dog was standing behind him, straddling the dog as he held it by the collar and holding himself against the door posts. Of course, Mark couldn't make any conversation. He called across the street for me to come over, said this guy wanted to talk to me. When I got there, the dog was barking so loudly I couldn't hear anything. I cupped my hands around my mouth and shouted, "I like dogs." Mark said that was the only time in the campaign that I lied.

Our signs were a distinctive feature of our campaign. We bought two four-by-eight plywood sheets, painted them in the New Democratic colors, and added my name and an arrow pointing east that said: To Ottawa. The person living at the top of the 25th Street bridge, a very strategic location in the riding, happened to be a strong supporter and allowed me to put one of these signs up on that corner. We rigged up the other sign so it was movable and could stand alone. When I saw that the signs were beginning to work, I borrowed a truck from a friend and every night we would move that sign to a new location. Within a month I began to hear, "Father Ogle has signs all over the city." We had two signs.

As the first year wore on, the Progressive Conservatives also nominated a candidate, Dan Meyers. I did not know Dan, but I made a point of meeting him and I told him that we would fight a good fight. As the campaign went into its second year, I saw on television one night that Otto Lang had also decided to run in Saskatoon East. I couldn't believe it. I knew from knocking on doors that he couldn't win, that he couldn't even come second. I told my campaign workers that we were running against the Progressive Conservatives and that Otto was going to come in third, which was, in fact, the outcome of the election. I couldn't understand why Lang was running in Saskatoon East when he had the option of running in Humboldt-Lake Center. I didn't know if he had a chance in Humboldt-Lake Center, but I knew he didn't have a chance in Saskatoon East.

A tragic event that occurred in Saskatoon in the spring of 1978 was to have a direct impact on the campaign. A Mountie by the name of Brian King was shot by two young men when he stopped their automobile. When the shooting was reported on the news the next morning, it upset the whole city. Brian King was well-known and liked and the killing of a policeman was disturbing in itself. I continued to knock on doors, but for days after that there was only one question, "What's your stand on capital punishment?" My stand on capital punishment was clear. I was against it. When Dan Meyers announced that he was for capital punishment, I knew that I was now running on a very emotional, highly explosive issue, one that was particularly sensitive in Saskatoon at this time. Since there was no way of handling it politically, I reverted to handling it pastorally. I went to see the Kings. The King house, which was actually in St. Philip's parish, was full of flowers, RCMP and relatives. I met Brian King's mother and we had a long talk, during which she mentioned that she was against capital punishment. She saw no point in having other mothers' sons killed because they had killed her son. Her position gave me courage, as did that of Marie King, Brian's widow. Then I went to visit the mothers of the two young men who had committed the crime. I found that their homes had also been devastated by this event. Their sons had left in the morning to go to Lloydminster, with no intention of getting into trouble. But the following night it had happened. Now, their lives and the lives of their families were completely destroyed. One of the mothers, a very pious Christian who spent most of her time raising a family of eight, also worked at Friendship Inn. I looked at all these sorrowing women and I realized that I was dealing with just that—evil and sorrow—not a political issue at all. The question was how to handle the human problem.

The following Sunday in church I preached on the commandment, ". . . thou shalt not kill . . ." I talked about the three mothers and about what an evil killing was, but that it didn't make it right to kill someone else. As people were leaving the church that morning, one man came up to me, very angry, and said, "What's the idea of talking politics in church?" I knew then that the line between politics and church was very fine.

One day I was knocking on doors with Elaine Stevens, one of my most faithful helpers in the campaign. A huge man appeared at the door, wearing a sweaty shirt, jeans and a baseball cap. It was obvious he had had a few beers. Another guy in the same condition came out from behind him and said, "What's your stand on hanging?" Knowing I wouldn't get anywhere with these guys, I answered, "Hanging what?" They came at me: "You're a church man. You should know what it is. An eye for an eye and a tooth for a tooth." I shouted back, "Don't quote the Bible to me. Have you ever committed adultery?" They shut up and I continued, "Listen, those that commit adultery are supposed to be taken outside the city and stoned to death." There was silence. A few years later when I told this story to a Brazilian bishop, he said, "Yes, if that was still done, we wouldn't run out of adulterers. We'd run out of stones."

During the time that capital punishment was the main issue in our campaign, another tragic incident intensified my feelings on the question. Two kids went home from school for lunch one day to one of the boys' homes. While they were there, one of the boys found an old gun in the basement and accidentally shot and killed his friend. He then got a piece of rope and hanged himself. I'm sure he hanged himself because he thought that's what happened to people who shot other people.

The capital punishment issue persisted throughout the campaign. It's a very simple issue for people who don't think about the complexity of society or the futility of multiplying acts of violence. It was a difficult issue during the campaign; my position, however, did not change.

In the fall of 1978, we realized that the election was not going to take place until spring and we had almost another year to go. That in itself was very depressing. I knew we had to maintain our momentum; we had to assure people that we hadn't died in the water. It was sign time again. We hauled in the sign from the top of the 25th Street bridge and added another board underneath it. The plan was for me to draw a new cartoon on that board every week. I didn't know at the outset if I would have the energy or the wit to last the whole winter, but I made it. Every Friday afternoon I drew that cartoon, a facsimile of Charlie Brown and his friends. People used to watch for it as they drove up the bridge. It became a Friday afternoon event for a lot of people. Sometimes, if it wasn't finished when they drove by, they would come back in the evening to see what it said. The cartoon was always very simple and the message humorous. Once, after a blizzard, it said, "Somebody's giving this country a snow job." It was basically a $10 weekly expenditure for the new piece of board, but it kept the campaign alive. Three or four days before the end of the campaign, I received a letter from an office in Cleveland, Ohio, accusing me of breaking the Charlie Brown copyright. I suspected that some of my political opponents were behind this, but I wrote back. I told them there might have been some pictures that looked like Charlie Brown, but there were also some pictures that looked a bit like me and there were certainly some pictures that looked like my opponents, because we all have round heads. "I'm just a missionary priest from Latin America," I added, "and we don't have enough money to run this campaign. If you people would be interested in making a donation to the campaign, it would be much appreciated." That was the end of the correspondence. My lawyer said I gave them a real snow job.

When I saw how effective signs were, we raised enough money to build a flatbed trailer with a large box on it that looked more or less like a television set painted NDP orange. I drew cartoons on this screen weekly and we pulled the trailer through the constituency. It was like having 10,000 more signs. Once I drew characters that looked a bit like the king and the knight in The Wizard of Id. The knight was saying, "Vote Ogle for better weather" and the king was saying, "So true." There was no political content in the messages and the humour appealed to people. I sensed that people wanted politics with a bit of humanity and the cartoons introduced that quality. I think they influenced the outcome by drawing people who had never voted New Democrat before.

Saskatoon East was the perfect constituency to campaign in because it's small enough to be a bicycle constituency. I began to ride my bicycle everywhere. A large poster on the bike identified me. Whenever I went out knocking on doors, I rode my bike and I'd always tie it to a tree

89

or a post on a main avenue, so people would know I was around. Simple technique that it was, I felt that it, too, brought me close to the people. During Exhibition week, I rode my bicycle in the Traveller's Day parade and the Pioneer parade. It was great. I could ride back and forth from side to side and talk to people. I was continually spotting someone I knew. I could shout hello to them by name, which gave the impression that I knew everybody. While I was riding my bicycle, talking to people, my opposition was following along in a limousine. I know that the image you project is as important as who you actually are. The image I was trying to project was that of somebody ordinary, like them, who was interested in them and in their lives.

The part of the campaign that I enjoyed most was the creative work—writing a theme song with musicians, designing newspaper and television ads, having fun with creative people. This campaign, however, required as much endurance as creativity.

Many difficulties arose because the campaign dragged on for so long. Early in 1978, when we thought we had only two or three months till the election, we rented a nice office in the center of the riding. When the election was not called, we knew we couldn't afford to maintain the office. We turned it over to two provincial NDP candidates who were running in the election Blakeney had called in Saskatchewan. The provincial election was a good exercise for me. It gave me a chance to see from the inside how it's done, what the candidate has to do, what the manager has to do, what it means to pull votes and what is required to win an election. Up until that point, I had not had a campaign manager. As it turned out, I never did have one. We had a few people in charge of different sections, but I oversaw it all.

The executive of the constituency allowed me to move my campaign headquarters into an old house in which I had partial ownership and that's where we stayed throughout the rest of the campaign. Some faithful CCF-NDP veterans spent a lot of the winter in that house, copying the results of the provincial campaign. A provincial NDP vote does not necessarily equal a federal NDP vote, because many people who vote New Democrat provincially will vote Conservative or Liberal federally. But it was a start. It was useful information. The person who organized the statistical information-gathering was Helen Moon, now deceased. She was an ardent New Democrat. She had difficulty relating to other people and other people had difficulty relating to her, too. But of all the political people I met, she was the most astute. She always appraised a political situation accurately. People wouldn't listen to her, but she was always right and she knew it.

Dr. Alan Boulton served as my official agent. He was in charge of campaign expenses. We never received any help from the national office of the NDP, either in funds or personnel. I suspected that they didn't think I could win and they were helping those who had a better chance. When my campaign was over, we were not in debt. Saskatoon East New Democrats had paid their own way.

That old house wasn't very convenient. The basement leaked and there were other problems with it. The campaign came together well, though, and on election day, May 22, 1979, we were pretty confident that we had a win. You can never be absolutely sure though, so I worked hard that day visiting those people who were pulling votes and encouraging them to keep going until the very last moment. I had bought two new suits and I changed into one of them before going to the campaign office at 7:30 p.m. We waited expectantly for the polls to close. We had a television set tuned in to CBC and we knew eight minutes after the polls had closed that they were giving me the election. By 8:30 it was official. Then the excitement broke out. People had put so much time and effort into this election. The old house just shook for a while. Then I had to leave to go to the radio and television stations for interviews. I met Otto Lang at CFQC. He had made his appearance and was leaving. "I'll pray for you," he said. "If you need help, get in touch with me." I appreciated that very much and I thought it very generous for a man in his position to say that to me at that time. The press in general said it was one of the cleanest campaigns they had ever covered, which made me very happy.

When the evening was over, I went back to the seminary where I was living. I had won the election, but it was not a great sensation. It was just another step into an unknown future.

CHAPTER 6

ON TO OTTAWA

The morning after the election I went over to the old house that we'd used for our campaign headquarters and joined in the clean-up. It took a few days to wrap up the campaign. All the while, I was thinking I should go to Ottawa and meet some people in the party. During the campaign, apart from the time that Broadbent came out to the Saskatchewan Provincial Convention, I received regular mail-outs, but had no real contact with the federal New Democratic Party. My suspicion was that they thought Ogle might be a nice guy, but he doesn't have a chance, so we can't afford to help his campaign.

I bought a plane ticket to Ottawa, not knowing that members of Parliament have their fares paid. I knew nothing about the privileges of being a member of Parliament. When I took some letters to the post office, the clerk told me that I didn't have to stamp my mail anymore because I now had the "franking" privilege, which meant I could send mail free of postage.

I arranged to stay with a cousin in Ottawa. I can still remember arriving at the House of Commons and being afraid to go in. Although this was to be my work-place now, I did not feel worthy to be there. I walked across the lawn feeling like a little kid going to school on the first day, wondering how I was going to get in. Much to my surprise, the guard at the door recognized me and welcomed me.

During my first days in Ottawa, I met Ed Broadbent and House Leader Stanley Knowles. Stanley Knowles was like a father to newcomers. He immediately set about getting me an office and told me about the privileges that went with the office, including free long- distance telephone calls and free flights to one's home constituency. He told me I would be reimbursed for the fare to Ottawa.

During those first few days, I also visited an old classmate from canon law, Monsignor Maurice Theoret, who was now the parish priest at Old Chelsea, Quebec. I asked him if there was any possibility that I might live at Old Chelsea. His reply was, "If you hadn't asked me, I would have asked you." St. Stephen's parish in Old Chelsea, Quebec became my Ottawa home. It was a great blessing. Old Chelsea is about 15 miles north of Ottawa in the Gatineau Hills. The rectory is an old brick building, probably 100 years old, and the church is at least 100 years old, surrounded by a graveyard. Living there made it possible for me to celebrate mass every day and live my priestly life, as well as doing my work in the House of Commons. I could come back to Old Chelsea at the end of the day and feel as if I were 10,000 miles from Ottawa. At Old Chelsea I could always find peace.

Three weeks after the election, the federal caucus held a three-day meeting at Mont-Ste-Marie, a resort about 50 miles north of Ottawa, in Quebec. The election was considered a success by the New Democrats, as well as the Conservatives. The NDP had gone from nine to 32 seats. That meant that the majority of us at Mont-Ste-Marie were meeting one another and learning the basics, like how a caucus runs. Stanley Knowles briefed us on how to set up an office and staff and other practical matters.

During that first caucus meeting, everyone was invited to say what they thought was going to be important in the coming Parliament, and what they personally were interested in. I said the New Democrats should develop a much stronger position on international issues and take a new position on immigration. That went over like a lead balloon. The New Democratic Party had really grown out of provincial politics and, although there are people in the party who are very concerned about international affairs, that concern has been overshadowed by preoccupation with securing the labour and farm vote. After two days of discussion, Broadbent assigned critic roles. Andrew Brewin, the former external affairs critic, had come out to see me prior to the campaign and had expressed the hope that I would win the seat and take over his role in the House. External affairs was my choice of roles, but Broadbent assigned that role to Pauline Jewett and asked me to take health. That worried me, because of my pro-life stand. Apparently, Broadbent never thought of that. Over the next six or seven months, certain people in the party voiced their displeasure over having a pro-life person in the role of health critic. Rather than changing the assignments, Broadbent took the criticism.

An incidental recollection I have from that first caucus meeting is of smoke as thick as in the back room of an old pool hall. The smoking continued until Lynn McDonald was elected and laid down an ultimatum. No smoking in caucus meetings or no Lynn McDonald in caucus meetings. She won.

Having been assigned the health role, I thought the first thing I should do was to go and meet the minister of health. That happened to be David Crombie, the neat little mayor from Toronto. David had entered Parliament a few months before in a by-election. He was very cordial at our first meeting and has become a close friend since. At the time, he was as green in his role as I was in mine and it was a relief to be able to admit this to one another. The person who really knew what was going on was the Liberal health critic, Monique Begin. She used to run over both of us in the House because she was strong, aggressive and experienced, having previously been minister of health.

Some of the press were following our meetings at Mont-Ste-Marie. At suppertime on the second night, Mike Duffy from the CBC came over to me and apologized for a story that he had done during the campaign. The story had used pictures of me saying mass and Duffy knew I took a lot of flack over that story. I was impressed by his apology.

That first caucus meeting was held in early June and Parliament wasn't called until Thanksgiving. I don't know what Joe Clark thinks about that now, but it seemed a mistake to me, not calling Parliament. His government never got started, just never got out of the chute. For me, the summer was a time of waiting, of not knowing what to do. I was getting paid now, which came as another surprise. I set up a constituency office in Saskatoon and completed a report on youth and drugs, but essentially I was marking time that summer of 1979.

The main feature at the Saskatoon Exhibition that summer was a show by Bill Cosby. I was given two free tickets, so I invited my sister-in-law, Joan Ogle. We had the two best seats in the house and it was the best show I have ever seen. I laughed so hard that night, I literally cried. Someone had told me at the caucus meeting, "If you forget the folks in the back seats, the folks in the back seats will forget you" and that night at the Cosby show I was aware of the impermanence of this privilege, of sitting in these seats. The year before someone else had sat here. And, next year, someone else might be sitting here. You can never be comfortable in the privileged seat, because you may not be in it for long. The thought occurred to me that I would really be more comfortable in a back seat with the folks.

My first public act as a member of Parliament was completely unplanned. John Diefenbaker had died on August 16, 1979. I never met him in the House of Commons, but I had met him several times in Saskatchewan, before I was elected. He had made elaborate funeral arrangements for himself. His body was to be brought west on the train and buried at the University of Saskatchewan, which happened to be in my constituency.

Diefenbaker's body was sent out by train, MPs were flown out and bussed from the airport to the university campus. The burial site was a few hundred yards from St. Pius X Seminary, my Saskatoon residence. Some of the television camera crew made a point of including me in shots, and that became my first media exposure as an MP. I met Joe Clark for the first time at Diefenbaker's funeral. He gave the eulogy.

Because of the long time-lapse between the election and the opening of Parliament, Broadbent's staff suggested that I take a national tour as health critic. They arranged for Bill Blaikie, another new member who was social affairs critic, to go with me. I didn't realize then how dangerous this tour would be. I didn't have enough knowledge or experience to handle it properly and the briefing we got prior to the trip was not sufficient. Bill and I worked hard at preparing a good press conference. We booked the press room at the House of Commons and sent out press releases. We were all set. Our press conference was scheduled the same day as the press conference on Diefenbaker's will. They had the room first, and it was packed with journalists. When it came time for our press conference, the room was empty. It was a dull note for the start of our tour. We went on to Toronto, where we visited several health care institutions and had a press conference. The press walked all over us because we just didn't know our stuff well enough. Because Bill Blaikie is an ordained United Church minister and I am a Roman Catholic priest, the press began to call us "The God Squad," a term that stuck with us across the country. Part of the difficulty I had on the tour, in addition to feeling ill-prepared, was that every place we went I was taken to an abortion clinic. I don't know if this was done intentionally or insensitively, but I had little experience handling the press or difficult situations and I did not manage either well.

The purpose of the tour was simply to get our names before the media, to get some profile in our critic roles and, as such, it wasn't a bad idea. But they sent us out too early and they should not have sent out two new MPs. One of the two has to know how to handle the press and how to take the flack.

Parliament was finally called the Tuesday after Thanksgiving. I wanted to celebrate the opening of Parliament with my family. A number of relatives and friends were able to come. We started the celebrations with mass at St. Stephen's parish and from there we went to the House of Commons, where I had arranged for a banquet room. It was a good party. I think the family enjoyed it. I have a very strong sense of family and I was deeply troubled by the fact that most of my uncles and aunts in Rosetown were still not speaking to me, a fact that did not change.

Members of Parliament are allowed to invite their immediate families for the swearing-in. Since I had none, Stanley Knowles stood by me as I was sworn in by the Clerk of the House, Alistair Fraser. It was a thrilling experience to write my name in the book that records all the members of Parliament. Alistair Fraser mentioned that in one of the old books you can see Louis Riel's signature. That's as far as Louis Riel got. He won the election in Manitoba, made it to Ottawa and signed the book, but they never let him sit in the House.

The 31st Parliament finally began the middle of October 1979, with the standard reading of the speech from the throne in the Senate chamber. It was exciting to see all of this for the first time. Broadbent asked me to be the first speaker for the New Democrats in the debate on the speech from the throne. This is considered an honour and it usually goes to a new member. After introductory remarks, I delivered a speech on health. I quoted Tommy Douglas and Emmett Hall, and I used the parable of the good Samaritan. "It's an old story," I said, "and a new story. The same story about three groups of people. The first group consisted of thieves who came upon this person. Their principle of life was what is yours is mine, so they took all he had. The second group of people," I continued and somebody said, "It's the Conservatives." "The second group of people," I persisted, "consisted of the priests and the Levite— officially good people going down to the temple to pray. They saw the man, half-dead. Touching him would make them unclean and, according to the laws, they would not be allowed to pray then. Their principle of life was what is mine is mine. The poor Samaritan did not know all these rules. All he knew was that there was a person in distress, a person in need. So he stopped, picked him up, put him on his animal and looked after him. The last principle of life was what is mine is ours and that is what I believe."

My first speech in the House of Commons obviously had the tone of a homily and even later I often cited the Scriptures and church documents in my speeches. In general, I think I was respected for that and gained a bigger audience that way.

My staff had prepared that first speech and written it out for me. You are supposed to speak without a document in the House of Commons. It's a rule that's broken all the time, but it is the rule. In my experience as a public speaker, I had found that I operated best if I had a few key words, that was all I needed. I tried to follow the speech my staff had prepared, but I couldn't do it. It was impossible to follow the speech and look alive. From that time on, my staff would prepare a speech and I would reduce it to four or five key words that I could work from.

The death of John Diefenbaker meant there had to be another election in the riding of Prince Albert. Stan Hovdebo, the NDP candidate who had lost to Diefenbaker in May, was running again. The party asked me to go west and help with the election, which was to be held in December. I went and spent a couple of weeks campaigning, doing exactly what I had done for most of the preceding two years.

Because I was a priest, the party seemed to think I would have a great influence on Catholic voters. In that campaign I was taken to four or five towns where I felt I was not helping the cause. The traditional Catholic vote was Liberal and the fact that I was a Catholic priest and

97

a New Democrat was not going to change anyone's mind. It took a long time for the party to realize that.

Stan Hovdebo won the election. I was back in Ottawa at the time. We had a direct telephone line and were listening to the results. He came to Ottawa and had eight days as a member of Parliament before the House fell.

After the Hovdebo campaign, Bill Blaikie and I finished the health tour with a swing through the Maritimes and Newfoundland. We were a little better at it now, but I still felt uncomfortable because I was too inexperienced to do it well. Between campaigning for Stan and finishing the health tour, I only spent a few days in the House of Commons during that 31st Parliament.

My initial impressions of the House of Commons were, I suppose, quite similar to other people's. The House almost has the feel of a church and sitting there officially adds to the solemnity. As you go there day after day it becomes more commonplace, but the first time I sat in the House of Commons officially, there was an awesome feel to it.

The last days of the 31st Parliament were historic days in the sense that the fall of that Parliament abruptly changed the course of our history. Mr. Trudeau had resigned as leader of the Liberal party and as leader of the opposition that autumn, which meant that the Liberals would have to pick a new leader. In the last days of that Parliament, we heard the budget speech and I learned how that is handled. It is a fixed debate, which can only go on for a limited number of days. The minister of finance reads the budget speech and makes a motion that it be carried by the House. Then the leader of the opposition, or the financial critic of the opposition, gets up, gives a speech and presents an amendment to the budget motion. Finally, the third party gets up and makes a sub-amendment to the amendment. The sub-amendment cannot be written until the debate is in progress, because you don't know what the amendment will be.

When the time came for the New Democrats to write their sub-amendment, there was a lively debate in our caucus about whether or not we should write an amendment that could be supported by the Liberal party. Traditionally, the sub-amendment is worded in such a way that it can only be supported by the party that makes it. But, this House was so evenly divided that the Conservatives were counting on the six Social Credit Members. And, there was always the possibility that if someone was missing from the House the government might fall. If the New Democrats proposed a sub-amendment that the Liberal party could support, it could bring down the government. It was decided that we would write a sub-amendment that the Liberals could support, although it was certainly not a unanimous decision. Finance Minister John Crosbie read

98

the budget and moved its acceptance. Then Herb Grey, Liberal finance critic, gave his speech and made the amendment for the Liberals.

Before Bob Rae the New Democrat finance critic, could make his speech, the sub-amendment had to be written. Bob Rae's seat was immediately in front of mine. Everyone was gathered around, watching Bob write the sub-amendment. I did not understand much of what was going on, but I was concerned about producing a clear statement. I remember taking the piece of paper from him and rewriting it just a bit and handing it back to him. He took the paper and read the amendment as follows: "Mr. Speaker, I therefore move, seconded by the Honorable Member for Winnipeg-North Center, Mr. Knowles, that the amendment be amended by changing the period at the end thereof to a comma and by adding immediately thereafter the following words: and this House unreservedly condemns the Government for its outright betrayal of its election promises to lower interest rates, to cut taxes and to stimulate the growth of the Canadian economy without a mandate from the Canadian people for such a reversal." Bob Rae sat down and we knew that the process that would bring about the fall of the government had been set in motion.

Christmas time in Ottawa includes festivities sponsored by the political parties, and that night happened to be the Liberal Christmas party. I don't know exactly what took place there, but the Liberals obviously calculated that they could bring down the government and they persuaded Trudeau to take on the leadership again.

The next morning we had our regular caucus meeting, where we discussed who was going to speak during question period. The mood was quite casual, as if it hadn't occurred to anyone that this might be the last question period. It was decided that Stan Hovdebo would give his initial speech that evening on the budget. We were told that there would be a vote that night. That's all that was said.

The main item on my agenda for that December 13 was a meeting with Broadbent to discuss the abortion issue. Fonz Faour, a pro-life MP from Newfoundland, and I were to meet with Broadbent in his office after dinner to talk about how we, as pro-life supporters in the New Democratic caucus, would handle the issue.

Fonz and I decided we would have lunch together in the West Block. We had just picked up our lunch in the cafeteria and as we were sitting down, Heward Grafftey, a Quebec member of Joe Clark's cabinet, came over and tore into us as if he were going to knock us down. I never saw anyone in the House of Commons become so violent. He knew then that the Conservatives were probably going to lose the vote. He knew how many PCs would be missing and that the number was enough to lose it for them. He was blaming the New Democrats for bringing on this calamity. He talked about the fact that he had just started in government and here he was probably going to lose his seat, which he did.

Business continued as usual in the House that afternoon. Question period was marked by a mood of nervous excitement—like kids before a Christmas concert. Everybody was jumpy. Everybody knew that something was going to happen that day. I stood in the House all afternoon and talked to Stanley Knowles and Lorne Nystrom about what would happen if the government fell. Stanley had told me earlier that there was no possibility of this Parliament ending so soon. But now he saw that it could. I felt strangely secure inside myself, even though I dreaded the thought of another election. I phoned my sister Mary Lou, who was in charge of my Saskatoon office. She had been watching it all on television and she too, sensed that it was going to come down. She was quite gloomy about the prospect of another election, but she said she had bought a new pair of campaign boots and she was ready to go again. I took my staff out to dinner that evening in the parliamentary restaurant. The mood in the restaurant that night I would describe as pre-battle. There was an almost crazy exhilaration.

After supper I had the appointment to see Ed Broadbent with Faour, and even in Broadbent's room, which is always a welcoming place, there was this strange mood. We talked about the abortion issue and I felt that Broadbent was very open to both Fonz and me. We talked about positive ways that we could handle it and both suggested to Broadbent that the absolute position held by some New Democrats should be modified, difficult as that would be in a convention setting. We argued that the party lost many votes every election because of that position, which was in effect held by all three parties, but which had somehow been labelled an NDP position. Then the phone rang and the message was that Hovdebo was about to speak. We shook hands and, as I wrote in my notes, "we headed out in our spitfires."

Stan spoke for 27 minutes, followed by Roger Simmons, a Newfoundlander. He gave one of the funniest speeches I ever heard in the House, mostly poking fun at John Crosbie, who had brought in the budget. It was 9:45 when he finished and the vote on our sub-amendment was called. The party whips started bringing in Liberals—one was even brought in from hospital on a stretcher. The whole scene was like a circus. I went over and talked to Gene Whelan, who had been through it all before. He said there was less tension than there had been in '62 when the government fell. The final count was 139 to 133. The six-vote split reflected the fact that the Social Credits abstained. If Clark had been able to work out a deal with the Social Credits, he could have saved his government. Their main objection was to the 18-cent gas tax that Crosbie had proposed, and they wouldn't budge on that.

The Speaker called the House to order. He said the sub-amendment was carried, and since it was 10 p.m. the House would ordinarily stand adjourned. Then he went on to say that he had received indication that the prime minister wished to gain the floor for the purpose of making a brief comment to the House. Prime Minister Joe Clark got up and said, "Mister Speaker, I rise on a point of order. The government has lost a vote on a matter which we have no alternative but to regard as a question of confidence. I simply want to advise the House that I will be seeing His Excellency the Governor General tomorrow morning." With that, the 31st Parliament came to an end.

The dissolution of Parliament sent us all back to our ridings to fight another election. For me, it meant starting from scratch—getting re-nominated, setting up another team, raising money, finding new campaign headquarters, and knocking on doors. I was plagued by planter warts on my feet at the time and I dreaded campaigning in sub-zero weather, walking on sore feet. There was also much less enthusiasm for this election. People were annoyed at having to go through the whole exercise so soon after the last election. When people say, "Don't worry. You'll do all right," instead of saying, "I'll get out and help you," you know you're in trouble.

In this campaign Doug Richardson ran in place of Otto Lang and Dan Meyers ran again for the Conservatives. I knew it was going to be either myself or the Conservative candidate in front, with the Liberal third. That became clearer as we went along. I had a rule of thumb which I called the "four and ten" rule. When I was knocking on doors, I kept a mental count of how much support I thought I was getting. If I was getting four out of ten, I knew I was winning and if I was getting fewer than four out of ten I was in trouble. In this campaign, I was getting fewer than four out of ten. Towards the end though, I felt that we had picked up support and were going to win.

In one sense, the campaign was very different from the first one. Some of the public meetings that I participated in during this campaign were brutal. The first campaign seemed to have a kind of gentlemanliness about it and this campaign did not. It was rough and hard and I was the one who was under attack now. It was like knock the rooster off the roost. I think that's the way people respond. They're harder on the incumbent than on the challenger. The mood of the campaign was not pleasant, but we struggled through the winter and we kept on working until February 19. Voter turn-out for this election was low. I managed to win, though with a reduced majority, and keep the same proportion of the total vote. After the election, I was exhausted. My brother and I took a month-long holiday in Phoenix, Arizona. After that I was ready to go for the 32nd Parliament.

The New Democratic Party had picked up a few new seats and had lost some members. Fonz Faour and John Rodriguez had lost, as had Father Andy Hogan, the only other priest in Parliament. I was reminded again of how brutal an election is and how fragile one's hold is on a seat.

Broadbent told me there was opposition within the party to my being the health critic, because of my pro-life stand. He asked if I would mind letting someone else take the health critic role. I was relieved to be out of that and to become one of the critics in external affairs. Pauline Jewett would maintain her role as the first critic in external affairs and I would be critic on international aid and human rights. I was very pleased with this assignment. It was a role in which I could feel comfortable.

By this time, I had discovered that members of Parliament were ordinary people. Once I had grasped that, my attitude toward Parliament changed. I was not as overawed by everything. I was also much more familiar with the way Parliament worked. I could see there were different ways of being noticed in Parliament. One was to be the hot-shot questioner. Every morning, when caucus members were fighting for questions, you would think that question period was going to change everything. But question period is a very insignificant part of Parliament. Many times I would ask people what question period had been about the day before and they couldn't remember. The hype that came with television made people think it was important. But I had seen that an MP who appeared on television could lose as quickly as one who hadn't, so I decided that I would do my duty by asking questions when I could, but that my energy would be chiefly focused elsewhere. I felt the best thing I could do was to know my area well and work behind the scenes. My goal was to advance in the House of Commons an awareness of Canada's role in the Third World.

When Pierre Trudeau returned as prime minister, knowing that he had one more Parliament, he picked his own agenda. That agenda was the patriation of the Constitution and establishment of a Bill of Rights. I don't think either of those items was a high priority in the minds of most Canadians, nor had the election been fought on those grounds. The patriation of the Constitution caused a considerable amount of tension in the NDP caucus. Ed Broadbent supported patriation, as did a number of members of the caucus. Others were concerned about the process or about the difficulty of supporting patriation without looking like Trudeau supporters. Some sided with their province's position of pressing for more rights for the provinces.

I certainly had concerns about the process. Rather than starting with a rational, comprehensive draft, the Constitution, as I saw it, was created by a patchwork method of action and reaction, and response to pressure.

It seemed to me a very haphazard way of creating a permanant framework for the functioning of our country. It also appeared to me that the people who would gain the most from this patchwork Constitution would be lawyers.

Ironically, despite my lukewarm attitude towards the Constitution, I had a hand in drafting it. For months our justice critic, Svend Robinson, served on the Constitution committee, but when it came to inserting reference to God in the preamble, the caucus sent me into the committee.

Another of my reservations about the Constitution was that it did not protect the life of unborn children. I had trouble, however, with the Campaign Life group, who lobbied against the Constitution. While I shared their desire for a provision in the Constitution protecting the life of unborn children, I disagreed vehemently with the way they went about their campaign and the way they attempted to discredit the Constitution and the Bill of Rights because that provision was not included. They also put heavy pressure on me to vote against the Constitution. I considered that option. But it seemed to me that Canada should have its own Constitution. A Bill of Rights also seemed to have merit. It might not protect the life of the unborn, which I thought it should, but it would include many other human rights. I was faced with the common dilemma of deciding whether or not to support an imperfect package.

As the Constitution debate drew to a close, I could see that one vote here or there wasn't going to change the outcome. The Constitution was going to come to Canada. That gave me the freedom to make a symbolic gesture, which would at least make people ask, "Why did you do that?", which they still do. Within days of the final vote, I made the decision to abstain on the vote. My abstention was intended to indicate that I was not voting against the Constitution, but neither was I supporting it, because it lacked a provision I felt it should contain. I explained my intention to the caucus and prepared a press release to be issued at the time of the Constitution vote, December 2, 1981. At first, Broadbent was nervous about our split on the constitutional vote. As it turned out, Svend Robinson, who had been the NDP representative on the Constitution committee, voted against it, as did others. The final count was 246 yeas, 24 nays.

Unfortunately, I didn't make full use of the opportunity afforded by my abstention. According to the rule of the House, you can get up after the vote and explain to the Speaker why you didn't vote. Abstentions are so rare in the House of Commons that I had never seen that done. I should have been up on my rules, but I wasn't, so I missed the opportunity to record the reason for my abstention. At the end of the session, I did go out to the press scrum that was taking place in front of the House and a few of the national press people gave me some time. Mike Duffy was one of them. "I owe you one," Mike said, and let me explain to the people of Canada, on television, why I had taken this unusual stance.

The abortion question didn't go away once the vote on the Constitution had been taken. It was a constant problem for me. Interestingly enough, I was never harassed by the pro-choice people. They knew what my position was and they never tried to interfere with it—probably because they knew it wouldn't change. I had discussed the question many times with pro-choice members of Parliament and other people. The question always boiled down to a difference in language and understanding. One side focused on the rights of the unborn child to the exclusion of other factors—the future of the child, the well-being of the mother, family support. The other side focused exclusively on the mother—her circumstances, her well-being, her future. They saw the fetus as an intrusion into her life. There seemed to be no common ground for discussion.

The people who kept after me were the Campaign Life people, the militant wing of the pro-life movement. They were holding out for a total ban on abortions. Having observed the aggressive, implacable attitude of these people in numerous meetings when all three parties were present, I concluded that they were a hindrance to the pro-life movement. They didn't understand that it takes a long time to change laws, and that it's better to get a little change than no change at all. These people, along with people who didn't like the New Democratic Party, showed up wherever I went. They would argue that my being NDP was a sign that I was not sincere as a priest, because the New Democratic Party had passed a convention resolution calling for the removal of abortion from the Criminal Code. I always replied that I had made my pro-life position absolutely clear prior to being nominated, that I was against the party position and that I continued to act according to my personal conviction in the House of Commons.

There was only one bill regarding abortion presented in the House all the time I was there. It was a private member's bill, brought in by Bill McKnight (PC—Kindersley-Lloydminster). The debate, which took place November 18, 1980, lasted only an hour. Certain members of the NDP caucus did not want me to speak on that bill. But House Leader Stanley Knowles said that as long as I noted in my speech that I was going against the party position, I had a right to speak in the debate. Given this opportunity, I took a very strong pro-life position. In my Commons speech, I quoted from my nomination speech of September 17, 1977, "I will defend human life from its conception until its natural end." I went on to say: "This means I am opposed to: first, abortion; second, euthanasia; third, capital punishment. And although I do not have it included in the document from which I read at this time, I am also against death from starvation, from war or from any other act in which the human right to live is violently taken away from some other person. The human rights which I support are: first, the right to be born; second, the right to adequate food, housing, medical care and education; third, the right to live in at least frugal comfort within one's cultural tradition; fourth, freedom of conscience, worship, expression, political participation and peaceful dissent; fifth, equal treatment in public job markets and courts regardless of sex, age, ethnic origin, marital status, religious or political beliefs, social and economic status; sixth, the right to social assistance when age or other circumstances make self-support inadequate; and seventh, the right to die with dignity. I believe that human rights are all of a piece; ignore one right and you jeopardize all the others. That is why a single-issue approach to rights will not work. If we are really pro-life, we have to protect human life from conception through to death. This requires an active life-long concern for a just social system.''

Further on in that speech, I expressed my belief that the individual is unique on the face of the earth and has rights not because the House of Commons confers them, but because of the uniqueness and dignity inherent in human nature.

What used to bother me most in regard to the whole question of abortion was the fact that the medical profession, which did all the abortions and made all the money, was generally silent on the subject. I thought the medical profession should have been held much more responsible for its part in the confusion.

I think abortions will continue, with or without legislation. Legislation does make a difference, though. Once an act becomes legal, it gains acceptance. Making an act legal, though, does not make it moral. The death camps in Europe during Hitler's time were legal; they were not moral.

Another life issue, capital punishment, was debated during the years I was in the House of Commons. It came up on what is called an allotted day, when the opposition can bring a motion of non-confidence to the House and it will be the business of the day. On that particular day, June 11, 1981, the leader of the opposition, Joe Clark, brought a motion to the House of Commons asking that a committee be set up to restudy the question of capital punishment. I felt, and I was not alone in thinking this, that Clark was forced into this by his caucus, because Clark was and is an abolitionist. He voted against capital punishment at the time of the open vote, July 14, 1976, which abolished capital punishment by a vote of 130 to 124. It looked as if the group in his caucus that was trying to remove him as leader was using the capital punishment motion to embarrass him. He opened the debate by presenting reasons for striking a committee to restudy the issue.

The New Democrats asked me to lead the response for our party. I began by suggesting that Mr. Clark had been pushed into a position he wasn't comfortable in and I alluded to a similar situation—when Pontius Pilate found himself forced to speak for a position he personally did not accept. That set the roof bouncing. The Progressive Conservatives and the Liberals had practically all left their seats, but that brought them back. I can still see them, coming down from behind the curtains almost in a swarm, as if they were going to attack me physically. The record of the House for that day notes numerous interruptions to my speech. The tumult reached the point that Stanley Knowles, the NDP House Leader got up and asked the Speaker to try to restore order.

My opposition to capital punishment was based on philosophical grounds and on personal experiences. I told the story of Brian King, the Mountie who had been shot in Saskatoon, and said I had become convinced, as had the families involved in that tragedy, that more deaths would not help. The motion to establish a committee was defeated, ending one of the most raucous debates I experienced in the House of Commons.

In August 1981, Mark MacGuigan, the Secretary of State for External Affairs, took a small parliamentary group to China. As NDP critic of international development, I was asked to be part of the group, which also included the PC critic, Doug Roche; the chairman of the external affairs committee, Marcel Prud'homme; the president of CIDA, Marcel Masse; and several senators.

It was my first trip to China and I found the country fascinating. Fifty years ago China was one of the major famine areas of the world. Famine had run in cycles in China and millions of people had died from hunger. From what we saw in 1981, it looked as if China now had enough food for its population, which seemed like a modern miracle. We certainly didn't see all of China, but we saw no hungry people in the cities or in the rural areas we visited. I wondered how they were managing to feed one-fifth of the world's population.

It would be too complicated to try to analyze how they had accomplished this transformation, but a few factors became clear to me as we travelled. First of all, the old class structure had been forcibly dismantled. They got rid of the class that owned the land and set up a centrally controlled communal system, under which everyone worked on the land to grow food. The new system retained the old, labour-intensive farming methods. China is basically a big garden. The country, for the most part, is non-industrialized and food is hand-grown. We passed through ten distinct agricultural areas and everywhere it was like watching gardeners out working the land.

The Chinese made a point of telling us, everywhere we went, how long the land had been in use. In one area they said the land had been farmed 3,000 times and in another place they claimed that the land had been used 8,000 times. There's very little land in North America that has been farmed 100 times. Where I grew up in Western Canada, the land has been broken less than 100 years and it's only used every second year, which means it has only been used 45 times. The Chinese have obviously managed to keep their land fertile, which is more than we can say. The Bamboo Curtain permitted them to carry on the traditions of power and hand labour. We were taken to a place on the Yangtze River where there was an irrigation system that had been created by cutting a canal through a mountain. A huge wooden gate regulated the flow through the canal. The opening and closing of the gate was controlled by ropes and hand power. The water that came through the channel irrigated an area about 200 miles long and 60 miles wide, without a single pump. It was all gravity irrigation. The land had been irrigated by this system for 2,000 years. It remains to be seen how agricultural production in China will change now that the Bamboo Curtain is lifting and the Chinese are becoming more familiar with highly industrialized technologies.

The Chinese had a specific request to present to us. They were looking for a way of upgrading their university education. During the Red Guard revolution, many of the Chinese universities had been closed for a period of almost ten years and many Chinese professors had been killed or exiled. The impact of this persecution was now being felt in a shortage of teachers and university professors. They were hoping that Canada would provide assistance for Chinese students to study in Canada. The part that fascinated me was how careful they were to assure us that the students they sent would be the best. They provided statistics on the number of students that started at the bottom of the system and how drastically it was reduced by the time it reached the top. The numbers were absolutely staggering. There's just no way we can grasp the numbers they are dealing with in China.

The education minister's office was in a dilapidated building, by western standards. We had been to see several ministers and their offices were no better. The minister of education was sitting behind his desk, wearing an open-collared shirt with the sleeves rolled up. He smoked all through our meeting, adding to the already full ashtray on the desk. We were invited to sit on couches in front of the desk. Orange pop and tea were served and for the first half hour there was casual conversation about our trip. By this time, we were familiar with the ritual. Suddenly, the pleasantries stopped and a succinct, hard-nosed deal would be proposed. This happened every place we went.

The minister of education told us about his job. Education, like agriculture, is a centralized system. He was responsible for all the education in China. We started asking numbers and, again, were staggered by the figures he gave us. He had more people in his school system than the entire population of the United States. He had more people in his kindergarten classes than the entire population of Canada. Whenever I'm tempted to complain about having too much work to do, I think about the Chinese minister of education.

Before leaving Canada, we had asked external affairs to arrange as many meetings as possible with church people for those of us who were interested—mainly Doug Roche, Senator Lowell Murray and myself. The Catholic Church in China is not in conformity with Rome and relations between Rome and China have been strained for many years.

In Beijing, the capital, we were to meet the priests at the cathedral. We found the cathedral, which was built in the 1650s by Jesuit missionaries. Inside, it looked very much like a Catholic church in Canada in the 1940s. The liturgy, books, statues, the whole atmosphere were pre-Vatican II. The mass was said in Latin. Our conversation with the two priests who met us was carried on in broken Latin—their Latin was much better than mine. I asked about the difficulty over the appointment of the bishops. I was particularly interested in Bishop Tang, the new archbishop of Canton, whom I had met a few months earlier when I was in Hong Kong with the North-South Task Force. One morning I had said mass at a Jesuit college and been invited for breakfast afterwards. Most of the old priests sitting around the refectory table were Irish but the one sitting beside me was an old Chinese priest. He didn't say much, although he spoke English. When we finally got talking a bit I found out that he was Bishop Tang. Pope John Paul II had just appointed him the new archbishop of Canton and he was on his way to the Philippines to meet the Holy Father. That appointment exacerbated the strained relations between Rome and the Chinese National Church. The basic difficulty seemed to be the question of how the Chinese church could be part of the universal Church and still be Chinese.

The glimpse of China I had in 1981 put development in a new perspective for me. The size of the country and the population were overwhelming. Yet the Chinese had achieved, not without suffering and abuse I'm sure, an astounding degree of stability and basic human requirements for their people. It seemed they had accomplished the impossible.

2. Bob with siblings

1. Mother, father and baby Bob (1930)

3. Bob (2 yrs) and baby Marguerite (1931)

4. Bob, Marguerite, Charles and Sparky (1935)

5. Fort made out of relief straw - Buster the dog (1938) 6. Sunday afternoon in Rosetown - Ogle family 6

7. High school graduation - June 1946

8. Winner of oratorical cup (1946)

9. Day before leaving for seminary (Sept. 1, 1946)

9

10. Leaving for seminary   10

11. First-class trip to seminary (l to r) - Norm Andries, Bob Pravda, Des Leeper, Benny Provost, Bob, Charlie Gibney   11

12. Home-made cassock   12

13. "Tex" singing Streets of Laredo - at seminary

14. Bob's ordination as sub-deacon (l); James P. Mahoney's ordination as priest (r) - St. Paul's Cathedral, Saskatoon (June 7, 1952)

15

16

15. Bob's ordination as priest - St. Theresa's Chapel in St. Joseph's Convent, Rosetown (May 30, 1953)

16. Ordination service by Bishop Francis J. Klein

17. First mass in Rosetown - Father Basil Sullivan, Bob and Father Gerard Provost (May 31, 1953)

17

18. The new priest (1953)

18

19. Rector Bob with spiritual director, Father Joe Bisztyo (centre front) - St. Pius X Seminary

20. Walking in Calgary (1958)   21. 40th birthday - Brazil (1968)   21

23

23. Christmas - Brazil (1968). (l to r) Sister Elizabeth Ann Murphy, Ida Raiche, Diane Lieffers, Father Jack Sissons, Father Don Macgillivray and Bob

22. Frei João Vogel, OFM   22

24. Language class - Petrópolis   24

25 The bottom-of-the-class language group 25 26. Anisio 26

27. First mission team from Saskatoon to Brazil - (l to r) Father Bernard Dunn, Cécile Poilièvre, Father Don Macgillivray, Ida Raiche and Bob

27

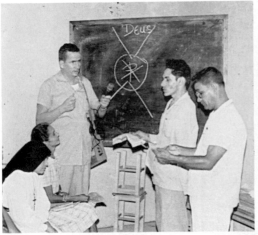

28. Working with Fermentistas   28   29. Plunge into the pastoral - União dos Palmares 29

30. A street in União dos Palmares   30

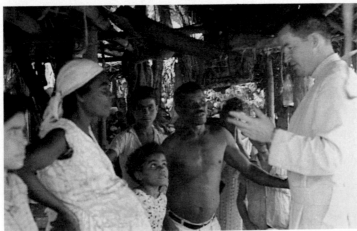

31. Visiting a home   31

Completed village (1970)   32

33. Jorge and Bob - Brazil

33

Benedictine sisters - Curitiba, Brazil   35

34. School mural   34

36. Mass with Archbishop Arturo Rivera y Damas - San Salvador   36

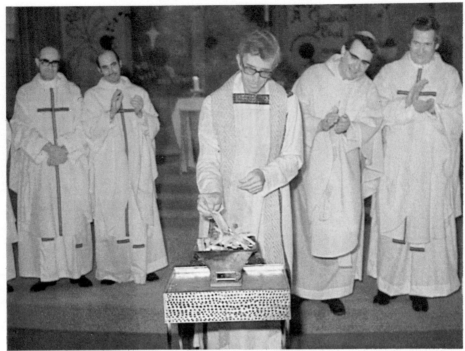

37. Father Don Macgillivray burning the mortgage at St. Philip's

37

38. Bob, Dom Miguel Camara (Archbishop of Maceió) and Sister Ann Lafferty - St. Philip's 25th anniversary

39. 25th anniversary celebration mass, St. Philip's (May 26, 1975)

38

39

40. Bob campaigning
40

41. Bob and two best friends?
41

May 19, 1979

Dear Voter:

On the 22nd you will have to make your choice. It will not be easy. My opponents have run good campaigns. Now you must vote your conscience. I invite you to vote for me at Poll *69* at *Brevoort Park School*

Shalom!

Fr. Bob Ogle

213 - 8th St. East - 61

42. Message on back of "holy" card
42

43

43. The Parliamentary orator

44. With Mary Lou in constituency office   44

45

46

47

45. Swearing in new member (1979)

46. With Ed Broadbent

47. Parliamentary Inter-Church Committee -
(l to r) Bob, The Rev. Walter F. McLean
Archbishop Arturo Rivera y Damas,
Stan Hudecki

48

With Tommy Douglas at teachers' convention in Saskatoon

49. NDP caucus after 1980 election

49

50. North-South Task Force report press conference - (l to r) Maurice Dupras, Bob, Herb Breau, Doug Roche (Dec 17, 1980)

52. Great Wall of China - (l to r) Bob, Mark MacGuigan, Doug Roche (1981)

51. Skating on the Rideau Canal, Ottawa

53. Meeting with Castro (1982)

4. Protesting cruise testing (1983)

54

55

55. Checking notes from Central American trip (1982)

5. Opposing abortion, 1983 NDP Convention, Regina 56

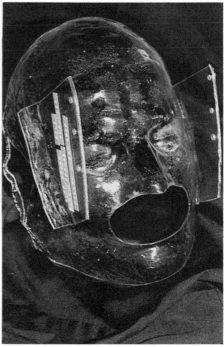

7. Peace demonstration, Saskatoon (1983)

5758. Radiation therapy mask (1986)

58

59. With Pope John Paul II (1982)

CHAPTER 7

NORTH-SOUTH

On October 22-23, 1981, world leaders gathered in Cancun, Mexico to examine the North-South question—the whole web of issues concerning economic relations between the developed countries of the North and the developing countries of the South. Pierre Trudeau was elected chairman of the conference and, although the conference collapsed for lack of American support, Trudeau's concern with these issues continued.

Early in the 32nd Parliament, Trudeau had established a number of task forces to study areas which were to be the subject of legislation. One of them was a North-South Task Force. The NDP caucus named me to this task force, an appointment with which I was very pleased.

The chairman of the North-South Task Force was New Brunswick Liberal Herb Breau. Edmonton-South PC Doug Roche was vice-chairman. The other members were Maurice Dupras, a Liberal from Labelle, Quebec; Girve Fretz, a PC from Erie, Ontario; Doug Frith, a Liberal from Sudbury; and Jim Schroder, a Liberal from Guelph.

Doug Roche and I had been friends for years, but the rest of the people on the task force were new to me. In our first discussions I could see that we spanned the political spectrum and I remember wondering if I could ever get close to these people. Eventually, they all became close friends. Because I was the only person on the task force who had ever lived in the Third World, and because they could see I had a very strong interest in it, the other members of the task force were quite open, from the start, to my experiences and observations. Over time we learned how to hear each other and I think we helped each other understand more about North-South issues.

Our mandate was to propose policies in the area of food and food production, energy, trade—including export earnings and payment balances—and development issues, including official development assistance.

Gathering information on which to base our recommendations required travel to the areas under study. On those fact-finding missions, we met many people who were extremely knowledgeable in their field. When we were at the United Nations in August 1980, for example, we met Raphael Salas, executive director of the United Nations Fund for

Population Activities and Andrew Young, the U.S. ambassador to the United Nations. Young, who had been a close friend of Martin Luther King, talked about aid. He said the hardest thing to do is to give aid to somebody, which is exactly my sentiment. "Around here," he said, "people look at aid as a way to stop Communism or stop the arms race or to make money or set up a deal. People just don't give aid for aid." I remember him saying, "Aid is for aid" and I insisted when we did our final report that we incorporate that statement, "Aid is for aid."

In Washington we talked with top U.S. officials about their aid program. We visited the International Monetary Fund and the World Bank, each time talking to top-level officials and obtaining top- level information from them. The list of witnesses in the task force report indicates the extent of our consultations.

Task force reports are frequently tabled, shelved and forgotten. When the North-South Task Force report was tabled December 17, 1980, the initial printing of 10,000 disappeared almost instantly. Requests for copies came in from across Canada. The report was reprinted and the second printing ran out as well.

Although it's hard to put a barometer on attitudes, I do feel that in the almost six years that I served in the House of Commons, people at least became more aware of the North-South subject. We knew the North-South idea wasn't going to be easy to get across. The term meant nothing to most people, and it was hard to convince people that they should be concerned about other countries. Shortly after I began to work on the North-South Task Force, my sister, Mary Lou, who was running my Saskatoon office, received an angry phone call one night from someone who wanted to see me. She said that I was working on the North-South Task Force and that I would probably be home on the weekend. The person at the other end of the line said, "Yeah, he's like all other politicians. Never thinks about his home. There he is now working for Regina!"

I firmly believed that what was happening in the Third World was going to have a great influence on Canada, whether Canadians liked it or not. It was clear that trade and manufacturing were going to move, Canada's markets were going to shift to the Third World and immigration was going to become a greater pressure. Markets that Canada had thought secure were going to disappear and countries that had been net importers were going to become major exporters. Many examples could be cited. When we started the Task Force in 1980, no one would have believed that Korea was going to become a car manufacturer, or that its cars could become competitive in the North American market. Of course, that has happened. And the same thing that happened in Korea is happening in Malaysia, Hong Kong, Singapore and other Third World

110

countries which weren't supposed to be able to do this. International corporations, too, will continue to build their factories where they can get cheap labour. And, cheap labour is in the Third World. They will also pick up and move to another country when conditions change. Whether the House of Commons paid any attention to this or not, it was going to happen. That's why I felt it was necessary to keep pushing it as a subject. We needed to understand what was happening. The whole thrust of the North-South Task Force was to try to get away from the aid mentality, to show that our relationship with the Third World in future would revolve around trade and that we would have to deal with world-wide movements of people.

Before any legislation can be approved by Parliament, particularly legislation in an area as complex as this, people have to be informed, there has to be a supportive mood. International finance and world trade are such big, complicated issues that nobody understands them completely. But we wanted some of the facts to become common knowledge. In 1980, for example, the Third World debt seemed impossibly large and it has multiplied many times since. That's the kind of information people need to have. Third World and North-South questions have more or less disappeared in the Mulroney government, but this indifference will not eliminate the issues.

Canada itself has many of the characteristics of Third World countries, and we need to be alert to the danger in that. We may have water and food and health care, but international corporations run the economy of Canada just like international corporations run the economy of Venezuela or the Congo. Decisions that profoundly affect our economy are made outside the country. Our standard of living may be higher, but our branch plant economy resembles that of a Third World country.

While serving on the North-South Task Force, I was also a member of the external affairs committee and a subcommittee it struck to study Canada's relations with the Caribbean and Latin America. Again, our first task was to gather information. This entailed several trips to the Caribbean and Latin America.

Several of the trips to the Third World countries I made as an MP came neither through the North-South Task Force nor the external affairs subcommittee. The Socialist International, an organization that brings together more than 70 socialist parties and organizations around the world, presently including the ruling parties in France, Spain, Sweden, Australia, New Zealand and Peru, was meeting in Grenada in July 1981. Ed Broadbent was, and still is, vice-president of the Socialist International, representing the Americas. Since he could not attend the meeting, he asked me to go in his place.

Grenada's Prime Minister Maurice Bishop had come to power not by an elected vote but by popular uprising, and the Socialist International was concerned about the situation. The secretary of the SI asked me to try to determine whether Bishop's party had moved too far left for the Socialist International.

The island of Grenada is a small, extremely poor Third World country. It has a population of about 113,000 people, which is smaller than the population of Saskatoon. It was called the Spice Island by the British, who used it as a place to grow spices because it was closer than their sources in the Far East. Bishop's plan was to build an airport so they could fly in tourists. The existing airport terminal was about 50 feet long, a plywood shell with two-by-fours exposed on the inside of the building. The landing-strip was very dangerous. Built by the British during the war as an anti-submarine base, it was too small to accommodate jet aircraft.

When I arrived in Grenada, an airport official phoned external affairs to have a car sent out to drive me to my hotel. The island was like a toy country. It was only 10-miles-wide by 15-miles-long and even though it had only 113,000 people, it had a Department of External Affairs, a Department of Education, a Department of Transport and so on. The limousine service from external affairs turned out to be an old car and a driver who treated me like royalty. The hotel was in St. George's, on the other side of the mountain ridge that makes up the island. The drive took about two hours, over a road that was about six-feet-wide and full of ruts, donkeys, chickens, dogs and women carrying water on their heads. It was a Third World scene I had experienced many times before.

The hotel was a Holiday Inn, owned by a man from Montréal. The convention was held in a building that had been built to attract convention trade from outside the country. That trade had not yet materialized and the country was still so poor that there wasn't enough food for the delegates. The conference hosts forced the hotel to give us one meal. For most of the two-day convention, sessions went right through meal hours. Delegates just didn't eat. It was the first time I'd been in a place that was so up against the wall.

The speakers, particularly Bishop's people, were quite impressive. Most of them were graduates of Oxford, Cambridge or the London School of Economics. Listening to them was like listening to Shakespearean theatre. They spoke without any notes and their speeches were masterpieces of prose and oratory. I found this fascinating. These men were obviously highly intelligent and well-educated. They were also revolutionaries. At least they called themselves revolutionaries. Anyone not used to revolutionary rhetoric would have been terrified listening to them. During one of my conversations with Bishop, he said to me, "The reason the Americans are so afraid of our revolution is that it's

the first time there has been a revolution of Blacks who speak English.''
I think he had a point.

The Grenadians were very fearful of an invasion. They said an American fleet was practising off the coast and had already taken a practice run at an island off Cuba that resembled Grenada. They seemed a bit paranoid to me at the time, but they were right about what was going to happen to them.

Concern about Bishop's take-over surfaced a number of times. Bishop kept responding that Grenada didn't need to have an election like they had in the U.S., because there was more democracy in Grenada than they'd ever have in the U.S. His argument was not totally satisfying, but one evening I got a glimpse of what he was referring to. Out in a parish, as the districts of Grenada are called according to the old British system, I observed a meeting in a church basement where people were discussing how they were going to spend the country's health budget that year. There wasn't much money in the national health budget, but it was being allocated by people in a church basement! The size of the island permitted it. It was a different kind of democracy. They weren't electing a representative and sending him off for four years to make all the decisions. They were making the decisions themselves.

The Grenadians' hopes were pinned on that airport. We were driven out to see the construction. At that time the earth-moving was about half done. Since there wasn't a single level spot on the island, they had to make one. Off one end of the island there were a number of finger points that reached out into the sea. The plan was to knock down some of the mountain and fill in the space between the fingers.

The Grenadian in charge of the construction was a graduate of McGill. Most of the construction workers were Cuban volunteers. I went to visit the Cuban camp and found the workers living in very primitive conditions. At the construction site, they were using old Italian and Spanish Caterpillars and bulldozers to do the levelling. Part of it was being done by a dredging outfit from Miami, Florida. A British crew was there to put in the landing-lights for the runway, which was going to be a one-way strip. Planes would have to come in, land, turn around on the runway and go back to the terminal. It was obviously going to be a small, civilian airport. Rumours that it was a Communist-run project to build a military base were patently absurd.

In my conversations with Bishop, I suggested that it would be a good idea to have an election so outsiders could see that he had come to power by the will of the people. He kept repeating that there was more democracy in Grenada than there is in countries that have elections. I could not get him to see that image counts as much as reality.

While I was in Grenada I made a point of going to see the Catholic

113

bishop, Bishop Charles, who was a Trinidadian. I had heard that Maurice Bishop had put some of his opposition in jail and I asked the Catholic bishop about this. He said it was true and that he and some Anglican churchmen were monitoring the situation to make sure there was no further abuse of human rights. The bishop said he didn't know what was going to happen in Grenada and he didn't know what to do because they hadn't taught him in the seminary how to handle a revolution. I thought it was just as well, because he seemed to be doing fine, working it out day by day.

At the end of my stay in Grenada I was to catch a plane to Barbados and then home. The plane was supposed to leave at 6 a.m. and they told me the car from external affairs would pick me up at 4 a.m. A number of other delegates were to be picked up too. At 4 a.m. I emerged from the hotel into a very dark tropical night. The car was waiting. The driver went from one home to another, where the other delegates were staying, but nobody was up. The driver didn't wait. After several of these futile stops, we started out across the island. Again, ten miles took two hours. Even at that time of the morning, people were already out. The road was cluttered with people and animals.

When we got to the top of the mountain, the sun was just breaking over the South Atlantic. It was a beautiful sight. And the air was full of the smell of cloves. We made our way down the other side and finally arrived at the airport. There I recognized one of the dynamic speakers from the day before, a Grenadian. He saw me and we shook hands and I had the feeling that I have had so often on meeting a Third World person in their own country. I sense in them an embarrassment, as if they're thinking, "You've seen better things, and here is my country and this is all we've got." It's the embarrassment of poverty. This man had brought his mother to the airport. He was sending her off to Boston, where his brother lived. His mother had never been on a plane before and he asked if I would sit with her and see that she got on the right plane when we arrived in Barbados. I said I'd be glad to do that.

The airplane that was to fly us out of Grenada was a Banderanti. It was the whole Grenadian air force—one airplane—a Banderanti that had been made in Brazil. At 6:10 a.m. a tall Englishman with a long moustache came into the building. He looked in his mid-50s or 60s. He was wearing short pants and stockings and looked like an RAF pilot. He invited us out to the plane and we followed him onto the airstrip. The Banderanti doesn't have individual seats; it just has benches. So I sat next to this old, black lady and belted her down and waved to her son. Everything seemed under control. The Englishman and his co-pilot climbed into the plane, closed the door and went into the cabin. They started up the two engines, both of which caught, to my surprise. Then

I saw the pilot reach up and turn off the two switches and both engines stopped. Immediately, I envisaged repairs. They would have to replace a part and the closest place one could be found was in São Paulo, Brazil. The pilot came back and told us we'd have to get off. No one was in the tower yet and he couldn't take off until the tower radioed ahead that we were coming. Now, all that had happened was that the man who operated the radio tower, which was a little wooden box on four stilts, had slept in. So we got out and my friend, who was part of Bishop's government and who was now more embarrassed than ever, sent someone off on a bicycle to get a radio operator. In 15 minutes or so this person appeared on a bicycle, looking very tired. He climbed up a wooden ladder into the tower. He must have got a message to where we were going, because we were escorted back to the plane for a successful take-off.

In January 1982, I travelled through the Caribbean and Central America with the external affairs subcommittee: Maurice Dupras, Flora MacDonald, Walter McLean, Ken Robinson, Jim Schroder, Stan Hudecki and Jack Murta. The purpose of the trip was to evaluate Canadian aid projects in Haiti and the Eastern Caribbean, and Canada's economic relations with Central America and Cuba generally. Half the group went to Haiti, the other half, of which I was part, went to Trinidad and Tobago. We then joined forces and were briefed in Costa Rica by the Canadian ambassador, who lived there and represented most of the Central American region. From there we continued to Nicaragua. As we touched down in Managua, I said jokingly, "Well, we're back in NDP country." A few months later someone in external affairs confided that my remark had been wired to Canada.

We had a very full visit in Managua. Although the Canadian Embassy in Costa Rica had arranged for us to meet with a good cross-section of Nicaraguan society, I also felt they were steering us in one direction. They wanted us to see things the American way. After hearing numerous spokesmen for the American position, I wanted to hear something else. But whenever we wanted to diverge from the agenda they had laid out for us, we were told no, we had to stay with the group. Fortunately, Walter McLean and I had connections through the church and, in Nicaragua as in other countries, we were able to pursue these connections and through them have access to other information.

A friend of mine, Father Bill Smith, a Scarborough priest from Toronto who now works for the Canadian Catholic Organization for Development and Peace, came to the hotel where we were staying in Managua. He had been a missionary in Latin America and was on a year's sabbatical, studying landholdings in Central America. He suggested that there were many things we could see in Nicaragua besides the outline that had been given to us. While the rest of the delegation visited one of the newspapers, *La Prensa*, which I had visited before, Bill Smith and some of his Nicaraguan friends took us to some of the Christian base communities up in the mountains.

Another person who came to see us privately at the hotel where we were staying in Managua was Sister Peggy Healey, an American Maryknoll Sister. A colleague of hers was one of the four women who had been murdered in El Salvador. I had visited the community where she worked and noticed that the people looked upon the dead Sister as a saint. They talked about her as if she were still alive, still part of the group. Peggy had a big influence on several members of our delegation because she was so authentic, because she believed so strongly in what was going on in the country and had committed herself so entirely to the people in the country.

I was also able to contact some Nicaraguan Jesuits whom I'd known before, and they, too, gave us a very different interpretation of the American line. One Jesuit who was particularly helpful, has remained a close friend to me. Xavier Gorostiaga is an economist who was, at the time, director of the Institute of Economic and Social Investigations, which is a branch of the government. He was quite familiar with Canada as he had undergone a Canadian speaking tour during Ten Days For World Development and has many contacts in Canada. He had supported the revolution and was now working very hard inside the government to try to make the revolution work. These informal meetings brought us much closer to the ground and provided more accurate information about what was happening than we were able to get from government officials.

We had one official church visit with Archbishop Miguel Obando y Bravo. We met the archbishop in his home, which was quite an elaborate house a few miles outside the city of Managua. Of all the people we met over a period of ten days or two weeks, our group felt that Obando was probably the most rigid. He was ideologically rooted and absolutely incapable of dialogue. He was very sharp with me when I asked him about a report that Bishop Remi DeRoo had prepared for the Canadian bishops after visiting Nicaragua. He told me that no one had any right to make a report on another country and priests should stay out of politics. After the interview, I had to try to explain how a person of this level in the church could be so closed. Of course I couldn't explain it. All I could say was that we were not seeing the whole church here, we were seeing one personality.

By the end of our stay in Nicaragua, we had met literally hundreds of people. One of our final meetings was with President Daniel Ortega Saavedra. He was in his 30s then, passionately committed to the revolution and to Nicaragua. He made it quite clear early in the conversation that he had spent 12 years in the hills and that we weren't going to tell him what to do. He had put too much of his life into the revolution. Generally, when we went into a meeting such as this, Maurice Dupras, who was acting as chairman, would introduce us and then invite us to ask questions of the person with whom we were talking. Ortega refused to follow this procedure. He insisted on hearing all the questions before responding. He then replied to all the questions in the form of a speech. He was very anxious for Canadians to understand what the *Sandinistas* were trying to do and he felt that Canada could and should play a role in supporting the process of change in Nicaragua. He explained the history of the revolution and how he had been involved; how they had taken the name *Sandinista* from Sandino, a revolutionary who had tried to expel the Americans in 1930 and had finally been killed by them; and how the *Sandinistas* had finally ousted General Anastasio Somoza-Debayle in 1979. He explained that the first two policies the revolution tried to implement were universal education and universal health care. The difficulty was lack of financial and technical resources. Somoza had left less than $3-million in the banks of Nicaragua. But the *Sandinistas* were determined. They continued to try to establish these programs despite American attempts to undermine them. Ortega saw that what they were doing was a threat to the U.S. because other countries might follow the Nicaraguan example of trying to take charge of their own development, rather than allowing it to be controlled from outside. Like the Cubans, Ortega wanted a dialogue with the United States, but he was not optimistic about American willingness to entertain this possibility. He was convinced that the Americans would not allow any country to make a new start, to change in any way that was not to the advantage of the U.S. In his view, it was the poorest countries that would suffer most from the American determination to obliterate the Nicaraguan experiment. Ortega wanted Nicaragua to have relations with North America, Europe, the Eastern Bloc and the Third World. He used the analogy of a stool. These were the four legs of the stool. If any one of them was cut off, the stool would fall over.

One of the highlights of that trip to Central America and the Caribbean was meeting Fidel Castro. Prior to the session with Castro, we met with Cuban Vice-President Carlos Raphael Rodriguez. Rodriguez had been with Castro from the beginning. He had been a university professor and although he spoke English well, our formal discussions were conducted in Spanish. We sat at a large table, our delegation on one side, his on the other. The discussion was translated by a woman, Fidel Castro's personal translator. She was the best translator I've ever seen in a situation like that. She not only translated both languages back and forth, she also seemed to look and act like the person whose speech she was translating. You could pick up their mood by watching her.

My documentation, which had been prepared by the Cubans, listed me as *Reverendo* Robert Ogle, which is the formal way to address a clergyman in Spanish. Our delegation also included Walter McLean, the PC member for Kitchener-Waterloo, who is an ordained Presbyterian minister. He, too, was referred to as *Reverendo*. But during the talks, because some of the people on our side of the table would refer to me as Father Bob, the woman who was translating realized that I was a Catholic priest and he was a Protestant minister. The next time she addressed me, she called me *Padre* rather than *Reverendo*. Vice-President Rodriguez instantly caught this and interrupted the discussion to ask me if I was a Catholic priest. I said I was and he seemed pleasantly surprised. On the way out of his office after the meeting he asked me again if I was a Catholic priest. He couldn't believe that a Catholic priest would come to talk to Cubans. I turned to him and tapped him on the chest, which is a Latin way of making sure that you get heard, and I said, "How is it that you went to a Jesuit high school and turned out to be a Communist?" He laughed. He could tell I was kidding him and he laughed again as we went down the corridor to Castro's office. Each of our delegation was introduced to Castro and when it was my turn, Rodriguez said to Castro, "Fidel, this person is a Catholic priest." Castro said, "Are you a Catholic priest?" I said I was and then I tapped Castro on the chest the same way I had tapped Rodriguez. I asked Castro how it was that he had gone to a Jesuit school and turned out to be a Communist. He didn't flinch at this. He just put his finger up against his nose, and the translator put her finger up against her nose. He stopped for a moment and then said, "Yes, I went to the Jesuits and the Jesuits taught me two things. They taught me morality and they taught me discipline."

If I had to sum up in two words what I saw in Cuba, I would say: morality and discipline. The idea of everyone having a place to live, something to eat, a job, education and health care, I would call the social morality of Cuba. And this was brought about by discipline. You couldn't just do what you wanted. To make this program work for everyone, you had to do what you were told. Later, when we had another chance to talk to Castro, I picked up the idea of this Jesuit discipline. I said, "You know it works for awhile, but it won't work forever because after awhile people will say no." I talked about the problems in Quebec where the Church had tried to enforce morality and discipline. I had visited several high schools in Cuba and I told him they reminded me of the old Catholic schools I had known. I was afraid that Cubans, too, would eventually rebel against that form of discipline.

Our talks with the Cubans were very friendly. They were trying to find a way to negotiate with the Americans and they were really hoping that Canada might be able to facilitate this. They didn't want to invade the U.S., they didn't want to convert the U.S. They just wanted the Americans to let them be Cubans and do things their own way, a liberty the Americans seemed unwilling to grant them.

In our briefing session, the Canadian Embassy official in Havana estimated that of Cuba's ten-million people, about a million were totally in favour of the Castro regime, about a million were against it and about eight-million were in between. That ratio, I thought, could probably be applied to most countries.

We had a very informative visit with the archbishop of Havana, Jaime Ortega, a man in his 40s. He had studied in Montréal and felt a close connection to Canada. He told us that of the few priests still working in Cuba, many are Canadians. At the time of the revolution, many of the Spanish priests and nuns left and the French priests from Quebec remained. He was quite open in talking about the church-state relationship in Cuba. He said it could be better, but it certainly could be a lot worse. Prior to the revolution, he said about five per cent of the people were actively involved in the church and after the revolution about five per cent were involved, but it was a different five per cent. Before the revolution it was from the upper class and after the revolution the five per cent came from the lower classes. He said the church now was much more active, much more vital.

We met some of the Canadian priests and were able to arrange for them to meet Castro for the first time, which they appreciated. Some of the sisters who came with the priests to the reception at the Canadian Embassy were dressed in lay clothes and Castro was quite surprised to hear that they were sisters. I heard him say to them that he thought that was a very good idea because now they looked like the people.

The Americans claim that the presence of Cubans in Nicaragua proves that communism is spreading and has to be stopped. There is, however, a much simpler and more factual explanation for the presence of Cubans in Nicaragua. Because the Nicaraguans had no resources of their own after the revolution, they asked for help. They wanted Spanish-speaking technical advisors, teachers and health workers. Nicaragua literally opened its door to the world. Canada or the U.S. could have responded to that call, but didn't, at least not officially or to any substantial degree. There was some response from various countries, but the greatest response was from Cuba. They were Spanish-speaking and they had been doing the same work for some time in their own country. Cuban teachers and health workers came to Nicaragua and spread all though the country. When we were there, there were still Cubans in Nicaragua. The people I met in the church and in other sectors in Nicaragua made it abundantly clear that the revolution had been fought to bring justice to the country and its first objectives were to provide the basic human needs of education and health. The revolution was not based on a political ideology. It was not a Communist take-over. The revolution had been supported by many people, including the business sector, who were anything but Marxist.

We met with members of the business community in Nicaragua. They were rather patronizing and treated us like children. They sat us down in such a way that we couldn't leave the room and then lectured us about their position. They had supported the revolution, just before Somoza fell, but they were disappointed that they weren't in control now that Somoza was gone. They had to acknowledge, however, that the *Sandinistas* did permit them to continue in business and most operations in Nicaragua were still privately owned.

Castro had apparently given the *Sandinistas* some advice. After the revolution in Cuba they had mass public trials for the mayors, police chiefs and others who had persecuted the people. Those who were convicted at the public trials were executed. He indicated to the Nicaraguans that he thought he should not have done that. The Nicaraguans, either following Castro's advice or on their own judgment, had no public trials. Many of those who had been persecuting the people were jailed for awhile and then released. Tomas Borge, one of the original *Sandinistas* and one of the few who is still alive, has told the story which I've heard from many sources, of the time he met his former torturer in jail after the revolution. The terrified torturer asked Borge what he was going to do to him and Borge said, "I'm going to love you." Many of the torturers who carried out atrocities under the Somoza regime went to Honduras, where they were joined by foreign mercenaries and CIA plants and became known as the Contras, the group that is working to overthrow the *Sandinista* government.

Not visiting El Salvador was, in my view, a major flaw in the subcommittee survey, because at that particular time El Salvador was really the hotbed of contention in Central America. It's important to remember that even though Central America is a relatively small area, the five countries in that region are very different. North Americans tend to lump them together as one entity, Central America, but living in Latin America I discovered that each country has a very clear identity and that a person who lives in one country is very clearly identified as a national of that country. They are very conscious of their differences. This is hard for an outsider to understand because the histories of these countries seem so similar. Most Latin American countries were invaded by the Spanish, who married with the indigenous people. But in modern times their histories are very different. El Salvador, the smallest of the Central American countries, industrialized more quickly than the others, with heavy American investment. The country has had a hard time keeping any form of democracy. It has been taken over by the army several times. José Napoleón Duarte was tortured and expelled from the country. He lived in Venezuela for 11 years, then was called back in 1980, supposedly to head a form of democratic government and prepare for a general election. But the army was basically still in control. At the time of our tour in 1982, there was a civil war going on between those who supported the army and the Americans, and those who supported Salvadorean autonomy. The army and the central government were using death squads to wipe out the opposition. There was open fighting in the countryside, and thousands and thousands of people had been turned into refugees because it wasn't safe to go back to their homes.

Canada could not be expected to get involved in a civil war in another country. Canada doesn't even have much of an economic link to El Salvador. But I felt that we needed to clarify what was going on in El Salvador before we could advise the Canadian government. So in late February 1982, four members of the subcommittee went to El Salvador. Maurice Dupras led the group. Ken Robinson was the Liberal member, Flora MacDonald the PC and I represented the New Democrats. We met in Mexico City, where we were briefed by the Canadian Embassy staff, and then flew directly to San Salvador. There we were met by Canadian Ambassador R. Douglas Sirrs and his assistant, who had come up from Costa Rica to be our guides while we were in El Salvador.

My first impression of El Salvador was of a clean airport with very few people. We were taken into the city by bus on a road that had recently been built by the Americans. It was on the old road to the airport that four American religious women had been murdered the previous year. That was very much on our minds as we rode into San Salvador. We were taken to a deluxe hotel which could have been in any resort in the world, except for all the armed guards with sawed-off shotguns and rifles. Instead of a resort atmosphere, there was the scent of violence in the air. Each of us was assigned a room with a guard who sat outside the door 24 hours a day. The guards were 16 or 17-year-old high school students. I spent quite a bit of time with them. They each had a little Israeli machine-gun across their knees and all night long they'd sit there and do their homework—geometry and algebra and so on. They were nonchalant, and at the same time serious, about what they were doing. They had instructions not to let us use the elevators in the hotel. Any time we wanted to go downstairs, we had to go with two of them—one in front and one behind.

This air of violence and uncertainty was a new experience for me. We never actually witnessed any violence, but there certainly was evidence of it everywhere we went and sometimes shooting could be heard at night.

The purpose of our trip was to assess whether a free election could be held in El Salvador. We visited the different political parties, each of which was holed up in what amounted to an armed camp. At the official election bureau, they went through a lengthy explanation of why there couldn't be any invalid ballots. Every ballot was checked. That seemed beside the point. With so much fear and violence, how could there be a free election? Many people would not have the chance to vote because civil war was raging in the country. Many people had fled to refugee camps, which they were afraid to leave. Those were only some of the obstacles we saw to a meaningful election. The violence was taken so much for granted that the people who were talking about the election didn't even consider it extraordinary that 22 mayors had been killed in El Salvador that year.

As in any civil war, it's difficult to sort out the causes of the violence. But in general, in El Salvador, and this is inevitably an oversimplification, there is a group of people, primarily peasants, working class and intellectuals, who are calling for a redivision of land. And there is the other group, the wealthy and the military, who oppose it. No one would openly oppose redivision of land. It has always been promised, but the Right has no intention of carrying out the promise.

There was violence on both sides, but in general we felt more of it was coming from the Right. They were assassinating leaders of the other side whenever they could. If a mayor of a town supported land reform, that mayor would die. That was the kind of intimidation that was going on. Because of the intimidation, violence and open fighting in the countryside, thousands of refugees were pouring into the city, where church-run camps were struggling to look after them. We visited three or four refugee camps. They were full of women, old men and young children, living in very poor conditions, often just a lean-to up against a wall or in part of some church property, like an old college or seminary. Most of the men were still back in the countryside, in hiding. It was too dangerous for them to be in the refugee camps. The army would frequently sweep down on the camps and take men away. They usually didn't come back.

The American ambassador invited us to his home and treated us very cordially. He made it very clear that the United States was supporting the military and the Right, that the Americans weren't about to lose control of the country and that they were going ahead with this election.

When we met with General Garcia, the head of the army, the American press turned out in full force. General Garcia's position was predictable. According to him, the violence was caused by the guerrillas, who were all Communists bent on destroying the country. The army was going to save the country from communism.

From all our meetings with people in El Salvador, a story emerged of two strong groups. One side was the military, directed by very hard-line military officers who were fighting a war against Communists, with strong American support. The other was the legal aid group that had been set up by the archdiocese of El Salvador to seek information regarding the thousands of people who were disappearing, being murdered, found in ditches and so forth. Between these two highly emotional positions, there seemed to be no bridge. Nobody on the American or military side seemed to care about the human suffering.

The general tone, as we drove from one place to another, was one of fear and violence. There were soldiers on the streets everywhere. As we were driving from the legal aid office to see Duarte, an army truck passed us going quite fast. We could see five or six soldiers in the back of the truck with their rifles pointed down at a civilian, who was lying on the floor. I remember the feeling of helplessness, knowing that this man was probably going to be killed and there was nothing we could do about it. This was going on all the time. For the people we talked to, it was almost as common an occurrence as a bicycle going by.

When we arrived at Duarte's presidential palace, it was almost deserted. One of my colleagues commented, "You can see who has power in this country." No press showed up for our meeting with Duarte. Duarte, of course, was in a very difficult position. He told us that Salvadoreans were now living in a culture of violence, that in this milieu everyone hated everyone else. He was in the impossible position of trying to solve the problem. It was so complex that if anyone claimed to have a clear answer you'd know they were wrong.

That same evening we met Major Roberto D'Aubuisson, who was running for one of the elected seats on the interim commission that was to govern until the full presidential election was held. D'Aubuisson came to our room with three colleagues. The three others, we found out, actually lived in California and Florida. They were extremely well-dressed. They looked like people you'd meet at an expensive country club. The three colleagues spoke English well; D'Aubuisson seemed not to speak English at all. It was difficult to reconcile the well-dressed, genteel businessman standing in front of us with the reputation that went before him. D'Aubuisson had been in the secret service branch of the army prior to seeking this political position. He had been identified by the former American Ambassador Robert White as the person who organized the murder of Archbishop Oscar Romero. He was never charged, but it was generally accepted that he was behind the shooting. Everything D'Aubuisson said to us was intended to show great concern for all his suffering countrymen.

When it was my turn to ask a few questions, I adopted the Latin custom of asking about family. How did he come to have a French name, I asked. He really warmed to this, like most Latins, who love to talk about their family. He explained that his grandfather had worked on the French crew that made the first attempt to build the Panama Canal. After the failure of the canal attempt, his grandfather had gone to El Salvador, found land and stayed there. He talked about his brothers and sisters. He told me he had a sister who had been a nun and that she was now working as a social worker in one of the parishes in San Salvador. He made a point of explaining that she had obtained all the proper permissions to leave. It struck me as ironic that this man, who was reputed to have organized the murder of the archbishop, needed to make sure that I understood that his sister had obtained all the proper permissions to leave her religious order.

We always asked about land reform. The land is held by a few wealthy landholders and everybody else works as peasants. D'Aubuisson, like all the political figures, spoke of land reform, but without conviction or credibility. Land reform was part of every political platform. Various acts had been passed, but the actual redistribution always ran into insurmountable problems. The simple fact was that nobody was going to give up any land. They've been trying to do it for 200 years. Land division is always difficult. You couldn't do it easily in Saskatchewan either. The wealth in the country, as far as we could make out, is still tied to land holdings, although the few wealthy landholders have also invested in the businesses that exist in the country. Actually, most of the investment is American and the factories tend to be companies like Texas Instruments, producing technical equipment. The land— which produces coffee, bananas and cattle—is still real wealth in the mind of the upper class. Owning land is still a powerful status symbol.

We heard a lot during our visit to El Salvador from the right-wing military American side. Canadian Ambassador Sirrs set up meetings for us that would clearly give only that side. Fortunately, again, I had a few contacts with the church and through them we were able to gather more information. The Jesuits at the Catholic University of Central America were particularly helpful. The civilian university had been attacked by the army the summer before and had never reopened. The religious university run by the Jesuits was still functioning.

We met with Jon Sobrino, who is on the board of directors of the Catholic University and is considered one of the world's leading liberation theologians, and with Ricardo Stein, a social economist at the university. They had statistics and opinion polls and were able to give us factual information about what was going on in the country. In their view it was not possible to have a valid election at that time because of the violence, displacement and intimidation. More than 500,000 people were displaced, and that was a major portion of the country's population of 5.5-million. The opposition politicians were all in exile. The parties mounting platforms and candidates were artificially created to divide the Right into three parties. There were no real differences among them.

Sobrino talked about life for the people in his country. He said that oppression was the air they breathed. He was very emphatic about the futility of holding an election. He said it could not produce freedom of any kind and he predicted that people would continue to suffer. The truth of the situation had never been seriously sought, Sobrino said. Romero tried to come to a point of truth, but since his death there had been no truth in the country. The public official statements were not true. No one expected to hear the truth anymore. The campaign that was going on while we were there was not helping matters either. All three parties were praising the military and condemning the guerrillas. We were curious about the extensive use of public walls and spaces for campaigning. Such use of public space is common in Latin America and, although it had been banned in San Salvador, it was still being done. I was surprised, in fact, at the high level of campaign activity.

The archbishop of San Salvador, Arturo Rivera y Damas, was out of the country at the time and in his place we met with Monsignor Orioste, the vicar general of the diocese of San Salvador. He told us that although the elections were being touted as a route to peace, the archbishop felt they would not bring peace. He also said that many people would vote for fear of being killed, because not voting would suggest that they were Leftist. The assumption would be made that, "If you don't vote, you're a Communist."

Monsignor Orioste strongly supported the Puebla and Medellin documents on the Church's preferential option for the poor. He recognized that the traditional church had been close to the government and had used its connections to prevent divorce laws and protect Catholic education and other interests. Most priests and bishops now, though, he said, believed in a renewed church, a church that identified with the poor, but it was not yet possible to preach it openly. The persecution was too strong. He made a comparison between the church in Poland, which is under persecution in a sense, but where relatively few people have been imprisoned and killed, and his own church in a very small country where thousands had been killed. He told us there were 26 Salvadorean priests in exile, out of a total number of slightly more than 100.

Our last day in El Salvador was Ash Wednesday and I wanted to go to mass. There was a church about a mile from the hotel where we were staying and I was planning to go to mass there. Flora MacDonald wanted to come with me. We took a taxi to the church of Our Lady of Guadalupe. It was early morning and the streets were busy. There were soldiers with their rifles, little girls in their uniforms going to school, people driving their cars to work. When we got inside the church there were a fair number of people. The mass was the standard Ash Wednesday ceremony; ashes were distributed. It was just like any Ash Wednesday any place in the world. You would never have guessed that there was a war going on outside.

That same day we visited several refugee camps and there was always the feeling of "Where do you go next?" Refugee camps are the edge of despair. There's just nowhere to go, nowhere to turn. That's what I remember most from that trip—the feeling in the air that there was no solution. As long as the war went on, there was no possibility of a solution. Until they had a full ceasefire there could be no serious negotiations leading to the formation of a government that would represent both sides. Four years later, the talks still haven't begun because the Left, the guerrillas, will not meet in a town full of soldiers, and the military government won't withdraw its troops.

Our impression after talking with Duarte was that he would bend over backwards for negotiations, but that he would not be able to get negotiations started. General Garcia, the army and the American Embassy held the power. And they did not want to negotiate.

When we got back to Canada we recommended that Canada not send observers to the election. Based on what we saw and the information we were able to gather, our conclusion was that there could be no valid election at that time. Sending observers would not turn it into a valid election. We felt that by boycotting it, we would make a statement about what we believed was taking place.

When the constituent assembly election did finally take place March 28, 1982, voter turn-out was very high, even though the election offered no real options. There were a number of reasons for the high turn-out. For many people, voting was a sign of wanting peace. They had been told that the election would bring peace and democracy. That was the American line. As the people at the Catholic University predicted, the election brought neither peace nor democracy. The right-wing council that was elected was not able to control the situation. The civil war continued. The army got more military aid and kept up the battle against the peasants. And, the situation remains basically unchanged even though Duarte was finally elected president March 25, 1984.

Another reason for the high voter turn-out has to do with standard Latin American voting practice. I knew from living in Brazil that eligible voters are issued a voter's card, which has to be marked on election day. If they do not vote, they are barred from many other civil rights. For instance, they couldn't get a driver's licence or a passport if their voting card was not up to date. People often vote because they have to, as they say, keep their documents in order.

After assessing the situation in El Salvador with the external affairs subcommittee, I was asked to retrace my steps. The Inter-Church Committee on Human Rights in Latin America asked if I would help organize an all-party delegation to El Salvador prior to the presidential election in 1983 to assess the human rights situation there. Frances Arbour, the executive secretary of ICCHRLA, explained that they were having difficulty securing funding for the trip and we would have to pay part or all of our expenses. Walter McLean expressed interest in going. He had a good background in Central America and strong feelings about human rights, as well as many contacts with church groups. Stan Hudecki, who had been in Central America previously with the North-South group, was also very interested. The Liberal party whip didn't want him to go, but Stan told me he would go anyway. As plans for the trip were taking shape, I did something which I seriously regretted afterwards. I told Mrs. Hudecki and Mrs. McLean that there was no danger, that we would be safe in El Salvador. I neglected to take into consideration that when I was there with the external affairs subcommittee, which was an official government delegation, we were under security. This time there would be no security and I did not anticipate the danger we would be in.

The Inter-Church Committee briefed us well in Toronto prior to our departure on November 5, 1982. Our first stop was in Mexico City, where we were met by John Foster, a United Church minister from Toronto who is active in the human rights movement. He had arranged for us to meet a number of Salvadoreans who were in exile in Mexico City. The first day we met Hector Dada. He was an engineer and economist, one of the founders of the Christian Democratic Party in El Salvador. He had been minister of foreign relations in the first Junta in 1979 and a member of the second Junta in 1980, but he had left the country to try to negotiate from the outside. He gave us an outline of the recent history in El Salvador, including the murder of Archbishop Oscar Romero.

Stan Hudecki was very concerned about whether those who opposed the army and the government were Communist and I remember Dada's reply to this question: "There are many ways to be a Christian and there are many ways to be a Communist." I think that was Dada's way of saying that you cannot describe the complicated nature of contemporary Central America in such simple terms. It's not a black and white picture.

After extensive briefing in Mexico, we flew into El Salvador. We had with us a secretary-translator, Tim Draimin from Toronto's Jesuit Centre for Social Faith and Justice, who arranged meetings and translated for us. Immediately after we arrived in El Salvador on Saturday afternoon, he was able to set up a meeting for us with Archbishop Rivera y Damas. The archbishop explained the situation in El Salvador, the difficulties caused by the civil war and intervention from the United States, and the situation in regard to human rights. I asked if I might celebrate mass with him at the cathedral the next morning. He welcomed that and invited our group to come and sit at the front.

The following morning we took a taxi to the cathedral where Archbishop Romero is buried. The cathedral was damaged in fighting that took place in the square around it, and it has not been repaired. Thousands of people come every year to pay homage to the archbishop who spoke out so courageously against injustice and inhumanity and was assassinated while saying mass in a hospital chapel. The tomb in the cathedral has become a popular shrine.

When we arrived at the cathedral, I was surprised to see so many foreign journalists, even television crews from Germany and France. They were there because the archbishop's sermon on Sunday was their primary source of information. In his sermon, he reported on the events of the week, how many people had been murdered and how many had disappeared. None of this information was reported by the Salvadorean media. The archbishop had this information because the human rights group in El Salvador, some of whom have died since, had their office on the cathedral grounds. The relatives of the murdered and missing came there to report their tragedies and seek help.

The archbishop was vesting for mass at the back of the church when we arrived. I joined him and when we had put on our vestments, he invited the people who were with me to come and sit in the sanctuary, which they did. Later it occurred to me that they would have been directly in the line of fire if anyone had started shooting in the church.

In his homily, the archbishop explained to the people what had happened during the past week. He told of one incident in which heavily armed men, dressed in civilian clothes, had stormed a house and dragged out all the people living there. None of them had been seen again. He cited the week's total number of deaths and human rights violations. He condemned the injustice and the inhumanity, and called for basic changes in El Salvador. It was a very strong sermon. Afterwards, someone told us that he was particularly strong that day because we were there. He had some international support. We knew that it was very dangerous for him, or for anyone else, to speak out like that, because the death squads were everywhere and no one was safe from them.

We met that day with many people from different political persuasions and with different viewpoints on the general situation. Professor Ricardo Stein at the Catholic University of Central America helped provide background information and contacts. While we were at the university that Sunday afternoon, the buildings were buzzed several times by army helicopters. I was quite alarmed, but the people who lived there assured us that army helicopters frequently flew over at a low level as a sort of threat. They said they got used to it.

The Canadian Embassy official, who had been sent up from Costa Rica to accompany us, informed us that Sunday afternoon that we had received a threat. Someone had recommended that we leave the country immediately because our lives were in danger. We took this as a death threat. We went back to the hotel and then weren't sure if it was even safe to discuss it, because we thought our room was probably wired. We turned up the radio and talked very quietly in the centre of the room about what we should do. We decided to take our chances and stay as long as we had planned. We hadn't yet seen the Protestant groups we came to see.

We spent the next days visiting with Anglicans, Lutherans and Baptists. In general, they were doing the same thing as the Catholic Church—trying to protect the poor and those who disagreed with the military dictatorship. They were just trying to protect their lives and in doing so, many times they became threats, too, were persecuted and killed. Because these Protestant churches were smaller and didn't have the international voice of the Catholic Church, the outside world hadn't heard how they were being persecuted. That was one of the reasons we had been asked to visit them. The first Protestant church that we visited was the small Episcopal Church of El Salvador. The pastor, Victoriano Kimeno, told us that one of their priests and some of their congregation had recently been tortured because they were working for social rights and for the poor.

On the Monday, we went to the Catholic justice and peace committee legal office, which was right behind the archbishop's offices. The office manager, Maria Julia, explained that their mission was to provide assistance to the families of the dead and missing and to promote the basic doctrines of Medellin and Puebla, the documents that the Latin American bishops had produced. She explained that each month 60 or 70 people disappeared or were known to have been captured. Their relatives would report it to the justice and peace office. In the back of the office we could see some women and young people putting the names of their missing relatives on a list. They did this because it was their only hope that someone might look for those who had disappeared. Assassinations were obvious, Maria Julia explained. The body was found or witnesses described the event. The identification of bodies was sometimes done officially by the state, but more frequently by a family member's identification. The disappearances were harder to deal with.

That same day we visited several refugee camps that had been set

129

up by the Catholic Church in San Salvador. There were some refugee camps in the countryside, but most of them had been set up in the city on the assumption that they thought they would be safer there. There was a large refugee camp right behind the seminary, with people living in flimsy shacks and home-made tar-paper buildings. They were afraid to go back to the countryside where fighting was still going on. They were afraid to even leave the camp. They told us that one man who had left the camp was killed immediately. At another camp we visited, the refugees told how army troops had come in looking for "rebels." They terrorized the camp for five or six hours and then took away several men.

The second Protestant group we met were Baptists. We drove out to the Baptist Church one night in the back of a truck. I became very nervous when I realized that we were being followed. We were in a part of the city I didn't know and I felt very exposed in the back of that pick-up. To my great relief, we finally arrived safely at a little Baptist Church and were warmly welcomed by a small group of friends. Their pastor was one of the "missing" and so they had not replaced him. They didn't want anyone to become known as their leader because it was too dangerous. These Baptists were very grateful that we had come to see them and were going to take their message back to Canada. They told us that they looked upon the Church as the yeast of a new society, where there will be no violence and only peace. I felt very comfortable with their understanding of Church and the active role it should play in society to bring about peace. Not large in number, the Baptist Church had nonetheless suffered considerable repression and their new ministry had become a ministry of caring for displaced persons. It was very similar to what we saw in all the churches in El Salvador. The Church now found itself ministering to the dispossessed.

The Pentecostals we met also explained to us that they were living a war which they didn't want. They asked if we could get a petition to the people of the United States to ask them not to permit this violence and to look for peace through justice.

In addition to seeing church groups, we also had a long interview with José Napoleón Duarte. The meeting took place at his party head-quarters, a fortress-like building with armed guards scrutinizing the traffic below from the roof of the building. We drove up to the steel gate and waited. A small door in the gate opened and guards emerged. They check-ed our ID and gave the signal for the gate to be opened. As soon as we were inside, we were totally surrounded by guards with sawed-off shotguns and rifles. We were escorted up a set of stairs to Duarte's office.

Duarte is a graduate of the University of Notre Dame, Indiana, and he speaks fluent English. He also speaks passionately about El Salvador. Duarte is absolutely committed to saving his country, but he was in an

130

impossible situation, torn between the possibility of a sham election that might reinstate him as president and a right-wing takeover by D'Aubuisson and the military. No matter what happened, he was going to get caught in the middle. Duarte told us that he felt the U.S. position on El Salvador was a mistake. The American assumption that they knew what was best for El Salvador was not only paternalistic, it was inappropriate, according to Duarte. He said the U.S. didn't understand El Salvador. He was quite emphatic on that point.

My most vivid impression of that trip to El Salvador is of imminent violence. The streets were full of armed soldiers, but you see that in other countries. It was more than that. One of the people we had on our list to visit was American Ambassador Dean Hinton. His residence was a beautiful home in the area of the city that had formerly been owned by coffee plantation owners. The house was enclosed by a very high, reinforced wall. Marines stood sentry at the big steel gates. Once they were satisfied as to our identity, the door opened a few degrees and we slipped through. Inside, it was like a Texas ranch house, with a swimming pool at the back, a grand piano beside the swimming pool and Dean Hinton sitting there with his big dog. He gave us a very cordial welcome and his version of what was going on in El Salvador, which was quite different from what other people had told us. Then he presented the American solution. It consisted of a right-wing government, which would support the policies of the United States. Nothing else would do. No other kind of government would be acceptable. There would be an election to legitimize the installation of the right-wing in power and to make it palatable to the outside world.

At 6 p.m. Hinton announced that he had to go to a diplomatic cocktail party. He excused himself and got up to leave. Stationed around the back of the swimming pool where we were sitting were five or six men in civilian clothes, all carrying F-16 rifles. There was an atmosphere of super security. We got up to leave, too, and as we were waiting for our car, we watched Hinton leave the house. His bullet-proof Cadillac pulled up and two marines seemed to almost grab him and throw him in the back seat of the car. In front of Hinton's car was a jeep with five or six soldiers in it. Behind his car was another jeep, also containing five or six soldiers. When he was seated in his car, a guard slammed the door and someone gave the order, "Gate open." The first jeep rushed out and blocked the street, barring any traffic. Hinton's car slid through the gate, then the second jeep went out and moved in front of the Cadillac. It was like a dance. The second jeep started off down the street and the Cadillac followed. The gate slammed shut and all the marines and soldiers in the yard lowered their guns. A few of them, I remember, cleared the first shell out of the barrel. Suddenly, there was a bell ringing, the gate was open again and the Cadillac was back. I thought, and the soldiers thought, there had been an attack on the street. As it turned out, Hinton had forgotten his brief-case. It was a false alarm. But, for a moment, the fear in that yard was palpable. The marine beside me, an 18- or 19-year-old from upper state New York, said to me, "God, I've never been so scared in my life." That mood of fear and tension could be felt everywhere in El Salvador.

On our last night in El Salvador, we found out that we were going to have a hard time getting out to the airport the next morning. No taxi wanted to drive that 25-mile stretch. Even though it was a new highway, built by the Americans, no one had forgotten that the four American nuns had been shot on their way to the airport.

That evening we had a visit from Maria Julia, the woman who worked at the human rights office. She brought some documents on human rights cases that she wanted us to take back to Canada. And she told us that the Baptists were going to take us to the airport in their van. True to their word, two Baptists arrived early the next morning. We piled into the van, which had Baptist Mission painted on the outside, and took off. As long as we were in the city, everything seemed more or less normal. Children were going to school, shops were opening, soldiers were out on the street. But once we got outside the city limits and onto the airport highway, there was no one in sight. Just as we started onto the highway, two military police cars appeared. One pulled in front of us and one pulled up alongside us. We could see they were full of soldiers with automatic rifles and machine-guns. We couldn't get off the road, we couldn't turn around. We really didn't know what was happening or what to do. They made no move to stop us, so we kept driving. I remember thinking, "Could this be the end?" I was scared and I was furious with myself because I was responsible for getting Walter McLean and Stan Hudecki into this mess. We just looked at each other. There wasn't a thing we could do, except keep going. That was a long 25 miles. There was no traffic on the road. About half a mile from the airport, both military police cars pulled to the side and let us pass. Then, before we knew it, we were through immigration and on the plane. The stewardess was coming down the aisle, asking us what we wanted to drink. That night I was back home in Saskatoon.

I also made a second mission to Nicaragua in 1982. The NDP caucus asked me to represent Ed Broadbent on a Socialist International delegation to Nicaragua. The purpose was to find some solution to the Nicaraguan problem. The group was led by the former president of Venezuela, Carlos Perrez, and included representatives from Socialist parties in Germany, France, Sweden, Mexico and Chile.

Perrez knew all the political leaders in Central America and he had his own jet airplane. Both these factors helped get us to the people we needed to see. The group hoped to lay the ground-work for some kind of a peace settlement which would allow Nicaragua to get on with its program of development, rather than having to use most of its resources fighting a war. At the time, the Contras were building up strength in Honduras and Costa Rica for incursions into Nicaragua. Actually, in 1982 they weren't called Contras. They were still called *Somocistas*, which was much more revealing because most of them were old Somoza supporters. The Nicaraguans recognized them as Somoza's national guardsmen, jailers and torturers. The name *Somocista* was later changed to Contra and the Americans, of course, refer to them as "freedom fighters," all in an attempt to obscure their origins and intentions.

On one of the days during our stay in Nicaragua we flew to the Honduran-Nicaraguan border town of Jalapa in an old Russian helicopter. It was the first time I'd ever ridden in a military helicopter. It was like a gunship, with machine-guns sticking out of the side windows. The following week it crashed, killing 70, while airlifting children out of the war-torn border area. I remember looking down, as we were flying over the countryside, and thinking of it as a tortured land. It has been pitted by volcanic activity, battered and shaken by geological upheavals, stripped of its vegetation for sugar and coffee plantations and now ravaged by war. As our helicopter touched ground, we were surrounded by TV cameras and pressmen, soldiers, bullock carts moving produce and sundry. It was a scene of confusion.

The Nicaraguan military personnel along the border knew the Honduran soldiers on the other side by name and had a direct phone line with them. The Honduran soldiers were supposed to keep the Contras from crossing the line into Nicaragua. The Nicaraguan military officers also knew by name many of the Contras who were operating on the Honduran side of the border. The military described the general tension along the border and showed us on maps where the incursions were taking place. It was the first time I had ever been in a war zone. The enemy was less than a mile away and, as a matter of fact, the village we visited that day was attacked a few days later. The Contras would sweep through an area, killing a few people, burning a few farms or homes, and generally terrorizing the population.

The helicopter took us to another village a few miles from our first stop. It had been hit by the Contras a few days before our visit. We talked to several widows and mothers whose men had been killed in the raid. The message we got from people was a strong plea for some way to stop the war, without capitulating completely to the Contras.

It became very clear to us in our discussions with the ruling Junta, as well as through our own observations in the countryside, that the economy was in ruins. The country had been struck by floods, drought and earthquake, as well as by war. The *Sandinistas'* attempt to build a new, just society had been choked off from the very beginning by the Americans, who were using the Contras, or *Somocistas*, as they were still called, to further destabilize the economy and the morale of the country.

An interesting meeting I had during our stay in Nicaragua was arranged by our translator. It was a session with the Apostolic Nuncio for Nicaragua and Honduras, Archbishop Andrea Cordero di Montisemolo. He had formerly been in Papua New Guinea and he spoke very good English. I think he might have been assigned to Nicaragua because Papua New Guinea had a number of priests in government. The nuncio had worked out an arrangement under which the priests involved in the Nicaraguan government could continue to work in government, as long as they didn't appear publicly in a liturgical role. After talking with several of my priest friends in Nicaragua, I anticipated that the Pope's visit was going to disturb this working arrangement and make matters difficult for everyone.

While we were in Nicaragua, the National Assembly for the Council of State opened and we were invited as observers. At the formal opening of the assembly, we met the three priests who were ministers in the government. The National Assembly had been put together, pending a full election, by calling on each segment of society to send representatives. Thus, priests were involved as representatives of a part of society, i.e. the clergy.

Having surveyed the situation in Nicaragua, we began visiting neighbouring countries in our effort to start a process that would initiate peace negotiations. Our first stop was Costa Rica. President Luis Alberto Monge Alvarez was certainly interested in a peace initiative. Despite the traditional tension between Costa Rica and Nicaragua, the Costa Ricans were hoping that something could be done to stop the war before it got out of hand. That was the general message we heard throughout central America. Everyone was afraid of a conflagration and wanted to prevent it.

From Costa Rica we flew to Panama. At the time of our arrival, there was rioting in the city and we couldn't leave the airport. The Panamanians were afraid that one of us was going to get hurt or killed. We were met by guards at the door of the airplane and hustled off to a security room in the airport. There we learned that the riot was over water supply.

Perrez got on the phone to the president of Panama and asked for some helicopters to take us into the city. No helicopters were available, but they sent a paratroop plane. The guards took us from our room to the plane, which had only canvas seats against the sides of the aircraft. We were flown up over the rioting crowd and set down on a little landing-strip inside the city. There we were transferred to limousines and, with a motorcycle escort, whisked off to a hotel. We entered an underground section and were taken by special elevator up to the top floor, where we were locked in a luxury suite all day. We had food and a good view, but were not allowed to leave the room. The president of Panama, Ricardo de la Espriella, came to meet us and the discussion followed the same pattern as in Costa Rica. Perrez described our visit to Nicaragua, explaining that we had found a pluralistic society there and had been free to meet with everyone, from businessmen to refugees. The message we received in every sector, Perrez said, was that they wanted to negotiate a settlement. He alluded to the long-standing grudge between Costa Rica and Nicaragua and indicated that Costa Rica was prepared to talk.

It's difficult to judge whether our mission was successful. Some of the countries we visited formed the original Contadora group— Colombia, Panama, Venezuela and Mexico. Other Latin American countries joined later. (The name Contadora was taken from the island off Panama where they first met in January 1983.) Perrez's influence may have helped mobilize the leaders of these countries to work towards a negotiated settlement in Nicaragua.

At the end of the tour, most of our delegation felt that the peace plan was probably doomed because the Americans wouldn't support it. Most of the countries in Central America still depend heavily on American support in one form or another and they simply wouldn't be able to survive American opposition. As the Canadian member of the delegation, I was given a clear message to take back explicitly for Canada. People everywhere said that Canada should play a much larger role in this kind of negotiation because we didn't have vested interests.

Our last stop was Washington, D.C. We wanted to see if the Americans would consider a peace initiative. In Washington we were able to see Tom Enders, the State Department official responsible for Central America. Before taking on this post, Enders had been ambassador to Canada. I had met him once while I was on the Latin American subcommittee. Because Perrez, who was chairman of the group, couldn't speak English, the group leadership was turned over to me for this meeting. We detected in the Americans' remarks their discomfort with the Socialist International. It was remarkable that they agreed to see us and even more remarkable that what was scheduled as a 20-minute meeting lasted almost three hours.

Our proposal for negotiations met with solid resistance. The Americans had obviously closed the door on any formula that included the *Sandinistas*. They had to totally disappear if there was to be any peace. The Americans seemed to regard the *Sandinistas* as the incarnation of evil, and the country itself as a Russian base on the American continent. Their position was based on a black and white ideological model that bore virtually no resemblance to the facts. Forcing the situation into such a simplistic ideological mould was not only a distortion of reality, it made any practical attempt at dealing with the situation impossible.

Perrez tried to explain to Enders, through a translator, that if the Americans continued their efforts to subvert the *Sandinistas*, it would force them to seek help from the Soviet bloc which they really didn't want to do. After awhile I thought some of this might be getting through to Enders. It was hard to tell. He never abandoned the American position, but he seemed to listen more seriously after awhile.

We asked about Guatemala, which is probably the most vicious of all the Central American regimes. Enders thought things were improving in that country because there were fewer murders. That was a mentality I had frequently encountered at American embassies in Latin America. If the number of monthly murders went down, things were getting better. They never seemed to question the basic evil of it all.

Now, four years after that meeting with Enders and his staff, I have to admit that the American position has never changed. They never supported the Contadora peace initiative and they have continued to undermine the Nicaraguan government, basing their support to the Contras on an ideological myth. The old group of Somoza supporters, who are still looked upon by the Nicaraguans as bandits, thieves and torturers, have been reinforced by mercenaries and millions of dollars of American aid. They are not fighting for democracy and the Americans calling them "freedom fighters" will not make it so. American pressure has forced the *Sandinistas* more to the Left. Most of the aid they're getting from Cuba and Russia is going into the war effort.

In its case at the World Court, Nicaragua won a conviction against the Americans for mining Nicaraguan harbours. The court found that the U.S. had broken international law. And yet the Americans continue to intervene with impunity in the internal affairs of Nicaragua. It's a big bully pushing a little kid in the schoolyard. And worse, it's American determination to destroy another country's attempt to find its own form of democracy and provide its people with the fundamental human necessities of food, shelter, education and health.

The external affairs committee, of which I was a member, had been studying Canada's role in NATO and in disarmament, and was preparing a report on that subject in early 1982. Most of the people on the committee took a very traditional position on security and national defence. There were a number of us on the committee, however, who did not share their view. This small group included MPs from all three parties—Doug Roche and Walter McLean from the Conservative party, Paul McRae from the Liberals, Pauline Jewett, Terry Sargeant and myself from the New Democrats. As the committee report was approaching completion, the six of us got together and decided that we would write a minority report. Parliamentary procedure did not provide for a minority report from a committee, which is expected to reach a consensus. Even though the report would not have a right to exist technically, we felt that a good minority report, highlighting arguments that many Canadians accepted, might get media coverage and have some effect. We did produce and release a minority report over our six signatures, and it was taken up by the press and by peace groups across the country. I think that report presented the position that many Canadians feel Canada should be taking.

We quoted the first UN Special Session on Disarmament, which concluded with these words, "Mankind is confronted with a choice: we must halt the arms race and proceed to disarmament or face annihilation," and we pointed out that virtually no progress had been made in stopping the arms race. There had been no agreement on a complete test ban of nuclear weapons, no ratification of the strategic arms limitation talks (SALT II), no establishment of new nuclear weapon-free zones, no convention on banning chemical weapons, no reduction of armed forces and conventional weapons, no reduction of military budgets and no reduction in the international arms race. Even as I write today, virtually no progress has been made in any of these areas. Instead, governments ignoring their own words, pursue the arms race. Part of the reason for this is that governments continue to view security in narrow terms. As armaments accumulate competitively, countries become more intensely concerned about military security and security becomes more elusive. The difficulty of resolving the underlying political issues increases. The growing insecurity generates a demand for more armaments. Thus, the arms race spirals upward ceaselessly.

Security today demands something other than the acquisition of arms. One of the paradoxes of the modern world is that, although defence is necessary, the arms race itself is a threat to security. It is no longer enough to keep the peace; peace must be vigorously waged.

In our minority report, we argued that the "primary object of Canadian foreign policy must be the building of conditions for peace." To accomplish this, we said, would require a "strategy of suffocation," to stop the arms race. The strategy would include four basic elements:

- a comprehensive test ban to impede the further development of nuclear explosive devices;
- an agreement to stop the flight-testing of all new strategic

delivery vehicles;

      - an agreement to prohibit all production of fissionable material for weapon purposes; and

      - an agreement to limit and then progressively reduce military spending on new strategic weapons systems.

To back up this strategy, we recommended that Canada should support the campaign which was, and is, gathering momentum around the world for a global freeze on the testing, production and deployment of nuclear weapons and their delivery vehicles; that we should pledge not to strike first; pledge to devote one-tenth of one per cent of our defence budget to disarmament efforts; and that we should deny the United States permission to test the cruise missile system in Canada.

The report did not deny the need for security. It recognized our obligation to our NATO partners to strengthen the Western defence system. We differed from those who submitted the (majority) committee report only in the means to maintaining security. We felt that the military approach to security is no longer viable. It is an outdated approach. Security today and in the future must be based on finding ways to dismantle the stockpile of armaments and work at the real causes of conflict in the world. Our report was not a plea for unilateral disarmament. It was an argument for a mutual, verifiable disarmament, beginning with a freeze on expansion.

The cruise missile question seemed an important issue from a symbolic as well as a practical viewpoint. By allowing the United States to test new nuclear weapons delivery vehicles, such as the cruise missile, in this country, Canada contributes to the technological capacity for nuclear war and risks its credibility in speaking for peace. The conclusion drawn by the six of us and stated in the minority report was simply that Canada's choice must be to build security by comprehensive disarmament measures.

Although it may sound as if I spent most of my time travelling outside Canada while I was a member of Parliament, I never underestimated the importance of keeping close ties with the people in my home constituency. My sister, Mary Lou, continued to manage my Saskatoon office and handle all the day-to-day calls that came in from constituents. One of the most common calls at the office had to do with immigration. This is an area in which people encounter a great deal of red tape and their immediate impulse is to call their member of Parliament. Many times the member of Parliament can do very little because he cannot change the immigration laws and regulations. Canada's immigration policy is deliberately restrictive. I personally think that Canada has to look seriously at itself and its responsibilities in the world community in regard to the flow of immigrants. Pope John XXIII said that people without land have a right to land without people. As the population of the world expands and the pressure builds, particularly in small countries, the world community has to respond by opening doors. The political climate for doing that in Canada does not yet exist. Even though all Canadians, aside from the native peoples, are relatively recent immigrants, Canadians are not eager to accept more people who need space to breathe and live. It's a problem Canada is going to have to face.

My approach to maintaining ties with my constituency was to act as if there was always an election on. Every time I was home in Saskatoon, which was most weekends, I tried to visit 200 homes, or 200 doors, as we'd say. The purpose of visiting homes in Saskatoon was basically to say to people, "I'm still around," and to find out what was going on and what people's concerns were. Even in a short visit, we could get a sense of what people were feeling. I also made a point of regularly visiting senior citizen homes and places where people were confined because of physical handicaps. This might have been done more out of priestly than political habit—I just knew that people confined to bed or rooms appreciate having someone visit, chat and listen to their problems.

During the time that I was a member of Parliament, my Saskatoon residence was at St. Paul's Cathedral Rectory. On weekends, the parish priests would ordinarily ask me to preach and to take one of the Sunday masses. In this way I was able to continue functioning as a priest, at the same time that I was acting as a member of Parliament. I found that the ministry of the parliamentarian was very much an extension of the ministry of a parish priest, in the sense that I was usually dealing with human problems. The only difference was that the denominational categories were gone. I was dealing with people of all denominations and all religions and in that I felt very comfortable. It seemed a perfectly normal way to function as a priest. I've always felt that one of a priest's major functions is to bring about reconciliation in the lives of people. No matter where you worked as a priest—with children or teenagers, families or single people, working people or the unemployed—it was always an important part of your work. It was true in the House of Commons as well, particularly in the areas in which I worked. In trying to bring about reconciliation, I felt that my work as an MP was a natural extension of my work as a parish priest.

On the whole, I don't think my being a priest was particularly noticeable in the House of Commons. Only once did I perform an overt priestly act in the House. A prayer group of MPs of all denominations that meets once a week asked me to say a mass for Sean O'Sullivan, which they would invite members of Parliament to attend. Sean O'Sullivan had been a member of Parliament and afterwards had become a Catholic priest. He had been stricken by leukemia and was not expected to live long. Not wanting to overstep the bounds of propriety in the House, I wrote to the Speaker, Madame Jeanne Sauvé. She had no qualms about it, so I wrote to the English auxiliary bishop of Ottawa, John Beahen and he, too, approved. The Senate and the House of Commons were invited. More than 100 people from all political parties and from Christian, Jewish, and other faiths attended. Madame Sauvé and Senator Madame Lapointe read the Scriptures and I gave a short sermon. I'm sure I am the only MP who ever celebrated mass in the Centre Block of the House of Commons, but under the circumstances it seemed a very normal and proper thing to do. Since I have become seriously ill, the same group of parliamentarians requested a similar celebration for me. This time Father Sean O'Sullivan, whose cancer is in remission, was invited to be the main celebrant. I was well enough to be concelebrant at the liturgy on November 19, 1986, which was attended by members of Parliament and friends.

CHAPTER 8

RESIGNATION

All the time I was involved in politics, my relationship with the church was a constant concern. In my first nomination speech I had stated that I was going to be a priest before, during and after whatever happened in the political arena.

I had scarcely been nominated when Pope Paul VI died in 1977. With the promise of a new pope came hope that there would be a resumption of the vibrant activity initiated by John XXIII. Eventually, out of the conclave, a new pope was called forth who was the Archbishop Cardinal of Venice. The new pope, John Paul I, quickly became known around the world as the smiling pope and the early days of his pontificate created the expectation that he was going to pick up where John XXIII had left off. I remember the deep joy I felt at the promise of new life and movement for the Church. However, in less than a month those hopes were dashed. I saw the headlines in a Minneapolis paper: Pope Dead. I thought it was the old pope, that it was an old paper, but it wasn't. John Paul I was dead. There have been questions about how he died, but the fact was that he was dead and the Church was once more without a pope. A second conclave was called and the world waited again for another pope. I remember well the day that pope was elected. I was in Saskatoon. I walked in the rectory door at St. Paul's and two ecstatic priests informed me that a new pope had been elected and that he was Polish. At that moment I had a deep premonition that the election of this pope was going to mean trouble for me. Premonitions are not normally part of my life. I don't go on premonitions; I go on facts. But here, all of a sudden, I had a deep premonition that I was going to have difficulty with this Polish pope and that feeling never went away.

John Paul's first major move was to attend the Latin American Episcopal Conference in Puebla, Mexico. Paul VI had planned to meet with the Latin American bishops. Whether John Paul II would fulfil this commitment or not was undetermined for awhile, and then he announced what was to be the first of many trips. At that time, I was a nominated candidate and, having relinquished my parish assignment when that happened, I was, so to speak, between jobs. Through the Chelsea Journal, published by St. Thomas More College in Saskatoon,

I was able to get a press affiliation to go to Puebla and cover the Pope's visit. I later wrote an essay for them on *Pope, Puebla and Politics*.

The conference, which had been set back twice because of the death of two popes, was finally held in Puebla in early 1979. The theme and mood of the conference was encouraging the idea of the Church's preferential option for the poor. Because I knew many of the Brazilian bishops there, I had a chance to talk extensively with them about the conference and the direction in which the church in Latin America was moving. The first day the Holy Father was in Mexico, he met the Mexican clergy inside the cathedral and gave the talk that was to cause such a furor.

A number of journalists, some of whom were on the plane with the Pope, had attempted to find out the theme of his address. Knowing that the conference would be influenced by Latin American liberation theology, they had questioned him about that, but he wouldn't say anything. They were still waiting to find out what their stories would be about when he finally met with the clergy that Saturday afternoon. I was in the press room with the other journalists, listening and watching on television, when he came to the phrase, "priests should be priests and not social workers." The press room was empty within minutes. They just took off like flies, heading for the phones. The European press—Germans and French, Italian and British—were meeting Sunday deadlines. Later, the North American press carried essentially the same story: Pope Opposes Liberation Theology. I don't think he said anything like that and what he did say was used out of context. Given a Polish pope reading a Roman document to a Latin American audience in Spanish, I think one could anticipate the likelihood of misunderstanding. He was speaking in Mexico where the clergy do not have any political rights and, where according to the constitution, the church is not free to exist. The Pope's statement was not particularly important to the Latin American bishops, because it was not an issue for them. The involvement of priests in politics had been allowed to follow a natural course. When I first went to Latin America in 1964, there were many priests in politics. By 1979, I think there were next to none in politics. That change did not come about through any law or edict. It was a necessary response to the political changes that were taking place in Latin America. In 1964 there were still democratic systems operating in some countries. In Brazil it was fading fast, but in Argentina, Chile, and Peru, democracy was still functioning. Fifteen years later the military dictatorships had taken over in Latin America, forcing everyone out of politics. No socially conscious priest could be involved or would even want to be involved, because it meant supporting an evil regime. That's why the question of priests in politics was a non-issue in Latin America.

142

The way the story came out, though, made it sound as if the Pope had said he was against priests being in politics and that story dogged me throughout my political career. From then on, everywhere I went, every time I was interviewed, the question about priests in politics almost invariably came up. I always replied to that question that I was an adult and had a right to be a full citizen the same as anyone else, that the law of the Church permitted me to do this provided that I had proper permission, which I did. I wanted to remain faithful to the Church and the laws of the Church, which I knew because I was a canon lawyer. For that reason, I was very very careful at every step of the political process to ensure that I was complying with the laws of the Church and receiving the proper permissions to do what I was doing.

The Code of Canon law, which is the law of the Church published in 1917, clearly provided for priests in politics. There was no question about that. My concern was with Pope John Paul II's personal opinion. I had the feeling that he was going to change the general law of the Church. I was afraid that because his eastern European background provided no model of the democratic process, he would see no role for priests in politics and project his view on the rest of the world. The question was whether he would go so far as to press for changes to the long-standing canon law provisions or intervene in specific situations.

As I learned more about Poland, I saw further reason for John Paul's mistrust of priests' involvement in politics. Poland had been controlled by other countries for 200 years, having been carved up by Russia, Prussia and Austria in the 18th century. Through all of those years, it was essentially the church that kept the Polish people together, kept them alive. In fact, I've been told that the Polish verb meaning "to bishop" means to be against the government. You can see how entrenched a position is when it becomes part of the language. The role of the Polish bishop is to be against the government. Once I understood this, I understood where Pope John Paul II was coming from. But I felt that his experience and perspective did not apply to the North American situation. The issue never went away. Meanwhile, the Pope's own actions seemed to be becoming more political. This seemed inconsistent.

During my first campaign, some people accused me of being a bad priest because I was going against the Pope. Even though I said that I was doing it in accordance with church law and with my bishop's permission and fellow priests' concurrence, I could not always dislodge this objection. On the other hand, many people saw my involvement in politics as a good thing. Of course, political persuasion had a lot to do with how a person saw it, but over my years as an MP, people of many different religious and political persuasions told me they thought it was good that I was actively involved in politics. Many people saw it as an extension of what I had been doing all along, especially in my efforts to raise concern for the world's poor. When I was elected in 1979, there was another priest, Father Andy Hogan, in the House of Commons. Having someone else in the same position helped sustain me.

During that short Parliament of 1979, Father Bob Drinan, a Jesuit who had been a U.S. congressman for ten years representing a Massachusetts district, was preparing to run again for the fall elections of 1980 when he received a phone call from the superior general of the Jesuits telling him to withdraw. I've talked to Drinan about it several times since. The story he had heard was that the Pope had talked to Pedero Arrupe, "father general" of the Jesuits, and told him to get Drinan out of politics. There was another story that Drinan had voted for a bill that contained some money for abortions and that the American bishops had asked the Vatican to get Drinan out of politics. I don't know which story is closer to the truth. The first I heard about it was a phone call late one night at my Ottawa residence. It was the press again, wondering what I was going to do now that Drinan was out of politics. I didn't know anything about the Drinan story at the time and I told the press that I still had my permission and I would continue. Then, Parliament fell, a new election was called, I campaigned again and won my second election in 1980. But the press continued to ask how I could stay in politics when the Pope was against priests in politics. It wasn't just the media pestering me that I was concerned about. I didn't want to go against the Church and I honestly believed that what I was doing was right and proper. To set my mind at rest, I decided to take it upon myself to confirm my status and activity with Rome.

In April 1982 I was on a government delegation to Rome and I used the opportunity to see His Eminence Silvio Cardinal Oddi, the Prefect of the Congregation of the Clergy. This meeting was arranged through the auspices of Monsignor Pinto, an Italian priest who taught a short canon law course once a year at Saint Paul University in Ottawa. Father Frank Morrisey, then dean of canon law at Saint Paul University, phoned Monsignor Pinto in Rome and made the request on my behalf. Monsignor Pinto arranged a meeting with Cardinal Oddi for me and actually took me to the cardinal's home, joining us for dinner. Oddi spoke English well because he had been posted at the Nunciature in Egypt. Over dinner we got talking about my role and he simply said, "Do you have the permission of your bishop?" I said, "Yes," and he said, "You have no problem. Why did you come to ask me about it? You have no problem. That's what the code permits." Then he began to tell me stories about other priests who were and had been in politics around the world. He said he had encouraged priests in Egypt to get into political activity because the Egyptian government is predominantly Islamic and he felt there should also be some Christians in politics.

The meeting with Cardinal Oddi left me with a sense of relief. I felt confident that what I was doing was proper and had the approval of the man at the top of the Vatican Congregation of the Clergy. When I got back to Ottawa I reported this to the Apostolic Nuncio, Archbishop Angelo Palmas. Archbishop Palmas had invited me to his house for lunch several times and had been most gracious on these occasions. He always asked me about politics and things that were happening in the House of Commons. When I told him about the meeting with Cardinal Oddi, his reaction was very positive. He went on to ask me several favours. He wanted me to try to arrange a luncheon at his house with Clark, Broadbent and Trudeau. That never materialized, but I think his desire for the meeting demonstrated his interest in politics. He also had some questions about the New Democratic Party and I gathered the information he required. He was always non-committal in discussing political parties and issues. I had the general impression that he considered the New Democratic Party acceptable within the context of Christian values and principles.

At this time, the Code of Canon Law was being revised and was expected to be released shortly. Father Frank Morrisey was one of the canon lawyers working on the revisions. From him I learned that the canon in the new code, which pertained to priests and politics, had been left basically the same as it was in the old 1917 canons. Later we heard that the Pope had personally gone over the code canon by canon, changing that particular one to make it much more restrictive than it had been. I can't prove that story. But Morrisey had the original draft of the revised code prepared by the canon lawyers, and the final draft. That canon had been changed and was more restrictive in the final version.

The revised Code of Canon Law was promulgated at the end of 1982. I started to worry again: Did I have the proper permission under the new code? At Easter 1983 I went back to Rome, this time on my own, to see Cardinal Oddi again and clarify my position.

Each year at Easter, Cardinal Oddi went to Assisi. Not knowing that, I arrived in Rome only to find that he wasn't there. I caught a ride up to Assisi with some Canadian priests and we entered this beautiful city in a tremendous snowstorm. It was very, very cold and I didn't have enough clothes on. It was just like the old days, hitchhiking my way around South Africa or South America. Some Franciscans showed me where the cardinal's apartment was, at the back of the basilica. I waited at the guardhouse until his car drove in. The guard stopped him and said, "This priest wants to talk to you." Cardinal Oddi looked over at me and said, "You're the Canadian in politics, aren't you?"

I said, "I am."

He said, "What do you want here now?"

I said, "I want to talk to you about the new code."

He said, "Well, okay, okay. You come back..." and he gave me a time in the afternoon to come to his apartment.

When I arrived at the appointed hour, he received me very warmly again and then said, "I don't know what you came back for. You still have the permission from your bishop?"

"Yes," I said.

"Well, that's okay. That's fine by me," he said and then added, "Would you stay for awhile? I'd like to talk to you about another thing." And so we spent two or three hours talking about how the American people had received the pastoral of the American bishops on nuclear war.

That second meeting with Cardinal Oddi did not leave me feeling as reassured as the first time, even though he insisted there was no problem. Deep within my bones, I felt unease. Maybe Oddi hadn't read the new code. Maybe he didn't have the authority to make a judgment. He was too flippant about the way he reaffirmed my status.

A few weeks later, I received a letter from Cardinal Oddi which began:

"I write this personal note simply to inform you that opposition to your candidacy for re-election has been heard here in Rome. It is based on reports that you have sought to invite to Canada Father Miguel d'Escota, the foreign minister of Nicaragua. The information came to me from other than ecclesiastical sources."

The letter went on to urge me 'to be prudent in the stands you take." It warned that:

"Not a few of the faithful, at least, would be confused, regardless of your good intentions, by your alleged position on the visit to Canada of another priest who is an important member of a government which recently gave such an ambiguous welcome to the Holy Father."

I immediately responded to the cardinal's letter, explaining that d'Escota's visit to Canada was not a response to any personal initiative of mine. The external affairs committee, of which I was a member, had called upon the Canadian government to invite to Canada the external affairs ministers of the countries of Central America. This was done as part of our efforts to find peaceful ways of resolving the chronic problems in that part of the world. Two countries accepted the invitation from the Government of Canada and sent their ministers, one of them being Father Miguel d'Escota, the foreign affairs minister for Nicaragua.

During Father d'Escota's visit to Canada, he was accorded the usual official treatment, including several public functions, the first of which was a welcome dinner hosted by External Affairs Minister Allan MacEachen. I attended that dinner, as did the Apostolic ProNuncio,

Archbishop Angelo Palmas; Bishop Adolphe Proulx, representing the Canadian Conference of Catholic Bishops; several ambassadors from Central American countries; and a good number of Canadian senators and members of Parliament.

In my response to Cardinal Oddi's letter I also mentioned that I had called on the Nicaraguan ambassador to Canada immediately following the Holy Father's visit to Nicaragua and had vigourously protested the handling of that event.

The remainder of my letter tried to provide background on my goals as a member of Parliament and a member of the external affairs committee. It also contained this conciliatory gesture: "In the light of your wise counsel, I have asked the leader of my caucus to change my critic role to another area of responsibility within Canada so that there will be less danger of the faithful being confused. In addition, if Your Eminence would like to speak to me again personally on any matter, I could arrange to return to Rome sometime in the future."

I went to the Apostolic Nuncio, Archbishop Palmas, and showed him both letters. When he came to the part in my letter about his attendance at the dinner for d'Escota, he looked very uncomfortable. He said nothing. He quietly gave me back the letter and never saw me again while I was a member of Parliament.

I discussed both letters with my bishop, James P. Mahoney. I waited. Nothing happened. The summer passed. I decided I would do nothing about seeking the renomination until my bishop had been to Rome.

That September, while Bishop Mahoney was in Rome on his *ad limina* visit, he brought the matter up again with Cardinal Oddi. He received the same reassurances that what we were doing was proper and that I could continue. At that point, I made it known that I would allow my name to stand for renomination for the New Democratic Party in the Saskatoon-East riding. Even then I was still uneasy about it all. I was hoping the nomination would take place before the new code went into effect in mid-December, but that wasn't feasible. On January 28, 1984, I was acclaimed the New Democratic candidate for Saskatoon East.

My work as a member of Parliament continued in Ottawa. On February 21 a letter from the Apostolic Nuncio arrived at my parliamentary office. Since it was not marked personal or confidential, my secretary opened it. The letter was to inform me that the Sacred Congregation for the Clergy "after an attentive study of your case" has concluded that a dispensation of Canon 285.3 "is not esteemed justified..." The Nuncio wrote that this decision had been signed by Cardinal Oddi. The letter was telling me that I did not have permission to be involved in politics.

The most astonishing thing about the letter, apart from its message and its impersonal manner of delivery, was the statement that "just and reasonable cause has not been proved," when no request to demonstrate "just and reasonable cause" had ever been made. Indeed, repeated assurances had been given that the local bishop's permission was sufficient.

My first reaction was to the manner in which this notification was delivered. It seemed to me that it should have been marked confidential or been preceded by a phone call—anything to demonstrate some respect for the recipient and to give some indication of the gravity of the contents. In addition to trying to think my way through the implications of the announcement and how to present it publicly, I could not help thinking about the reasons for this sudden reversal of my authorization to work as a member of Parliament. My thoughts went back to the letter from Cardinal Oddi and the cessation of contact with the Papal Nuncio. The clue there seemed to be Father d'Escota and Nicaragua. Had Pope John Paul II imposed his opposition to priests in politics on the Sacred Congregation for the Clergy? Or was it the CIA that wanted me out? I had grown accustomed to being followed by the CIA. Their operations in Latin America at times were so clumsy that it was easy to spot them. Once, my bag disappeared briefly while I was in transit in the U.S. When I got it back, all my clothing and papers had been gone through and the suitcase had been packed with female lingerie.

The CIA certainly would not have liked the work we were doing to help set up the Contadora group or any of our efforts to find a peaceful settlement in Central America. But would those efforts be seen as sufficiently threatening to require removing me from the political arena? The Pope's opposition to priests in politics seemed a more likely motive.

Just who put pressure on the Sacred Congregation I will probably never know. When the letter arrived on my desk, my more immediate concern was how to deal with the situation. I knew that this Vatican ruling could be appealed. It was an administrative and disciplinary matter, not a question of faith and morals. I knew how to proceed with an appeal, but I didn't know how to do it quietly. The media would grab this item and it would appear as: Ogle against the Pope. I was not in politics to be against the Pope. That was not the issue, but that's what the issue would become in the media and in the public mind. It seemed imperative to limit the number of people who knew about the situation. I told Father Frank Morrisey and my bishop. It was an open week in the House of Commons and I was in Saskatoon. Coincidentally, Broadbent was in Saskatoon that week too, and I told him.

That was probably the most stressful week of my life. What to do? I felt very strongly that what I was doing in the House of Commons was worthwhile and was the right thing for me to be doing. And I felt that I was there according to the laws of the Church. Suddenly, the official necessary authorization was being withdrawn by Rome, not by the bishop who had the authority even under the revised Code of Canon Law. Under ordinary circumstances, the Vatican intervention could have been challenged. In my case, it would have been impossible for me to challenge it without creating a public controversy, which I didn't want. Finally, on the advice of my sister, Mary Lou, I decided to resign the nomination. I informed the bishop of my decision. I had no intention of resigning from politics permanently. I was only resigning the nomination in order to buy time for an appeal to be launched. But that distinction was never noticed. I thought it was clear, but it wasn't.

While Ed Broadbent was still in Saskatoon, he called to say he had to return to the East and asked me to do a speech at Meadow Lake for him. They would fly me up there and back. I was in a terrible state of turmoil, but I didn't want to let Broadbent down so I agreed to do it. The pilot was to meet me at the airport at 4 p.m. At 4 p.m. I was at the airport, looking around, expecting to see a 25-year-old guy in a flying jacket, peaked cap and sunglasses. After a while someone poked me and said, "You're Bob Ogle, aren't you?" I turned around and there was a short, rotund 65-year-old man in farm clothes and tri-focal glasses. He was Ed Gross, the pilot. We took off for Meadow Lake in his shiny new Cessna. As we hummed along on that beautiful, late winter afternoon, I learned a little about him, including the fact that he owned 20 sections of land. That didn't fit the New Democrat stereotype and I was curious. As if he could read my thoughts, he started telling a story about when he was a kid. His family had been extremely poor and one day his mother was very ill. They took her in an old wagon box to the nearest hospital. When his father got her to the hospital door, they said she couldn't be admitted unless he paid $16 and he didn't have $16. The mother died, and that's why, the farmer said, he became a New Democrat. It was a powerful story, and it reminded me again that universal health care is absolutely vital.

We arrived at Meadow Lake and through some misunderstanding, I suspect, stayed at a house where supper wasn't offered until it was time to go to the hall for the nomination meeting. The last time I had been in Meadow Lake was with my father and my uncle when I was four-years-old. A lot of farmers who lost their land to drought and banks during the Depression had moved north. Some had settled around Meadow Lake. One of them had bought some horses from my uncle and had never paid for them. The trip to Meadow Lake, one of my first journeys in life, was an unsuccessful attempt to collect for the horses. So I told the audience in Meadow Lake this story, told them about the log shack we went to and how the only thing they had to eat in the house was old fish. Fifty years later, Meadow Lake was a prosperous farm community. As usual, I talked about international development and how it related to them.

After the nomination meeting, we returned to the airport to find the Cessna covered with about two inches of hoarfrost. My little pilot had to climb onto the aircraft and, looking something like Santa Claus, clean off the wings. There were no lights on the airstrip, so we took off in the dark and got up into the air. It was an absolutely clear winter night with lights sparkling all over the prairie. We were about 50 miles out of Saskatoon when Battleford radioed us that Saskatoon was fogged in. In fact, we could see the fog coming. We turned around and flew back to North Battleford. It was 11 p.m. when we walked into the airport radio room and heard the message coming in from Saskatoon that the fog was lifting there. So we ran out, got in the plane and took off again. We were within ten miles of Saskatoon when we saw the fingers of fog spreading out over the earth. We had to turn around. It was midnight by the time we got back to North Battleford. The airport radio operator drove us into town. We couldn't find a place to stay because every room in the Battlefords seemed to be occupied by kids who were competing in the Saskatchewan Broomball championship. At 2 a.m. we finally got a room in an old motel and settled down, hoping that the fog would lift and we could leave in a few hours. I was very anxious to get back to Saskatoon, there was so much to do. At 6 a.m. I looked out and the fog had not lifted. I took my briefcase and walked out to the highway, hoping I could hitch-hike back to Saskatoon. From 6 a.m. until 9 a.m. I stood there in the fog, trying to hitch-hike out of North Battleford. It seemed symbolic of the situation and mood I was in— caught in a fog, trying to hitch-hike out of it and finding no way out. Finally I phoned Doug Anguish, the NDP candidate who had been nominated the night before. Doug came and drove me back to Saskatoon.

Knowing that five days later, on March 1, I would have to tell my party that I was withdrawing from the nomination, I prepared a press release and took a copy to Bishop Mahoney so he would know exactly what I was going to say if the media approached him for comment. As I was leaving the bishop's office, his secretary told me that Mary Lou was trying to reach me. I phoned my sister and she said, "Trudeau has resigned." With that, my situation changed again. I knew that the story of my resignation would now drop back to the 40th page of the newspaper. Trudeau's walk in the dark and his resignation would dominate the news for the next week.

In my speech to the NDP constituency meeting on March 1, I simply told them that I had received a letter withdrawing my permission to work as a member of Parliament and that I was resigning my nomination. There was a prolonged silence. No one knew what to say. I remember Jim Wilde, a Catholic, got up and said, "You have showed people how to live religion, not just on Sunday, but all through the week." Pat Atkinson, a woman activist, got up and thanked me for my service. Then there was a standing ovation. I felt that those people, in addition to saying thank you, were trying to tell me that they understood how hard it was on me. It was hard on them, too. My decision to resign the nomination, however, was presented as a way of buying time for an appeal.

I went back to Ottawa expecting that appeal to be launched either by Bishop Mahoney or by the Canadian Conference of Catholic Bishops. Frank Morrisey prepared letters on how the appeal should be done and I forwarded those letters to Bishop Mahoney. The NDP waited for three months before nominating another candidate, in the hope that the decision regarding my status would be reversed. Nothing happened. That's when I decided it was "game over." By that time the general impression was spreading that I had resigned from politics.

The realization that I was finished sank in slowly. I had never looked upon politics as my total life. I had looked upon it as a good experience and important work. I really felt that I was most truly a priest during my years as a member of Parliament. I was constantly aware of the need for reconciliation and the urgency of trying to bring people together. Working towards that as a member of Parliament seemed an extension of my priestly role. The documents of Vatican Council II and the social documents of the Church are still, to my mind, the most all-encompassing documents on social issues and I used these Church documents in most of my speeches. Other people used them too, but because I was a priest, people identified those positions with me and, I think, listened respectfully.

Apart from my personal feelings of regret and reluctance to give up my work in Ottawa, I was concerned, as a canon lawyer, about the implications of the Vatican decision for the whole Church. The Second Vatican Council had affirmed collegiality as the model for the Church. Local bishops are to have responsibility for what goes on in their part of the church. And here it seemed that the central authority was stepping in again and overruling the local authority. It seemed a flagrant disregard of local authority and a return to the old centralized system. As such, I felt it could establish a dangerous, reactionary precedent.

The Church has good reason to be careful about allowing priests into politics. I believe, however, that there are situations in which it can be a valid ministry and should be allowed. Making a discernment about a particular situation is a serious responsibility, just the sort of responsibility to be assumed by the local church, according to Vatican II. It is precisely in regard to such matters that the local church is most knowledgeable and able to make an appropriate judgment. In my case, the call came from the community—in another case it might be heard first by the individual. Once that call had been heard, it was subjected to consultation and discussion by the bishop, clergy and lay people in the diocese. After two years it was subjected to a very serious review and reaffirmed. I think that process embodied the Vatican II concept of collegiality. The procedure used by the Vatican in withdrawing my permission was in sharp contrast to the open, honest, comprehensive consultation undertaken at the local level.

Following my resignation I received letters from many, many people across the country, the majority of whom praised my work in the House of Commons and, in the next sentence, praised my obedience in resigning. I'm not sure if the praise for my obedience was altogether appropriate. All my life I have had a strong sense of obedience and respect for church authority. In this particular instance, however, it was not so much an act of obedience as an attempt to obtain a reversal of a decision which I thought was wrong without causing public controversy and embarrassment for the Church. When it became obvious that this was not going to happen, I withdrew, blaming myself in part for not having made a clear enough distinction between resigning the nomination and leaving politics permanently.

During this troubled period, the life of one person was very much on my mind. It was Pierre Teilhard de Chardin, the Jesuit theologian who was censored by the Church in the 1940s. He obeyed and disappeared from public view at that time, but his name and ideas are now known all over the world. Another source of guidance and strength was the passage in Scriptures which says that Jesus remained silent before the high priests. That had a very strong effect on me. The question for me, too, was how to conduct myself in front of the high priests. I resolved to remain silent.

This whole experience forced me to reflect on the subject of authority in the Church. The church I grew up in was a centralized, hierarchical, clerical church. I accepted that until my experience in Brazil showed me another model of church, which was a community model, a church of the people. My personal experience in Brazil also coincided with the Second Vatican Council, which endorsed this model, based on local authority and collegiality. The old vertical structure was to be replaced by a horizontal structure.

The new, horizontal structure—which of course was not really new, it was in the original church model—seemed to me to be much more practical. Surely the local bishops are most attuned to and knowledgeable about the needs of their own communities and best able to make decisions for them. The community-based model, I think, also shows the world much more clearly the Christian gospel. It is a Church that loves, that knows and cares for its own and cares for others. That's very important: that it cares for others, that it's not a power machine, and not obsessed with law. When it is based on love and rooted in community, the Church can be the cutting-edge, which is what I feel it has to be. The Christian has to be the one who's ready to take that first step into the future and take the abuse, which he or she will get for having done so.

It wasn't easy for me to adapt to the new model, the community Church, but once I had, I felt that I was on solid ground. The letter from Rome arrived like a letter from the past.

CHAPTER 9

LEAVING THE HILL

During the last year of my term as a member of Parliament, the uncertainty surrounding my continued political activity produced a great deal of stress and I began to get serious headaches. These headaches, which seemed to originate deep within my head, became so painful and so frequent that they began to interfere with normal daily functioning. Members of Parliament have access to the National Defence Medical Centre and I had been having annual checkups there. As the headaches became worse, I went to see the doctor I had been seeing at the centre. He attributed the headaches to stress and told me to take Aspirin.

Once it was known that I would not be running again, the NDP caucus kindly sent me on a number of parliamentary delegations to Europe. These were pleasant assignments that ordinarily would have been distributed to more members of the caucus. In March 1984, the month I resigned, I was in Strasbourg with one of these delegations to the European Parliament. My sister was accompanying me and we were anticipating a very enjoyable trip. But I was so seriously besieged by headaches that I was afraid something was happening to me—either a stroke or something equally threatening. On my return from Strasbourg I again went to see the doctor at the National Defence Medical Centre. I told him how bad the headaches were and that the Aspirins weren't controlling them. "Well, just take some more," he said. "Take 16 a day."

A few days later I was driving to Montréal and happened to hear Peter Gzowski interviewing a woman doctor who had just published a book called *Patient Beware*. She was talking about the danger of taking Aspirins. I remember her saying that every time an Aspirin is consumed, it makes the stomach bleed a little. And here I was taking 16 Aspirins a day. Aspirins had always been such a common remedy. Nobody thought of them as dangerous.

Holy Week was coming and I wanted to be back in Saskatoon for that week, which I generally celebrated at the cathedral. It is a tradition that the bishop and priests meet for the blessing of the holy oils on Monday in Holy Week. They usually gather for supper prior to the mass. That year at the supper the bishop spoke about a number of matters, such as the printed materials for the Pope's visit later that year. Then he introduced my case. He explained, in a very general way, the changes in canon law that had taken place and why there could be an appeal. He said he would consider this and go over it with the Senate of Priests and with the priests of the diocese. He wanted no media involved, he wanted the whole thing dropped from public view. If he were questioned, he intended to say only that he was considering an appeal. My reading of his remarks was that it was the end of the road. We weren't going anywhere.

The priests I was sitting with at the table that night had two very different opinions about what I had done. One group felt that I had done the proper thing by resigning and not making a fuss. Some of the priests, though, felt that what had happened was not right and that I should have fought it openly. This discussion didn't affect me anymore. What was done was done. And I could see that it was not going to be undone.

At the end of Holy Week, which I celebrated at St. Paul's Cathedral, there was an Easter festival. Many people came up to me and offered friendly support. One woman said, "You have been such a great example of obedience. When we see our church leaders act like this, it makes it easier for us little people." I knew she was saying that from the bottom of her heart, but it bothered me a great deal because I have deep reservations about how people value obedience over justice.

While continuing to function as a member of Parliament, I was very much aware that my term was coming to an end and I would have to think seriously about what to do next. Some people thought I should go back to parish work. Although I felt I could have done that, it didn't seem to fully utilize the unique combination of knowledge and experience I had acquired.

Back in Ottawa at the end of April I woke up one night with terrible chills, feeling sick all over. With a bowel movement came blood—and fear. I waited until dawn and phoned my sister in Saskatoon, who is a nurse. Mary Lou told me to get to a hospital immediately. Later I found out that she knew how serious the situation could have been and she was very worried. I felt so weak that it was four or five hours later before I managed to get up and get myself to the hospital. They quickly diagnosed a bleeding ulcer. They put an intravenous into my arm and two nurses started to roll my stretcher down the hall to take me to intensive care. I remember the ride down the hallway very vividly. As a priest I had spent a fair amount of time visiting people in hospitals, but this was the first time that I was in a hospital bed rolling down a hallway. It doesn't matter how many times you've seen it, the first time it happens to you is a very disturbing experience. All you can see are the lights in the ceiling going by. You hear snippets of conversation, people walking by or with you talking about their families or the hockey game or about what they're going to do on Friday night. It's as if you weren't there, as if you had dissolved into the bed. We arrived at the elevator, which was going to take us up to the intensive care ward on the sixth floor. One of the nurses was backing the bed into the elevator. The other was pushing from the foot of the bed. The one who was backing the bed in must have caught her heel on the edge of the elevator. She started to fall backwards and, as she fell, she reached up and grabbed the intravenous pole, which tore right out of the socket. As this was happening, I felt the needle rip up my arm. Just as I threw my arm back, she let the pole fall forward and it hit me square on the top of my head. Of course, it was an accident. The poor nurse felt dreadful and embarrassed. That was my introduction to hospital life. The second time I was admitted to hospital, with a heart attack about a year later, I was directed to intensive care. When I walked into intensive care there she was, the same nurse. What could I say except, "Hi, it's good to see you."

Fortunately, they have excellent medication for ulcers today and my first stay in the hospital lasted only a week. But it was the beginning of what was going to become for me a long seige of hospitals. Staying in hospital, of course, changed my routine drastically. I was confined to bed—a terrible, new experience for me. Because of this confinement, I began to watch television. This in itself was a real experience because it had been years since I last watched television with any regularity. The little rental set that hung over my hospital bed had cable and brought in some 20 channels. I flipped from one to the next and was amazed at what I saw. Here was a world that I really didn't know anything about. We were very conscious of television in the House of Commons, in the sense that proceedings were televised and we had to be "up" for it. There was real pressure to speak well, because people were watching you on television. Everyone seemed to believe that television has tremendous power.

When I began to watch television, two things jumped out at me. One was the fact that the fundamentalist religious groups had taken over great blocks of television time and were preaching a very right-wing political message, to the point of supporting Reagan's intervention in Central America in the name of religion. The second thing that shocked me was the triviality of much of the programming. There were good programs on some channels, but the general, popular fare was empty and mindless. It seemed to serve only as filler between the advertisements. It was mood stuff, meant to anaesthetize, desensitize. I realized that these were the programs most people watched and that the audience, whoever they were, must like this type of programming or it wouldn't survive. Or maybe, I thought, they had nothing to do with it.

Some of those programs create a powerful illusion —like Dallas and other sophisticated shows. Those programs now have an international following. They are shown all over the world. Viewers who haven't been to North America have no way of knowing that life in North America isn't all like that. Even North American viewers, I suspect, may begin to believe that life should be like that. I also found it fascinating that writers and directors have found a way of keeping such thin story-lines going, giving people just enough to keep them interested to get them to the next commercial.

The game show fits right into this consumer-oriented propulsion. The excitement lies in seeing if he's going to win, if she's going to get the car. Game shows seem to appeal to people who have lots of time to watch. It occurred to me that those people who are not working are probably least able to buy those items. Again, television is presenting them with an illusion, a life that cannot be, for them. It troubled me that people spend so much time in such useless, if not destructive, viewing. There was very little on TV that dealt with anything I thought important.

There was one exception, one series which I felt was entertaining and also carried an important message. That program was M*A*S*H. It was using highly sophisticated, very expensive format to good purpose. M*A*S*H talked about disarmament and the peace movement subtly, even silently. It said that war is stupid. Over the period of time that M*A*S*H originally ran, a generation of people began to question the value of war as the previous generation had not, and I think M*A*S*H contributed to that disenchantment. Mulling over all these thoughts about television as I lay in my hospital bed, I began to wonder if there might be a way to use this medium and this format to deal with other important issues, in particular questions of international development. The ulcer healed, but the headaches did not subside. Instead, they became more intense and constant. I feared that a very serious problem of some kind was developing in my head. The doctors continued to blame stress. They said that headaches were common and that I had to handle them one way or another. While I was still in hospital, they suggested psychiatric treatment. I had several sessions with the hospital psychiatrist. He asked me if I was harbouring feelings of anger or resentment. I told him about the Aspirins and the Aspirins causing the ulcer. I said I was mad about that and he said, "You have a right to be mad about that. Who gave you the Aspirins?" When I named the doctor, he said, "Well, I don't think I can write that down." That was the last I heard about psychiatric help.

Next I was told that the problem probably lay in my vertebrae and I was scheduled for physiotherapy. The National Defence Medical Centre has an excellent physiotherapy section and I had no objection to trying this. One day while I was going through the physiotherapy routine, the head pain became so intense that I collapsed. The physiotherapist was very upset; she didn't know what had happened. Next I was told that there was arthritis developing in my spine and I was given Tylenol instead of Aspirins.

I was scarcely out of the hospital and back to my office when David MacDonald, the former Conservative MP, and Bob Miller, a friend of mine who had worked with us on the North-South Task Force, came to see me about a religious TV channel that several religious groups were trying to start. As David described this proposed religious channel, it struck me that there might be a connection between what they were trying to do and what I had been thinking about. MacDonald's task was to involve all the denominations. The Catholics had not joined and the Jewish constituency was waiting. Even if they all joined, the next question would be where to obtain enough funding. It was obviously going to be a long haul.

The Canadian Radio-Television and Telecommunications Commission had originally proposed a religious network. The intent was to provide interfaith religious news and programming to all regions of Canada, and to prevent a deluge of American fundamentalist preachers from filling the existing void. The Catholic bishops were very hesitant about it for various reasons, one of them being that many of the Catholics in Canada speak French and the French networks already carried religious programming. Some of the other major denominations held back because of the financial investment that would be required. I kept in touch with the people who were trying to get the network going because I thought it was a good idea.

Early in May 1984, I joined the priests of the Saskatoon Diocese on their annual retreat. The retreat director was a liturgist, Father John Gallen, a Jesuit from Phoenix, Arizona. At the end of the retreat, I asked him what theologians and liturgists were saying about the phenomenon of people experiencing church via television. The fundamental question in my mind was whether or not people who celebrated the liturgy via television were a church community. During the retreat, I had watched the other priests gathered around the TV set for the Stanley Cup playoffs. They were completely engrossed in an event which was taking place in another city and were responding as if they were there. When Edmonton scored a goal, there was exuberance in Saskatoon. I was intrigued by this participation in an event at which you are not present. It could be a hockey game or a mass. You watch and you get involved, but you're not there. What kind of a community can be formed that way? Can any community be formed that way? Personally, I much prefer a community church in which the people know one another, pray together and help one another. I don't know if you can have community without that physical presence and contact. Gallen didn't have an answer to my question, but he thought it was one that needed to be addressed.

Still faced with the necessity of looking at my post-parliamentary options, I decided to seek counsel from my friends. My sister Mary Lou, who had left her nursing career to manage my office in Saskatoon, faced the same situation. I called together a group of people who worked in various fields—political, religious, literary, media, education—people who had known me in various contents and who I felt would bring understanding, creativity and intuition to the question. A few of them were unable to attend. The group that gathered in my Saskatoon office that evening in May were Elaine Stevens, Danielle Fortosky, Caroline Heath, Thirza Jones and Arlene Skaros. Their opinions regarding what I should do ranged from returning to pastoral work in the Saskatoon diocese to going on my own, speaking and promoting international understanding and development. Finally, one of the women said, "We know you well enough to know that you've already got an idea. What is it?" So I told them that I was thinking about trying to do something around international development through the media. This idea was warmly received by most of those present. I left that meeting with the advice, "Be yourself and follow your heart" ringing in my ears. Nothing new, but coming from that group it was a challenge. I knew I would have to make the discernment about my future.

The month of May 1984 afforded the unlikely opportunity of seeing most of the people I had known throughout my life. My family had a large reunion in Rosetown, attended by cousins, uncles, aunts and relatives from all over the country. My seminary class had a special gathering, and the entire seminary alumni had a reunion. I wrote in my notes one day in May, "Could this be a sign that you're dying—seeing all the people you know in such a short time?"

All the while I was looking forward and back, I was really undergoing an emotional crisis. I felt assaulted by many emotions, the strongest of which was anger. I was angry at what had happened and angry that I had no control over the situation. Feeling such deep anger was a new and confusing experience for me, perhaps because I hadn't experienced or observed anger at home, as a child. I didn't know how to handle it. On top of this difficulty was the pressure of feeling that I had to accept what was happening. So, instead of expressing anger, I began to swallow it, to suck it down inside me, where it continued to settle. Externally, I tried to look calm and unperturbed.

The feeling of powerlessness was also very hard to deal with. I thought about poverty and powerlessness. I had observed the state of resignation among powerless people. They would accept whatever happened without question as the will of God. I was reminded of an incident in Brazil. Sister Diane and I had been working in a base community in a very poor district of the town we lived in, part of the town that had no lights, no water, no streets, just mud huts. We had started bringing people together there with the Family of God lessons. The people enjoyed coming together and having an opportunity to talk about the Gospels and their own situation. At first they didn't know what to talk about, but then they became quite interested in why they didn't have things other people did and in talking about what they could do about this. We used to meet every Wednesday. The people always brought their children and so the little mud huts would be absolutely packed, not a breathing space in them, with all the adults and their children. There was one little girl in a family on that street who had long fair hair, which was very rare in that part of the country. They called her the little angel because she had light hair. We got to know this little girl very well. One Wednesday when we arrived, there was nobody around the house that had been offered for that week's meeting. We could feel a mood of extreme somberness in the air. We started to ask around and it didn't take long to find out what had happened. During the week there had been a measles attack on the street and some 30 children had died. The little girl with the blond hair was one of them.

What I remember from that night is the absolute frustration of trying to provide consolation. These people always accepted what happened to them with a shrug and the phrase, "God willed it." We said to them time and again, "God may will it, but he also wants you to do something." That night all I could say was, "God willed it." I had run out of answers. Why did these people, who already had suffered so much, have to accept this additional suffering? Simply because they didn't have the medical expertise or supplies to prevent it? That night I was forced into accepting their understanding of what took place because I didn't have any answers that would make sense to them or to me. I couldn't say to them, "Well, you didn't have the medicine, that's all." I couldn't. I had to say something that had at least a little bit of meaning to them. There could be no satisfactory explanation. They had lived with this kind of suffering so long they knew there is no easy way to be poor. They had come, in their sadness, to accept it. In a way it was easy for me to come in and try to shake them out of their state of resignation. But I had to learn that people who have been run over a hundred times grow weary and resignation becomes a way of life.

In my own situation in 1984, I was torn between outrage and resignation. While I believed that what had happened in my case was wrong, I also believe there are times when resignation is the only answer. I had a strong sense during this time of the passion and death of the Lord. He had been falsely accused and did not try to defend himself. He was beaten by the religious authorities of his time. I meditated often on that. It may sound presumptuous, but I found strength in the belief that I was living a bit of the mystery of the death of the Lord. I have always believed that every Christian has to live through the mystery of the death and the life of the Lord. Even strong spiritual motivation cannot always prevent anger. Having never been taught how to handle anger, I found it surfacing in me in spite of my best intentions.

As Parliament began to show signs of coming to an end, a special bill was advanced in the House of Commons calling for a peace institute in Canada. This was an idea that I had repeatedly promoted in past years and now it looked as if it was going to become a reality. In a long and intense series of meetings, groups interested in the peace movement tried to hammer out the groundwork for the peace institute. I did a lot of committee work on it in the month of June. Legislation establishing the peace institute was the last bill passed before the House adjourned for the summer.

On the last day of Parliament the House leader gave me permission to make a statement, since it appeared that this Parliament was coming to an end and my term was over. I thanked the House for the experience, kindness and friendship I had received and the House gave me a warm round of applause. The government did collapse shortly after that. John Turner was elected leader of the Liberal party and an election was called for September 4.

One of the advantages of knowing I wasn't running again was that it gave me a chance to finish my work in the House and leave things in an orderly fashion. My papers were the first from that Parliament to be deposited in the Public Archives.

The summer months were taken up with helping Colin Clay, an Anglican priest and chaplain at the University of Saskatchewan, who was running as NDP candidate in Saskatoon-East. I ceased being a member of Parliament September 3, 1984, the day before the election. On election day, I was standing by Colin Clay as the results came in. The Conservative sweep that took the rest of Canada carried the Saskatoon-East seat with it, but just barely. Colin Clay lost by only 400 votes. We had ten days to clean out our Ottawa office. I had done most of it in June, so it didn't take long to finish.

When I was out of the office and officially no longer a member of Parliament, the impact of it all really hit me. Any member of Parliament who has resigned or lost an election, knows how suddenly and dramatically one's life changes. Simple things like having a telephone, an office, a place to park your car, a schedule, are suddenly gone and you are literally on the street. Losing your job is becoming all too common an experience. People who have had a position in government, business, education or industry suddenly find themselves on the street. It is a shattering human experience. Other people have a difficult time coping with it and I did, too.

While I was still a member of Parliament, it had been announced that the Pope would be visiting Canada. The Canadian Broadcasting Corporation asked me to be a commentator during the papal visit. Thinking it would lead to more problems, I said no. The months passed. My political career was drawing to a close. No other doors were opening. One day the CTV network approached me and asked if I would join the team covering the Ottawa portion of the Pope's visit to Canada. I checked with my confrères in Saskatoon. They thought it was a good idea, so I accepted. That's how it came about that, on September 19, 1984, 16 days after the end of my term as a member of Parliament, I joined Lloyd Robertson, Tom Harpur, Pamela Wallen and Father Gordon Davies in providing the television coverage for part of the Pope's visit to Ottawa.

Actually, I enjoyed the evening of commenting on the Pope's visit. It was easy to do because I was familiar with the protocol and knew the people he was meeting—the diplomatic corps and politicians. The irony of the situation, however, did not escape me. And I felt some frustration, sitting there, commenting in a detached manner on the man in white, when I would much rather have gone up to him and said, "Could we please sit down for a minute and talk about my situation?" But there was no point in thinking about that anymore. There was work to be done.

CHAPTER 10
BROADCASTING FOR
INTERNATIONAL UNDERSTANDING

In my last days as an MP, I had visited various people whom I felt might have suggestions about how to proceed with my idea for promoting international development in the media. I spoke to Bernard Wood of the North-South Institute, Peter Dobell and Bob Miller of the Parliamentary Centre for Foreign Affairs and Foreign Trade, Lewis Perinbam of the Canadian International Development Agency, and Nigel Martin of the Canadian Council for International Cooperation—a body that encompasses all the non-government organizations working on development. Nigel's response was very positive and from that time on I began to work with the idea that the Canadian Council for International Cooperation might be the agency that could act as a sponsor.

In the fall, Ivan Head, President of the International Development Research Centre for which I had done the year's research nine years before, offered me an office. Léa Attrux, who had been my assistant in the House of Commons, agreed to work with me and we set up our office at the centre. From this office we arranged appointments and I began to meet people from the many non-government organizations involved in development. Some of them I met privately, others I met at their annual general meetings. The initial response to my idea of broadcasting for international understanding was cool. Some of them had been burned in the media. Others seemed to dismiss me as someone with good intentions who would find out that it just wouldn't work. This attitude didn't surprise me. Having worked with these groups when I was doing research, I knew they were relatively conservative and resistant to new ideas.

We decided to test the concept of broadcasting for international understanding. I invited people who were working in development, the church, politics, and media who had shown some interest in the idea. The meeting was held in November at the Parliamentary Centre for Foreign Affairs and Foreign Trade, and was chaired by its director, Peter Dobell. The Parliamentary Centre for Foreign Affairs and Foreign Trade is a private, non-profit corporation which specializes in providing expert assistance to parliamentary committees in the field of foreign affairs and foreign trade. About 30 people attended the meeting. I gave a short introduction, explaining that Broadcasting for International Understanding was to be incorporated as a non-profit organization and registered as a charity under the Income Tax Act. Its aim was to get more information on international development into the media—radio, television and print. We saw its role as education, animation and production. After my presentation, there was a good discussion. I left the meeting feeling these people considered the undertaking important and viable.

Before we could do anything, we had to have seed money. The first group to offer support was Our Lady of the Prairies Foundation in Saskatoon. It was enough to get us started and then other religious groups in Canada began to make contributions. These early supporters included the Grey Nuns of Manitoba; Sisters of St. Joseph, Peterborough; Sisters of St. Joseph, London; Sisters of St. Joseph, Willowdale; School Sisters of Notre Dame of Ontario; Scarborough Foreign Mission Society; Sisters of Sion, Saskatoon; The Ursulines of St. Angela's Convent, Prelate; Jules et Paul Emile Leger Foundation; Mennonite Central Committee Canada; CUSO; Presbyterian World Service & Development Committee; and the Canadian Catholic Organization for Development and Peace.

We approached CIDA to see if we could get any developmental money from them. It looked as if they would be willing to provide matching funds on a two-to-one basis, as long as it could be channelled through an existing agency. We were confident that the Canadian Council for International Cooperation would fulfil that role, and we continued to operate under that assumption until we received notification at the end of February that its board of directors had rejected the proposal.

Just as the CCIC door closed, another door appeared to open. African Emergency Aid, a non-government organization operating under the aegis of the CCIC and co-ordinating Canadian relief operations in Africa, was headed by a Mennonite, John Wieler, whom I had known over the years through the Mennonite Central Committee. His office was in the same building as the CCIC and we ran into him one day. He greeted me like manna from heaven and started to talk in an animated way about the possibility of our coordinating the publicity for this umbrella group. Within days, that board, too, rejected our involvement. We were getting discouraged.

A brief respite from the struggle of trying to establish Broadcasting for International Understanding was offered in November. The Inter-Church Committee on Human Rights in Latin America asked me to go to Uruguay as an observer at the Uruguayan elections. For three weeks prior to, during and after the election, I watched with fascination as Uruguay returned to a state of democracy. My first visit to Uruguay had been 25 years before, when Uruguay was known as the Switzerland of

Latin America. Then it was the gem of the continent. I had never imagined that such a beautiful place existed. When I returned with the external affairs subcommittee in 1983, Uruguay had been under a military dictatorship for 11 years and the whole country was a state prison. Now, in 1984, there were to be elections and it was like springtime. The election wasn't perfect, in the full sense of an electoral process, but the Uruguayans had started on the road back to the tradition of democracy, and it was tremendously exciting to watch.

Bill Fairbairn, who works in Toronto for the Inter-Church Committee on Human Rights in Latin America, was the other Canadian observer. The rest came from the United States, Costa Rica and Argentina. The majority of them were women, all intensely concerned about human rights. Interestingly enough, most of them were lapsed Catholics. They were happy to encounter a priest who shared their concerns about political repression, military dictatorship and human rights violations—not common concerns in their local churches.

The day of the election in Uruguay was a very exciting day for everybody. As observers, we were given cards to go into any polling booth in Uruguay and observe the process. Early in the morning, I went out with the observer from Costa Rica who spoke Spanish and could talk to the people. I remember one man she stopped to talk to—a tall, wrinkled man in his 50s or 60s. When she asked him what he thought of the day, he said, "It's the second-happiest day of my life." "What was the happiest?" she asked. His reply was unequivocal, "The day my wife gave me my first son." It struck me as such a human response, such a typically Latin response. There were long line-ups at all the polling stations and the excitement was palpable. The voting went smoothly; we saw no irregularities. When the vote count came in that evening, I was a bit disappointed that the other side didn't win. But that was incidental. The important fact was that Uruguay had returned to a way of life that it never should have lost.

Returning to Ottawa, I resumed efforts to find a sponsor for Broadcasting for International Understanding. My sister, Marguerite, asked if I had approached Saint Paul University. Funny how we always overlook the obvious. Of all the groups I had considered, my alma mater had not crossed my mind. The acting rector, Father Alexandre Taché, OMI, was interested. Within days the university had considered the proposal and had agreed to sponsor us. An arrangement with CIDA was worked out and we were in business. I went back on the road, conducting workshops and speaking in churches on Sundays.

Friends told me I looked sick and I was feeling poorly most of the time. My energy level was low, but I felt I couldn't stop. I had given myself a year to get BIU off the ground. If we couldn't make it fly within a year, I would take that as an indication that it would not go.

We knew there were organizations in Europe doing the kind of work we envisioned doing in Canada. So we decided to go see what they were doing. The plan was for Léa and her husband, Mary Lou and I to go to Europe in May. While I was crossing the country on the speaking tour, an open house was being organized in Ottawa for May 22. Our European trip was to begin the following day.

The open house, which was the public launching of BIU, was a success. Arni Fjortoft from Norway, who was secretary general of Worldview International Foundation, was scheduled to visit Canada at that time and had agreed to speak at the opening. The mood at the open house was warm and supportive. At last, it seemed, we were launched. We had two small offices at Saint Paul University Seminary. We had an institution to sponsor us and an agreement with CIDA that would provide matching funds.

The stress test portion of the medical examination I had had several months earlier was booked for the morning of May 23—the day we were to leave for Europe. I packed my bags, put them in the car and drove to the military hospital. I had been through the stress test a number of times and, although it could be unpleasant, I didn't find it particularly difficult or unsettling. They wired me up as usual and I started through the routine. I can't remember exactly what I was doing when the woman doctor who was standing beside me reading the cardiogram said, "You have had a heart attack or you're getting one." The world stopped. I thought this woman was saying, "You are dying" and I can remember very clearly saying to myself, "Thank God, it's over." The frustrations of the previous year had been so overwhelming that my body was saying, "It's not worth it. It's too hard. Just die."

Once I realized that I was not dying on the spot, my mind was flooded with the practical problems of how to scrap this European trip and concern for all the people whose plans would be disrupted. For me, it was back to the intensive care unit. That ward always struck me as the last place you should put a critically ill person. You're constantly being poked and monitored and checked and awakened. There's constant noise and the lights shine in your eyes all night. There's no possibility of rest. But that's where I was going.

During my 11 days in the intensive care ward, they discovered that I was suffering from a disease called polycythemia. Polycythemia is a disease of the blood. The bone marrow breaks down and is only able to produce incomplete red blood cells. Eventually, the spleen becomes enlarged and the condition frequently turns into a form of leukemia. This diagnosis came as no great shock. My mother had been a victim of the disease and several other members of her family have had it as

168

well. My mother was 56 when she died, which is not an uncommon age for polycythemia victims.

At the end of the 11 days, I was given a number of options as to how and where I wanted to deal with the heart problem. I elected to go back to Saskatoon. There, the doctors at University Hospital discovered that I had a blocked artery. They operated on it, using a procedure called angioplasty, in which a tube is introduced into the body through an artery in the leg and pushed up into the heart. There a small balloon at the end of the tube is inflated, in the hope that the pressure will open the blockage. In my case it worked. After surgery, I was very weak and was told that a three-month rest period was required. No work for three months. I spent July and August recuperating in Saskatoon, trying to relax. My heart caused no further problem, but the headaches continued and I basically never felt well.

Early in September I went east to attend a meeting of the Group of '78, a foreign policy think-tank started a few years earlier in memory of Andrew Brewin, a former member of Parliament. The group met at Stony Lake, north of Toronto, the site of Brewin's retreat. I spent three days there with that very interesting group of people, discussing Canada's present policy in external affairs. The group includes people from various political parties, religions and all backgrounds who share Andrew's ideas on the necessity of protecting human rights around the world and working strenuously and continuously for peace.

In mid-September I was back in Ottawa, picking up where I had left off with BIU. Léa Attrux had maintained the office while I was an invalid and now she had to go into hospital. I wondered if we would ever be able to marshall our forces.

We had acquired a writer and he helped keep the project alive at this critical stage. Stephen McLoughlin had appeared out of the blue. He had heard me on CBC Morningside, talking to Peter Gzowski about the notion of addressing questions of international development through a television comedy series. Stephen said he thought this was the silliest idea he'd ever heard, but later, when he started thinking about it, he decided maybe that was the only way it could be done. Stephen is a very talented writer. When he came to see me, I couldn't even offer to pay him. He volunteered his services and, over the next six months, wrote the prototype for the comedy series.

Our contract with CIDA called for three television program prototypes, which we could either rent or produce. We knew we could rent one in Europe. Our plan was to produce one low-cost program and one high-cost program—high-cost from our perspective, not high-cost by commercial standards.

In late November we made a ten-day trip to London, Amsterdam,

Brussels and Paris. In each of these places we made good contacts with development groups and production companies. In London we found a film series that we thought would be suitable and arranged to rent it. The People Trade was a study of the transfer of peoples in the Third World labour market. It showed people being moved from Sri Lanka to Arabia, as one example of the millions of people being moved around in the Third World to provide cheap labour. We felt that this series would be very educational for people in Canada, especially for people in the labour movement who always seem to see labour problems as very localized. This series presented labour issues in their true, world-wide dimensions, showing how labour issues in one country are related to those in another, and specifically showing the cultural and human trauma that result from moving people around the world to keep costs down and profits up.

In Oxford we visited the headquarters of Oxfam, an international development agency. In London we saw Protestant and Catholic church groups and several production companies. In Holland we found a very active, progressive group called NOVIB. This NGO, comprised of Catholics, Protestants and humanists, was offering a variety of creative programs. One was a puppet show for children, in which the children could see questions of international development in the problems the animals had. NOVIB had produced teachers' guides to accompany the series. Dutch children would learn about international development early in life. The people at NOVIB were interested in our idea of humorous programs for adults on international themes. That was one thing they hadn't tried. Anther idea they gave us was the possibility of drawing on the Third World news service based in Rome. We had never heard of it. Apparently many Third World countries feed into it. In Paris we visited several television and film companies that were doing Third World material. They were all intrigued by the fact that someone had come from North America to see what they were doing. It was their first contact with a comparable North American organization. Coming home, we felt we had collected a store of good ideas and contacts, as well as an agreement to rent a specific film series. We felt ready to fill a void in Canada that was already being filled by other groups in Europe. The two limitations we faced were a shortage of resources and illness. We needed more staff, as well as more money. And my energy level was as low as our cash inflow.

A short Christmas holiday in the Dominican Republic plunged me once again into my Latin American experience and provided another idea for BIU. Santo Domingo was very similar to northeast Brazil, in that it was based on a sugar economy. The land had been ravaged by cutting down the trees. The mentality of big production companies and cheap labour was all too familiar.

At San José de Ocoa there was a priest I had heard about many years before and never met, a man my age by the name of Lou Quinn. He had been ordained one year before me and spent his whole priesthood as a missionary in Santo Domingo. I would describe Father Lou Quinn as a cross between Zorba the Greek and Gary Cooper. We hit it off immediately. He was a very earnest liberation theologian missionary, working on the base community idea. He is also a tremendous developer, with roads and water aqueducts and agricultural projects to his credit. He has become known all over the country as the "developer." When we were there, he had a project going to reforest the mountainsides. The parish co-op has three nurseries in the valley around the little village of San José. When the peasants come down from the mountains, he has each of them take two or three little saplings to plant on their way home.

Quinn had been criticized several times by the bishops in the Dominican Republic for his strong developmental messages, but the Scarborough Foreign Mission Society insisted that he remain in the parish. Another priest was brought in to be the pastor. Quinn is a great musician. He plays and sings the Latin music, and I could tell he had a very strong connection to his people. Watching this colourful, dynamic man gave me an idea for another film series. A film on him, or others like him in other parts of the world, could illustrate the problems of development and how they can be handled in a human way.

On the way home from that trip, I thought about the possibilities of such a series. It seemed probable that other denominations would have missionaries who had gone to another country to convert people and had ended up identifying with the people, working to help liberate them in all aspects of their lives, including economic. We could produce 13 films—the usual span of a TV series being 13 weeks—based on these Canadian missionaries.

We contacted churches and groups we thought might be interested in this project. The results were encouraging. The Anglicans proposed the story of a missionary who had spent 30 years in Nigeria. He has now been called back to Toronto, where his job is to recall Anglican missionaries. As they see it, that part of church history is over. I could see a film on this person in the country where he had worked, explaining the change in policy. The United Church suggested a Japanese missionary whom they had invited to Canada. He was working in southern Ontario teaching Canadians how to grow more food on their land. The Presbyterians proposed the story of a nurse who had worked in Nepal for 40 years. Each of the denominations caught the idea of focusing on an outstanding person whose work was tied to the notion of development.

The missionary film series seemed to have potential. It would have to wait, though, for more funding. Our immediate objective was to produce the low-cost program prototype required under our CIDA contract. It was planned and produced at the University of Saskatchewan with the co-operation of Danielle Fortosky, the director of the audio-visual department of the College of Education. Your Turn Now was a program along the lines of the Donahue show. The discussion topic was whether Canadian agricultural methods should be exported to the Third World.

The panel consisted of Dr. C.M. "Red" Williams and Dr. Graham Simpson from the Department of Agriculture, both experts in the field of food production; Alfred Epp, a young Mennonite, who had worked in Bolivia and Belize developing agricultural programs; and Manana Tuoane, a doctoral student in agricultural economics from Lesotho, who talked about the dangers of trying to introduce changes in agricultural methods without taking cultural patterns into consideration. Rita Deverell, an actress and television producer from Regina, and I hosted the show, directing the flow of questions from the studio audience of about 80 people, all of whom had been invited because of some involvement in the issue. The edited program became the prototype of one format that could be used in development education.

Our major production—the comedy series prototype—was called Ain't No Paradise. It was written and produced by Stephen McLoughlin and filmed in Hull, Quebec, in a little theatre at the Maison du Citoyen, using professional actors from the Ottawa area. The main character in the story was based on an old White Father I had met years before in Northern Ghana. He was originally from the Ottawa Valley, but had spent all his working life as a missionary. He earned the distinction of converting a whole tribe. In his senior years he decided that he should be doing development work, which he was doing when I met him. Our original plan was to set the story in Africa, but we realized it would be too difficult to convey the African culture accurately. The alternative we settled on was a mythical island in the Caribbean. The culture of the Caribbean is a mixture of cultures and is more familiar to North Americans.

In the story, good-willed developers from the North encounter this old priest and well-educated people from the South. The drama focuses on the rock band benefit concert. It is revealed that while the rock concert is raising $100-million dollars, over $12-billion is being taken out of the same part of the world to pay the interest on their international bank loans. It becomes obvious that the rock concert does nothing to eliminate the underlying problem. Despite the serious message, the film is humourous.

The film had its premiere March 21 in the East Block of the House of Commons The invited guest list included members of Parliament, people from the media and friends in Ottawa. Buoyed by the favourable reception, we were eager to start peddling our prototype. Once again, illness intervened. My strength was diminishing and my headaches becoming even more serious. I went back to the military hospital, described my symptoms which seemed like rehearsals for strokes, and finally convinced them that I should have a brain scan. There was a waiting-list for the scan, so I went to California with a priest friend. It wasn't much of a holiday. The symptoms continued, I started to lose my co-ordination and the headaches were relentless.

The week I got back from California the CT scan took place and I was promptly admitted to hospital again. Several weeks of tests in Ottawa were followed by further examinations at the cancer clinic in Toronto, using the MRI machine, which gives a clearer pictures than the CT scan. At this point I was told that I had a "mass" in the back of my head. This was a new meaning of the word "mass" for me. The word which all my life had been a source of joy, took on a new connotation. It now meant a tumour that could be cancerous. They thought it could be operated on and again gave me the choice of where I wanted the operation performed. It was very strange, trying to make a rational decision about who's going to open your head and where it's going to be done. For me it was particularly eerie, because it was something I had always feared. As a child, when other children were afraid of the dark or the bogeyman or something else, I was always afraid that somebody was going to open my head. Here, now, it was happening. They had come to tell me that they were going to open my head and I had to choose where this was going to be done. How do you make a choice like that? Having been in the Ottawa hospital for three weeks, I knew the staff and was more or less comfortable with the situation. There seemed little reason to move. A brain operation is a brain operation, I thought. It either works or it doesn't. The day after I had made the decision to have the operation in Ottawa, Doctor Peterson, the neurosurgeon, who had been brought in from another hospital, came to see me. From the pictures they now had, he said, it appeared the mass was inoperable. I knew what he was saying. He was saying that I had a tumour that might kill me. This time I cried. The woman doctor who was working with him, Doctor Cora Fisher, held my hand, which I appreciated very much. Dr. Peterson's advice to me was: "You could live five minutes or 25 years. Live each day as it happens and be thankful at night that you had it."

I had always hoped that when death's door loomed, I would have an opportunity to celebrate the sacrament of healing with my friends— not as a frantic attempt to beat off death, but as a celebration of our belief in healing as part of the Christian tradition. In the Gospels, we always see Jesus healing people. In the Catholic tradition, that healing aspect of Christianity has often been shunted aside. Vatican II reinstated this healing dimension in the Sacrament of the Sick. When I was a kid, the sacrament was called Extreme Unction, and we always imagined it would be like getting a last zap. Now the sacrament is called the Sacrament of the Sick and the emphasis is on healing. I was praying for healing. If it was the will of the Lord, I was prepared to live on. I was also preparing myself for death. My reaction to the imminence of death was not anger or a feeling of being unjustly treated—I had faced death two or three times already. My thoughts were centred on how to prepare for my death. I decided I wanted to get ready with my friends, in a liturgical setting.

We had been planning to celebrate the Sacrament of the Sick. Invitations had been phoned to my Ottawa friends. Father Gordon MacLean, the RC chaplain at the military hospital, who himself had had a brain tumor removed, was to officiate. It just so happened that the day designated for the celebration was the day I was told that the mass was inoperable. That evening Father MacLean and I drove to the chapel at Saint Paul University Seminary, where about 80 people were gathered. Many of them were Catholics, but not all. I introduced everyone and explained why they were my friends. I told them the news I had received that day and told them how much it meant to me that they were with me for the celebration of this sacrament. There were scriptural readings and we sang hymns—joyous hymns—and I received the oils of the sacrament. After the liturgical celebration, we went to the Alumni Lounge and had wine and cheese. It was an exhilarating evening. I felt very sustained by the event and I felt that the people who had attended also had an uplifting experience of sickness, impending death and the power of healing.

Among my friends that night was a reporter, Louise Crosby. Although not a Catholic, she was very impressed by the ceremony and asked if she could write something on it. Expecting the story to get one inch on the 34th page, I agreed. I was very surprised to see a major article on the front page of the Ottawa Citizen, which was then taken off the Southam wire service and carried by many papers across Canada.

Drugs were only partially suppressing the pain in my head. Doctor Peterson said they were going to implant a "shunt" in my head. Implanting this shunt is quite a major operation. It involves inserting a tube into the ventricle containing the brain fluid and bringing the tube down inside the body to a place in the abdomen where the brain fluid can drain. My sister Mary Lou came to be with me for the operation, which took place on a Friday. My recovery was amazingly rapid. On Sunday, I was celebrating mass in the hospital chapel.

The only remaining treatment was radiation. Again I was given the

174

choice of where I wanted to undergo the radiation treatments. I elected to have them done at the University of Saskatchewan Cancer Clinic.

As I was recovering from the brain shunt operation in Ottawa, I was visited by a group of my former parliamentary colleagues. Hearing what was in store for me, some of them arranged for me to be flown to Saskatoon on a government "training flight." Seeing the possibility of a little publicity, I called Maurice Dupras and asked him to contact the other original members of the North-South Task Force. They met me at the Ottawa airport. Several of them and the task force staff accompanied me to Saskatoon, where I made a statement on the North-South situation to the media who were waiting at the airport. I said that the global issues we had talked about five years before were still unresolved and that it was more urgent than ever that they be dealt with peaceably. From the airport I was taken directly to the University Hospital by my bishop, James Mahoney, to begin another series of tests in preparation for the radiation treatments.

The tumour in the back of my skull, in the cerebellum, was leaning up against the brain stem, a very difficult place to get at. The doctors at the cancer clinic began to analyze the pictures that had come from Toronto and Ottawa and they took more of their own. The treatment required that my head be held rigidly in position each time, so the radiation would always enter my head at the same place. To ensure this accuracy of positioning, a mask was made to enclose my head during the treatments.

The series of 35 treatments dragged out over two months because the radiation machine broke down several times. The side-effects of radiation, which are becoming all too common an experience, set in. I lost my sense of taste and my sense of smell. I lost part of my hearing and some of my hair. The worst effect was the fatigue and nausea. Throughout the treatment period I was sustained by the exercise of recording the material for this book, by the prayers, letters, visits and phone calls from friends all over the world. I was also sustained by the hope that my strength would return and I could get back to Ottawa to carry on the work for international understanding and development. Even with death standing barely hidden before me, I still feel the urgency of work to be done. The South is calling. The North is calling. I have to use my remaining days, as I have tried to use my life, to build community, to bring people together.

APPENDIX

109. Without permission from their Ordinaries the clerics shall not act as agents for the goods and property of lay people, nor assume secular offices that impose the obligation of rendering an account, nor exercise the office of solicitor or attorney, except in the ecclesiastical court, or in the civil court when there is question of their own case or church. Clerics shall not take any part at all—not even as witnesses, unless they are forced to act as such—in criminal cases in secular courts, if it is a case in which the criminal may be punished with a grave personal penalty (**Canon 139**, § 3).

110. Without permission of the Holy See, the clerics are not allowed to compete for, or accept, the offices of senator or representative in those countries where this is forbidden by the Holy See; in other countries they shall not seek or accept these offices without the permission of their own Ordinary as well as of the Ordinary of the place where the election is to take place (**Canon 139**, § 4). In the United States it is not the custom for priests to seek any public office, and the Third Council of Baltimore, n. 83, forbids the priests to meddle in political affairs unless the defense of morality and sound principles is at stake. Some States exclude clergymen generally from holding any public office.[7] The Sacred Congregation of the Council in a declaration of March 15, 1927, ruled that the local Ordinary has the right and duty to forbid ecclesiastics by precept to engage in political activities when their actions are not in harmony with the instructions of the Holy See, and he has the right to punish them according to the rules of Canon Law if they violate his precept and after due admonition still refuse to obey.[8]

111. The clergy must keep away from all theatrical performances, dances and shows (especially in public theatres), which are unbecoming to the clergy, and where their attendance might cause scandal (**Canon 140**). Much depends in this matter on the customs of particular localities and on the general reputation of a play-house or a theatre. As a rule, people in the United States regard theatre-going as a proper amusement and recreation, and take no offense at the clergy's going to respectable places of amusement or recreation. The Code does not absolutely forbid theatre-going, but qualifies its prohibition.

---

[7] Declarations concerning secular public offices, cfr. App. III, 2, b.
[8] *Acta Ap. Sedis*, XIX, 138.

1983 Code of Canon Law
official English translation

Part I   Christ's Faithful

Can. 284   Clerics are to wear suitable ecclesiastical dress, in accordance with the norms established by the Episcopal Conference and legitimate local custom.

Can. 285   §1 Clerics are to shun completely everything that is unbecoming to their state, in accordance with the provisions of particular law.

§2 Clerics are to avoid whatever is foreign to their state, even when it is not unseemly.

§3 Clerics are forbidden to assume public office whenever it means sharing in the exercise of civil power.

§4 Without the permission of their Ordinary, they may not undertake the administration of goods belonging to lay people, or secular offices which involve the obligation to render an account. They are forbidden to act as surety, even concerning their own goods, without consulting their proper Ordinary. They are not to sign promissory notes which involve the payment of money but do not state the reasons for the payment.

Can. 286   Clerics are forbidden to practise commerce or trade, either personally or through another, for their own or another's benefit, except with the permission of the lawful ecclesiastical authority.

Can. 287   §1 Clerics are always to do their utmost to foster among people peace and harmony based on justice.

§2 They are not to play an active role in political parties or in directing trade unions unless, in the judgement of the competent ecclesiastical authority, this is required for the defence of the rights of the Church or to promote the common good.

Can. 288   Permanent deacons are not bound by the provisions of cann. 284, 285 §§3 and 4, 286, 287 §2, unless particular law states otherwise.

Can. 289   §1 As military service ill befits the clerical state, clerics and candidates for sacred orders are not to volunteer for the armed services without the permission of their Ordinary.

§2 Clerics are to take advantage of exemptions from exercising functions and public civil offices foreign to the clerical state, which are granted in their favour by law, agreements or customs, unless their proper Ordinary has in particular cases decreed otherwise.

Chapter IV

LOSS OF THE CLERICAL STATE

Can. 290   Sacred ordination once validly received never becomes invalid. A cleric, however, loses the clerical state:

1° by a judgement of a court or an administrative decree, declaring the ordination invalid;

2° by the penalty of dismissal lawfully imposed;

Can. 86   In so far as laws define those elements which are essentially constitutive of institutes or of juridical acts, they are not subject to dispensation.

Can. 87   §1 Whenever he judges that it contributes to their spiritual welfare, the diocesan Bishop can dispense the faithful from disciplinary laws, both universal laws and those particular laws made by the supreme ecclesiastical authority for his territory or his subjects. He cannot dispense from procedural laws or from penal laws, nor from those whose dispensation is specially reserved to the Apostolic See or to some other authority.

§2 If recourse to the Holy See is difficult, and at the same time there is danger of grave harm in delay, any Ordinary can dispense from these laws, even if the dispensation is reserved to the Holy See, provided the dispensation is one which the Holy See customarily grants in the same circumstances, and without prejudice to can. 291.

Can. 88   The local Ordinary can dispense from diocesan laws and, whenever he judges that it contributes to the spiritual welfare of the faithful, from laws made by a plenary or a provincial Council or by the Episcopal Conference.

Can. 89   Parish priests and other priests or deacons cannot dispense from universal or particular law unless this power is expressly granted to them.

Can. 90   §1 A dispensation from an ecclesiastical law is not to be given without a just and reasonable cause, taking into account the circumstances of the case and the importance of the law from which the dispensation is given; otherwise the dispensation is unlawful and, unless given by the legislator or his superior, it is also invalid.

§2 A dispensation given in doubt about the sufficiency of its reason is valid and lawful.

Can. 91   In respect of their subjects, even if these are outside the territory, those who have the power of dispensing can exercise it even if they themselves are outside their territory; unless the contrary is expressly provided, they can exercise it also in respect of *peregrini* actually present in the territory; they can exercise it too in respect of themselves.

Can. 92   A strict interpretation is to be given not only to a dispensation in accordance with can. 36 §1, but also to the very power of dispensing granted for a specific case.

Can. 93   A dispensation capable of successive applications ceases in the same way as a privilege. It also ceases by the certain and complete cessation of the motivating reason.

A LETTER TO BE REPRINTED AND CIRCULATED IN ALL PARISHES
OF THE SASKATOON DIOCESE, PREFERABLY ON SUNDAY SEPT. 25, [1977]

My brothers in Christ:

A man's priesthood does not take away his right as a citizen to run
for office. The Church recognizes this fact and has regulations to
cover it. Church law requires that the permission of the Bishop be
obtained before any priest can run for legislative office. This permission
is not to be given easily. When Father Robert Ogle applied earlier this
month, his request was carefully examined by the Bishop and most of the
parish priests of the city. With a clear understanding that there are
serious risks being taken when a priest accepts a political label, I
gave Father Ogle the necessary clearance.

At the same time, he received the support of our friendship. He has
been a faithful and hard-working priest of this Diocese for twenty-four
years, and has every desire to continue to serve the Church of Saskatoon
as a priest. I hope this desire will be understood and accepted by the
faithful. The priests of this diocese know that Father Ogle has stood
with other priests when they most needed support. He needs our friendship now. Whether or not we agree with his present decisions is beside
the point. He is in fact our brother in Christ and we are not about to
walk away from him.

Unfortunately, media reports of his nomination as a candidate have
created some blurring in the minds of many Catholics. Please try to
understand this: the support of friendship is not to be confused with
political support. I support Father Ogle's right to run in this election.
This does not mean that either he or his party has my vote. I am waiting
for the nominations of the other parties and a thorough discussion of all
issues. I will then decide on the best candidate and/or party and will
vote accordingly.
You can support your brother and still maintain voting freedom.

I knew my decision would cause lack of agreement in our community
and be a source of pain. This knowledge has weighed upon me heavily.
May I ask for your understanding and especially for your prayers.

Sincerely in Christ,

+ James P. Mahoney
Bishop of Saskatoon

4

HOUSE OF COMMONS
CANADA

FR. BOB OGLE, MP
SASKATOON EAST
OTTAWA OFFICE
HOUSE OF COMMONS.
OTTAWA, K1A 0A6
TELEPHONE: 613-996-4585

CONSTITUENCY OFFICE
301 220 THIRD AVENUE S.
SASKATOON, S7K 1M1
TELEPHONE: 306-665-6187

PERSONAL

O T T A W A
June 1, 1982.

Most Reverend James P. Mahoney,
Bishop of Saskatoon,
Chancery Office,
106 - 5th Avenue North,
SASKATOON, Sask.
S7K 2N7

Dear Bishop James:

Further to our conversation yesterday, I am writing to tell you about some of the events which surrounded my recent trip to Rome. I participated as a member of the official Canadian Government delegation assisting at the beatification of two Canadians, Blessed André Bissette and Blessed Marie-Rose Durocher.

In my meeting with you and the personnel committee on April 5th, you told me about the experiences that you had in Rome last year in regard to my status as a priest in political life.

Following our meeting of April 5th, I asked Fr. Frank Morrisey, Dean of Canon Law at the Pontifical University of St. Paul's, Ottawa, to prepare an interpretation of how he understood my situation. A copy of his letter is enclosed.

On the 18th of May, the day I left for Rome, Archbishop Angelo Palmas, Papal Nuncio, invited me to have lunch with him at his home. He was most gracious and cordial, and during the course of our conversation, we discussed my situation and Fr. Morrisey's letter, a copy of which I left with him. He agreed with Fr. Morrisey's interpretation and also suggested I should speak with His Eminence Cardinal Oddi in Rome.

In Rome on the 21st of May, I had the privilege of dining with His Eminence Cardinal Oddi. I was accompanied by Monsignor Pio Vito Pinto who is from Rome but teaches certain semester classes at the University of St. Paul's in Ottawa.

We spoke of many things relating to the modern Church and also discussed my role in politics. I gave a copy of Fr. Morrisey's letter to him as well as to Monsignor Pinto. They also agreed with Fr. Morrisey's interpretation. As I remember it, His Eminence Cardinal Oddi said, "You are fine in what you are doing. All you need is the permission of your Bishop."

....2

5

On my return from Rome, the Nuncio, Archbishop Palmas, invited me to lunch again at his home. He was very happy that I had seen His Eminence Cardinal Oddi, and that I had had an audience with the Holy Father. He asked me to keep in contact with him because he is very interested in what happens in the House of Commons.

As you know from my letter to you of February 4, 1982, I would like to have permission to place my name in nomination for the next federal election. I am happy in what I am doing, and I feel that it is a continuation of my lifelong desire to work in the area of social justice in the Church. As you know, permission to place my name in nomination in no way indicates that I will be nominated again, or that I will be re-elected.

You also know that without this permission I would not continue in politics.

I would ask for a decision as soon as possible because in all fairness to the New Democratic Party of which I am a member, they should be able to make other arrangements for a candidate as early as they can. I have informed the Party that I am awaiting your decision and that as I said in my nomination speech in September of 1977, "I wish to remain a priest before, during and after the event."

With my sincere best wishes and gratitude, I remain

Sincerely yours in Christ,

Encl.
c.c. Father Bernard DeMargerie
     Father Bernard Dunn

HOUSE OF COMMONS
CHAMBRE DES COMMUNES
CANADA

OFFICE OF THE LEADER
NEW DEMOCRATIC PARTY

0 1 SEP 1982

HOUSE C. . . . .S
CHAMBRE DES C. . .UNES

BUREAU DU CHEF
NOUVEAU PARTI DEMOCRATIQUE

O T T A W A
August 30, 1982.

The Most Reverend James P. Mahoney,
Chancery Office,
100 5th Avenue N.,
Saskatoon, Saskatchewan.

Your Excellency:

        I recently had the occasion to discuss with
Father Bob Ogle his plans for the next federal election. I was
delighted to learn that it is Fr. Ogle's desire to become a
candidate once again in the constituency of Saskatoon East.
However, I understand that prior to seeking the nomination,
Father Ogle must once again obtain permission from the Church.
It is for this reason that I am now writing.

        In your serious deliberations concerning the
possible candidacy of Father Ogle, I would like you to consider
the following points.

        First, Father Ogle has established an enviable
reputation as a man passionately concerned with the well-
being of mankind. Although he obviously works hard on behalf of
his constituents, all those who observe him in his work know the
depth of his feelings knows no provincial or national boundary.
He is truly a man following the most fundamental Christian moral
principle, namely that all men and women wherever they may live,
are to count equally in the eyes of God.

        The second point that I would like to emphasize is
that in his Parliamentary work, there is no member of the House of
Commons who better conveys a non-partisan approach to domestic and
international political matters. Fr. Ogle is equally quick to praise
or blame approaches taken by any one of Canada's three major political
parties. In so doing, I think he has demonstrated the unique
responsibilities of a priest who enters the very serious but very
partisan world of political life.

      . . . /2

I want to conclude with the simple assertion that
Father Ogle in his attitude towards public life is exemplary in
demonstrating by his every action what ought to be the real motive
for all politicians, i.e. he is involved in the real world of
politics because he wants to do things for people, not because
he wants to become merely a person people admire.

Needless to say, I hope your conclusion concerning
Father Ogle's desire to remain a Member of Parliament is in the
affirmative.

Yours sincerely,

Diocese of Saskatoon

CHANCERY
106 · 5TH AVENUE NORTH
SASKATOON, SASKATCHEWAN
S7K 2N7

March 9, 1983

Archbishop Angelo Palmas
724 Manor Avenue
Rockcliffe Park
OTTAWA, Ontario
KIM 0E3

Your Grace:

As you know, Father Robert Ogle is the sitting Member of Parliament for the New Democratic Party in the riding of Saskatoon East. Under the terms of the Code of Canon Law, I had given my consent, after consultation with the diocesan clergy, for him to be a candidate in the Federal Elections of May 1979 and February 1980. The consensus of the clergy at that time was that Father Ogle was an exceptional case as provided for in the law.

Early last year, Father and I agreed that we should discuss his future candidacy in the quiet time between elections rather than under the pressure of election fever, as had been necessary on the two previous occasions. With my approval he sought the opinions of Father Frank Morrissey, of His Eminence Cardinal Oddi and of yourself. He reported to me that he had received good hearings and, in fact, positive encouragement as far as his canonical status was concerned.

In September of 1982, at a meeting of the full presbyterium of the diocese, a formal discussion was entered into for the purpose of future discernment. Father Ogle was present and I was presiding. The interventions were many; the atmosphere was calm and deliberate. The clear consensus was that Father Ogle be permitted to allow his name to stand in the next federal election, expected in 1984 or 1985.

The priests who expressed reservations did so on the basis of principle. In every case they affirmed Father Ogle as a person and a priest; no one critized in any way his performance as a Member of Parliament. His actions and his stated positions were seen as fully in line with the Magisterium of the Church.

The release, earlier this year, of the Revised Code of Canon Law,

9

has caused a new problem. The canons which provided the basis for our earlier discussions have been removed from the Code. All of us in the diocese, especially including Father Ogle and myself, wish to be in full union with the Church. To this end, by this letter, I would ask, in the name of the Saskatoon Presbyterate, that Father Robert Ogle be given the indult he is seeking to be a candidate for the Parliament of Canada in the next federal election.

Thank you for your continued interest in this matter, and for whatever support you see fit to give.

Sincerely in Christ,

+ James P. Mahoney

James P. Mahoney
Bishop of Saskatoon

JPM:lc

UNIVERSITÉ SAINT-PAUL
223. RUE MAIN

OTTAWA, CANADA
KIS IC4

SAINT PAUL UNIVERSITY
223 MAIN STREET

FACULTÉ DE DROIT CANONIQUE
CABINET DU DOYEN

FACULTY OF CANON LAW
OFFICE OF THE DEAN

April 12, 1983

Rev. Robert OGLE, M.P., J.C.D.,
House of Commons,
OTTAWA, Canada.
K1A 0A6

Dear Father OGLE,

Further to your letter of March 3rd and to our recent conversations, I am pleased to give you the following information regarding the right of priests to seek elected political office.

As you are aware, Canon 285, 3, of the new Code of Canon Law now states that "officia publica, quae participationem in exercitio civilis potestatis secumferunt, clerici assumere vetantur."

This wording is quite different from that found in the various drafts of the Code; it no longer provides for special permission to be received from one's Ordinary. We can thus assume that the Holy Father gave special attention to this matter.

Nevertheless, it should be noted that this prescription is of ecclesiastical law (Canon 85) and, as such, is subject to the Bishop's power of dispensation (Canon 87). To date, I have seen no reference stating that such a norm would be constitutive law from which the Bishop cannot dispense, and therefore I find no restrictive clause in the new Code preventing the granting of a dispensation.

However, in the new law, the reason for granting a dispensation is stated to be the spiritual welfare of the person ("quoties id ad eorundem spirituale bonum conferre iudicet" - Canon 87). It would therefore be incumbent on you to show that such a dispensation in this particular case would be opportune for your spiritual welfare and that of others. This shouldn't be too difficult to demonstrate.

11

And so, to summarize, pending any authoritative pronouncement to the contrary, I believe that the Diocesan Bishop may dispense from the prescriptions of Canon 285, 3, and allow you to run for political office. The judgment as to the opportuneness of granting such a dispensation would depend on him.

Trusting that this information is of some assistance to you, and with my best personal wishes for the success of your important ministry for justice, I am, yours very truly,

Francis G. MORRISEY, O.M.I.,
Dean

Rev. Robert Ogle, MP.
Saskatoon East
House of Commons
Ottawa, K1A 0A6   CANADA

Dear Father Ogle,

           I write this personal note simply to
inform you that it recently has come to my attention
that opposition to your candidacy for re-election has
been heard here in Rome. It is based on reports that
you have sought to invite to Canada Father Miguel d'Escoto, the Foreign Minister of Nicaragua. The information came to me from other than ecclesiastical sources.
I thought it might be of interest to you since you are
probably deciding on the issues which will go into your
campaign.

           People see you, dear Father, as a Member of Par-
liament, yes, but also, and probably moreso, as a
priest. I urge you to be prudent in the stands you take
because, regardless of the disclaimers you may make, many
will view you as speaking for the Church. Not a few of
the faithful, at least, would be confused, regardless
of your good intentions, by your alleged position on the
visit to Canada of another priest who is an important
member of a government which recently gave such an ambiguous welcome to the Holy Father.

           I promise to keep you in my prayers and urge you
to pray for divine guidance in order to preserve the unity of the faithful and to seek the salvation of souls.

           With every blessing and best wish, I am,

                     Faithfully in Christ,

13

HOUSE OF COMMONS
CANADA

FR. BOB OGLE, MP
SASKATOON EAST
OTTAWA OFFICE:
HOUSE OF COMMONS,
OTTAWA, K1A 0A6
TELEPHONE: 613-996-4585

CONSTITUENCY OFFICE:
301 220 THIRD AVENUE S.
SASKATOON, S7K 1M1
TELEPHONE: 306-665-6187

May 26, 1983.   PERSONAL AND CONFIDENTIAL

His Eminence Silvio Cardinal Oddi, Prefect,
Sacred Congregation for the Clergy,
VATICAN CITY, Italy.

Your Eminence:

I am replying to your very kind personal note which I received on May 18th. I thank you very much for the concerns that you outline to me because I understand how serious a misinterpretation could be at this time. I do not know the non-ecclesiastical sources that you mention, but I would like to explain what actually did happen.

As you may know, I am one of the External Affairs critics for the New Democratic Party with a special mandate to cover Central and South America, international development and Canada's relations to the North-South dialogue. In this respect I have visited Central America four times in 1982, in January, March, November and December. Twice I was there under the auspices of the Canadian parliament, once as a member of an international group seeking a peaceful solution to the Honduran-Nicaraguan border crisis, and once under the auspices of the Inter-Church Committee on Human Rights in Latin America (an ecumenical group sponsored by the Canadian Conference of Catholic Bishops and leaders of the Protestant churches).

During my visits I met with many representatives of government, church authorities - Catholic and Protestant, university professors, journalists, refugees, United Nations personnel, development organizations, and many local people. I believe that the major problems in Central America are chronic and historic underdevelopment, outside interference, uncontrolled violence, and massive numbers of refugees. As critic in this area, I have constantly appealed for the stopping of arms shipments from whatever source to the area, for dialogue and a negotiated peace.

I believe that Canada as an English speaking country with no colonial involvement in Central America and a longtime friend of the United States, could act as a mediator in these situations. For that reason, during the last part of 1982 and the early part of 1983, I joined with other Members of Parliament from all parties on the External Affairs Committee to call upon the Canadian government

....2

14

to invite the External Affairs representatives of the countries in the area to
visit Canada. We also suggested to the Canadian Minister of External Affairs,
Allan MacEachen, himself a devout Catholic, to visit the area since he has
never been there. Two countries accepted invitations from the government of
Canada to discuss Central America, the Foreign Affairs Minister for Mexico and
the Foreign Affairs Minister for Nicaragua, Father Miguel d'Escoto. I had been
introduced to Father d'Escoto on one occasion in Nicaragua but I never had any
meetings with him. We were informed this week that Mr. MacEachen may visit the
area in September.

In Canada, I met Father d'Escoto at several public functions, the first of which
was a welcome dinner organized by Mr. MacEachen on Monday, the 14th of February,
1983, at which were present the Apostolic Pro-Nuncio, Archbishop Angelo Palmas,
a local bishop, Most Reverend Adolphe Proulx who represented the Canadian Conference of Catholic Bishops, several ambassadors from Central America and other
areas, Canadian Members of Parliament and Senators, as well as distinguished
members of the press.

I am not surprised, your Eminence, that someone has used this visit against me.
I am well aware of the difficulties of being properly interpreted by people. One
of the reasons I entered politics was to support pro-life and oppose abortion.
I have in my campaigns, in my public speeches, and in my voting record, consis-
tently opposed abortion legislation in Canada. Unhappily, the practice of abortion is still being extended. There are few Members of Parliament who openly
oppose it. However, many people accuse me of not doing enough to stop it and
yet I know that this is one of the main reasons why I am in the House of Commons.

Immediately following the Holy Father's visit to Nicaragua, I called on the
Nicaraguan Ambassador to Canada and protested vehemently to him about the whole
event. Furthermore, in the light of your wise counsel, I have asked the leader
of my caucus to change my critic role to another area of responsibility within
Canada so that there will be less danger of the faithful being confused. In
addition, if your Eminence would like to speak to me again personally on any
matter, I could arrange to return to Rome sometime in the future.

I appreciate the offer of your prayers, and I will likewise pray for you and
also for divine guidance in my own situation.

I have discussed the contents of your letter as well as my response to you with
both the Apostolic Pro-Nuncio, Archbishop Palmas, and my own bishop, Most Reverend James Mahoney.

I hope that I am open to whatever the Lord asks of me.

Sincerely yours in Christ,

Father Bob Ogle, M.P.
SASKATOON EAST

15

NONCIATURE APOSTOLIQUE

APOSTOLIC NUNCIATURE

N. 16618   Ottawa, February 17, 1984

Dear Father:

       I am directed by His Eminence Silvio Cardinal Oddi, Prefect of the Sacred Congregation for the Clergy, to convey the following to you:

       «The Sacred Congregation for the Clergy after an attentive study of your case has come to the following conclusion:

       1. - The applicability of Can. 90 is not seen because the existence of a «just and reasonable cause» has not been proved, nor the one of Can. 87 because there is no evidence that «a spiritual welfare» would result from it and to whom it would be profitable.

       2. - Consequently, the Bishop of Saskatoon must be informed that in the present state of things, a dispensation of Can. 285,3 in favour of Father Bob Ogle is not esteemed justified on behalf of the Holy See, nor of the Ordinary, even in the eventual case he had been authorized for it.»

       Hastening to inform you of what precedes, I am writing to the same effect to your Bishop, the Most Reverend James Mahoney, by disposition of His Eminence Silvio Cardinal Oddi.

       Please accept, dear Father, the expression of my devoted sentiments in Our Lord.

+ Angelo Palmas

Apostolic Pro-Nuncio.

Father Bob OGLE, M.P.
Saskatoon East
House of Commons
OTTAWA, Ontario
K1A 0A6

724 MANOR, OTTAWA (CANADA)   K1M 0E3

16

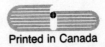

Printed in Canada